FINE
kettles of
FISH

A Treasury of Seafood
Chowders, Bisques, Soups & Stews

This is dedicated
to my mother and father,
to my daughters, Missy & Elizabeth,
to my brother,
and to my husband, Bud.

DEBORAH BENOIT MCGARRY
FINE
kettles of
FISH

A Treasury of Seafood
Chowders, Bisques, Soups & Stews

Illustrations by Kurt J. Wallace

Cape Cod · Nantucket · Martha's Vineyard
New Bedford · Plymouth

Published by
The Peninsula Press · Cape Cod 02670 USA
Donald W. Davidson
Publisher
The publisher is solely and fully responsible for the contents
of this edition, including any errors and omissions.

The illustrations by Mr. Wallace used in this book were published originally in 1984
as part of
The Gourmet's Guide to Fish and Shellfish
produced and prepared by
Quarto Marketing Limited
and published by
Quill, an imprint of William Morrow & Company.

An extensive effort has been made by The Peninsula Press,
by Quarto Marketing Limited, and by William Morrow & Company
to contact the creator of the illustrations in this book.
At the time of publication, however, none has met with success.
Any person knowing the whereabouts of Kurt J. Wallace
is encouraged to contact the publisher.

Cover image reprographics by
PRINTASTIC, INC.
South Yarmouth, MA 02664

Visit The Peninsula Press online:
www.capecod.net/peninsulapress
To e-mail The Peninsula Press: booksetc@capecod.net

Library of Congress Catalog Card Number: 97-066603
McGarry, Deborah Benoit
    Fine Kettles of Fish: A Treasury of Seafood Chowders, Bisques, Soups & Stews
    The Peninsula Press, ©1997.
    Includes illustrations copyright ©1984 by Kurt J. Wallace.
ISBN 1-883684-15-3

First edition
Manufactured in the United States of America
1 2 3 4 5 6 7 8 9 / 05 04 03 02 01 00 99 98 97

Table of Contents

My Apologies   vii

A Guide, Not the Gospel   9
Portions · Bowls · Kettles · Spoons & Ladles · Sieves
Blenders & Food Processors · Mortars & Pestles · Ingredients · Measurements

The Five Essential Elements   15
The Base Flavors · The Stock · The Durable Textures & Flavors
The Delicate Textures & Flavors · The Fish
ഉ Rules for Making Soops or Broths ഭ
— HANNAH GLASSE —

The Cooking Liquids   19
Broth · Dashi · Bouillon · Stock · Consommé
The Various Kettles of Fish

Cooking with Finfish   29
The Freshness of Fish · Cuts of the Fish · How to Dress a Fish
How to Cut Steaks from a Dressed Fish · How to Fillet a Fish
ഉ Fish Chowder ഭ
— HERMAN MELVILLE —
Eels · How to Skin & Dress an Eel

Cooking with Shellfish   91
Clams · How to Shuck a Clam
ഉ Clams and Quahaugs ഭ
— JOSEPH C. LINCOLN —
Mussels · How to Scrub & Debeard a Mussel
ഉ Mussel Soup ഭ
— ALEXANDRE DUMAS —
Oysters · How to Shuck an Oyster · Cooking Oysters
ഉ The Wellfleet Oysterman ഭ
— HENRY DAVID THOREAU —
Scallops · Cockles · Abalone · Conch · Squid · How to Clean a Squid
Lobsters · How to Clean a Lobster · Crawfish
Shrimp · How to Peel & Devein a Shrimp · Crabs · How to Clean & Pick a Crab

Cooking with a Variety of Seafoods   221
                         ဆ A Pretty Kettle of Fish ଝ
                            — THE BOSTON TRANSCRIPT —

Things that Go *Splash!* in the Water   273

Finishing Touches   277

Bibliography   282

Index   285

Acknowledgments & Credits   288

My Apologies

If confession is good for the soul, then it must be good for the soup as well. And so, I must begin with a confession.

Having spent all of my life (so far) on this peninsula called Cape Cod, I was raised in a household nourished by generations of Yankee cooking and upbringing. Basically, that meant that the word *chowder* was used more often than *stew*, and *stew* was used more than *soup*. After all, soup was something that came from a can while chowder and stew came from the kettle, a tool of the heart and hearth alike. These were the ultimate comfort foods, recipes that were at once simple and rustic.

In our household, then, as with households throughout Cape Cod, Nantucket & Martha's Vineyard, chowder consisted of 5 basic ingredients: some sort of fish, potatoes, onions, milk, and salt pork. The only variations might come from the day's catch (or the freezer's bounty) of finfish or shellfish, the use of cream rather than milk, and the substitution of butter for salt pork. Otherwise, the only seasoning was black pepper; the only other thickener, crackers. And both of these were added, to taste, at the table.

But there were two other unquestionable tenets, and they were these. First, every chowder made today is good, *but* any chowder made yesterday would be even better. It might even be best tomorrow, but — then again — it might not last that long. Second, adding any other ingredient was nothing less than an act of heresy, especially if that meant such things as flour, celery, or (*heaven forbid!*) tomatoes.

After all these years, however, I must admit — no, I must *confess!* — that I have been more than simply provincial; I have been wrong. As delicious as my family's chowders might have been (and continue to be), to maintain their universal supremacy would mean more than being self-centered it would be an act of denial. Not just the denial of the worthy contributions of others, but also the denial of those things to my own palate.

Looking back, I can now understand that our household's disdain for tomatoes in a kettle of fish had nothing to do with the folks in Manhattan or the fish in nearby Rhode Island. After all, we always loved the spicy, red-brothed recipe made by the Portuguese fishermen from Provincetown to New Bedford. The problem (it now appears) is that none of those recipes was a *chowder* to us, but a *soup*. But what in heaven's name was wrong with that? After all, if semantics were going to stand in our way, then how come we just thought it was odd (and not wrong!) that oyster *stew* had nothing in common with any beef stew we had known?

After all these years, I finally found the courage to admit this to myself and to confess it to others. In doing so, I'm not only liberating this mind once bound by the waters surrounding the Cape & Islands, but also allowing it to change to those channels that flow into every watery corner of the globe.

To those who live and fish along the Outer Banks and the Pacific Northwest, along the Gulf Coast and the Great Lakes, throughout the Mediterannean, the North Sea, and the South Seas, and wherever the waves rise up to meet the wind, please accept my apologies for any of my wrong thoughts in the past and enjoy with me now the bounties that our waters and our kettles have to offer.

DEBORAH BENOIT MCGARRY
Cummaquid, Cape Cod
March, 1997

A Guide, Not the Gospel

Portions

The ingredients for the recipes in this book have been proportioned to prepare a kettle of fish that yields 4 generous servings. At first glance, some lists of ingredients might not appear to provide that, but you must keep in mind at least three factors. First of all, some kettles of fish, such as consommés, are not intended to be robust servings and will probably be served with something else substantial, such as a salad. Second, other kettles of fish, such as stews, generally contain a greater proportion of fish and vegetables to stock. Finally, most of these kettles of fish are served with breads or crackers that are filling in themselves.

Bowls

Obviously, if you serve up your kettle of fish in a large mug, you need not worry about the items in this heading; however, some recipes beg to be presented in a wide, shallow bowl rather than a deep one. Regardless of whether you use your favorite mug or your finest china, though, always keep in mind one of those scientific laws you learned back in 8th Grade; namely, that heat is transferred from hot objects to cold. And that means that all the work you've put into bringing your kettle of fish up to a serving temperature will be lost if you ladle your creation into a stone cold bowl. Before you can say *oops!*, your family or guests will have a cold meal.

The remedies for this are simple. First of all, you could keep your bowls in a warmed oven until serving. Second, you could fill each bowl with boiling water from a tea kettle just minutes before using, then drain and quickly dry them at serving time. Finally, you might use the sort of tureen which is heated like a chafing dish.

In any event, a heated bowl is not only a *definite* plus, but a *definite* must for your presentation.

That said, this book *does* have a few recipes for cold soups. In that case, you might fill the bowls with ice water or chill them in the refrigerator.

Kettles

Whether you call them pots and pans, Dutch ovens, or stock pots, I still call them kettles. And those I have in my kitchen are nothing fancy. All that I ask is that each has 2 side handles, a cover that fits, and a heavy bottom that won't wear out or scald the contents.

Two of my kettles hold 4 quarts each, and I often strain my stock from one into the other, rather than into a heatproof bowl. The other kettle holds 10 quarts and is ideal for making large stocks from unwieldy pieces of frames and shells.

Spoons & Ladles

Aside from being particular about the ingredients that I put into my kettles of fish, I am also fussy about the utensils that go within, as well. Because the sound of metal banging and scraping inside a kettle can be downright annoying, the handle of a metal spoon left in a simmering stock can become just as hot as well. The way that I avoid both of those situations is simply to use a good, old fashioned wooden spoon, and I have several in my kitchen.

By the same token, I never use a rubber spatula in my kettles. These tools are fine for forcing solids through the mesh of a sieve, but they can easily melt in a hot kettle of fish. Moreover, a rubber spatula tends to pick up — become stale with — the flavor of a recipe. Try as you might, you *can't* rid the spatula of that staleness; however, it can take on a life of its own and pass that staleness along to some other recipe. The remedy? Don't use a rubber spatula.

Another essential for your kitchen must be a collection of ladles. As with a rubber spatula, a 1-ounce or 2-ounce spatula is an ideal alternative to a pestle for forcing foods through a sieve without damaging the mesh. For serving your food, though, you'll want a ladle that can contain at least 6 ounces, if not 8. Keep in mind that 8 ounces is equal to 1 cup. Finally, you really ought to have in your kitchen a ladle that holds 12 ounces, because it will make the transfer of food from one kettle to another a much quicker process.

Sieves

Long before I learned anything about cooking, I thought that *sieve* was simply a boating term, as in: "The dinghy leaks like a *sieve.*" After I learned about cooking, though, I not only discovered the true meaning of a sieve, but also that bigger *is* better! A large sieve not only will cover the mouth of a bowl or a kettle, but also will allow you plenty of room to drain liquids, as well as strain solids. You ought to have at least 2: a fine mesh and a medium mesh. In every event, respect that mesh and always take caution not to damage it with your pestle or ladle. Whenever you are using a sieve to puree cooked solids, your motion should not be a single, forceful one, but a gentle, up-and-down maneuver.

The best — and most expensive sieves — are the ones in the shape of a cone, which chefs refer to as a *china cap* or a *chinois.* They are wonderful, but not necessary. In fact, if you have a traditional food mill with a hand-cranked blade that forces the solids through a heavy mesh, that will often provide at least a good start toward a purée. In fact, there is nothing wrong with straining your stock first through a colander before giving it a second straining through a sieve with a finer mesh.

Blenders & Food Processors

When you first work with the recipes in this book, you'll probably be tempted to substitute an electric appliance for one of the old fashioned hand methods. *Hey,* it's still a free country! So, do whatever you wish.

As for myself, I try to avoid these kitchen tools unless I'm certain that the consistencies of the food are thin enough not to burn out the motors in these home models. While professional cooks have access to those appliances with industrial strength, the consistency of some recipes might cost you a gift from some Christmas past.

If you do intend to use a blender, keep these tips in mind.

First of all, blend in batches and never fill the container more than 1/3 full at any one time. Otherwise, the contents might be just too much for the capacity of the motor or the container. Second, start the blender on the lowest speed, pulsate, and work your way up to the level you want. Otherwise, the contents might suddenly spurt up and out! Finally, if you're blending hot — or even just warm — food, be sure to wrap a towel tightly around the lid of the container so that the food doesn't spew out and cause a burn. As always, an ounce of prevention is worth a pound of cure.

As for food processors, I've found that they don't always assure me either the uniform size or the attractive look that I can achieve in preparing some things by hand with a good, sharp knife. Sometimes a processor mushes things up; other times it leaves big chunks; and often it churns out a combination of both. That sort of processing is okay for solids that I plan to strain and discard, but not for those I want to cook with any sort of predictability or even serve to my family or guests.

Mortar & Pestle

For those of you who simply might not understand this term, this pair of tools consists of a container (*mortar*) and a crushing tool (*pestle*) that come in a variety of sizes according to the task at hand. The smaller ones are wonderful for mashing garlic or grinding together herbs and spices; the larger ones, for blending together sauces, such as aioli.

You will find them made of all sorts of materials from plastic to wood to china to marble. Though the plastic might be easiest to clean, and not absorb some otherwise essential oils, other materials provide a mortar surface of rougher texture against which you can work the foods. Often, though, your choice might be dictated by your budget. The *molcojete & tejolote* of Mexico has a nice texture made of black stone, and the *suribachi & surikogi* from Japan has an inner surface that is ribbed. Lacking these qualities, your mortar & pestle can be given some assistance with a simple sprinkle of salt to create some resistance among the ingredients.

Ingredients

I am not so naive as to believe that there is absolutely no use in this world for canned and bottled goods; however, if you don't draw the line somewhere you just won't discover much difference between a quick canned soup and a more time-consuming soup made with canned ingredients. So, I like to begin with the assumption that vegetables, such as tomatoes, carrots, and corn; herbs & spices, such as parsley, pepper, and garlic; and the all-important fish and shellfish are items fresh from the market, the garden, or the water.

And I believe that the same must be true of the cooking liquids, be they broths or stocks. Say what you will about the bottled stuff, I could *always* taste the difference. Just as important, meanwhile, must remain the distinction between fish and fowl, and these recipes are for fine kettles of *fish*. (Just to save you from looking back to this reference, let me forewarn you that one or two recipes do, indeed, combine flesh and fish, but they are few and far between.)

About the only place my feeble mind seems to allow a canned liquid is when it comes to using canned, evaporated milk in the place of fresh, whole milk. Part of that is my upbringing in these matters of chowder, but the other part is simply the true efficiency. Since the 1920s, Americans have brought home this canned variety that has had some 60% of its water removed, and it remains far superior to any of that powdered stuff. Given its availability, evaporated milk provides a sensible enrichment to a kettle which already might have either water, a watery stock, or even cream.

Measurements

Finally, let me lend a word here on consistency. In Cooking with Finfish you will find a brief discussion on Simplifying the Terms for cuts of fish; however, let me speak here to the other ingredients.

Because this book remains a *guide*, I have left you quite a bit of leeway in adjusting these basic recipes to your own tastes. This, however, just might drive some folks crazy, but I assure you that the reaction is not intended.

For starters, there are various ways of measuring the quantity of fish. Some fish and shellfish are sold by the pound; some (such as, shucked oysters), by the liquid measure; and some (such as, shrimp), by the count. With the exception of large and/or whole fish, the ingredients for finfish are listed by ounces of fillets, rather than pounds. Most shellfish are listed by the count, regardless of their size, and you are left to decide the quantity based upon your own tastes.

Similarly, a vegetable is listed as an unsized item; that is, I present it simply as *1 onion* rather than *1 large onion*. And unless the size of the piece is critical to the recipe, the cut is left without a dimension. Most important is the consistency among ingredients for cooking time.

Finally, I am a firm believer in allowing you to rely upon *your* own judgment. That means that some ingredients which others might measure by *dashes* or by fractions of teaspoons, I have simply left *to taste*. After all, if you can't accept the taste of what you are cooking, how can you expect others to do so?

Now, let's get ready to cook.

The Five Essential Elements

Creating a fine kettle of fish is no different than preparing any other sort of meal: it's part art, part science, and mostly a matter of taste. And though this book is simply meant as a guide to creativity and not the gospel outright, there are some ground rules that ought to be pointed out. These things are not anything I discovered on my own, but only came to understand through collecting recipes over the years. Time and time again, I'll encourage you not only to replace *this* fish with *that*, or one vegetable with another, but also to be imaginative and truly create a fine kettle of fish that's to your own liking. But always remember that in all matters of taste, what appeals to you might be nothing more than garbage to someone else, and sooner or later you'll discover that you can lead a guest to the soup bowl, but . . .

Simply keep in mind that every fine kettle of fish in this book can be reduced to 5 essential elements: the base flavors, the stock, the durable textures and flavors, the delicate textures and flavors, and the fish. Though these will differ from culture to culture, as well as from category to category, you'll soon recognize their respective counterparts and understand just how changing a proportion of each can mean the difference between a chowder, soup, stew, or bisque.

The Base Flavors

Be it butter, oil, or some sort of rendered pork, this is where the flavor begins. Though you might never have stopped to think of those ingredients as anything other than lubricants to keep the rest of the base flavors from sticking to the bottom of the kettle, each contributes in its own way to creating the first layer of flavor. Add to it the essential oils that come forth from other base ingredients such as onion, garlic, or pepper and you'll have begun a truly fine kettle of fish.

The Stock
More likely than not, the stock will bring to the kettle a distinct flavor of its very own; however, there is no rule which prohibits you from substituting clear water in its place. By the same token, you might add some other liquid, such as a tasteful wine or beer.

For the purposes of this book, however, I have ruled out two categories of stock (liquid). The first includes those that are commercially prepared and sold in cans, bottles, or even buillion cubes. All too often, the preservatives and flavors in those products simply add to your kettle the same indescribable, but recognizable flavor that you'll find in a can of soup. As far as I'm concerned, there's no sense in continuing with your own efforts. The second category includes the stocks made with chicken, beef, and veal. In the one or two recipes that also include chicken or pork along with the fish, these stocks do seem appropriate; however, my goal is to encourage you to make your own stock. The process is relatively simple, the stock can be made in batches and frozen, and the taste is far superior to anything else. And more likely than not, you'll be getting the flavor from some parts of the fish that you probably would have simply thrown out otherwise.

The Durable Textures and Flavors
These are the sort of ingredients that have at least two qualities which distinguish them from the others. First of all, they both require and withstand some prolonged cooking in order to become tender. Secondly, the extraction of their flavors does not require the sort of heat applied to ingredients providing the base flavors. Among these will be such vegetables as tomatoes, mushrooms, and squash . . . but not necessarily in the same recipe.

The Delicate Textures and Flavors
Unlike the durable ingredients, the delicate ones are those that tend to lose their body and flavors with prolonged cooking. Cream that thickens at first will become grainy, egg yolks that thicken will curdle, and starches that thicken will break down. Meanwhile,

fragrant herbs, such as basil, will relinquish all taste and possibly disappear, while pungent ingredients, such as garlic, simply become mellow and sweet.

The Fish

Finally, you'll add the fish to your kettle in the later stages, because the tender flesh tends to break down more quickly than in other sorts of recipes. By the same token, you'll probably be adding fish that is cut into rather uniform chunks and cubes, rather than in thin strips of fillet. That said, I must admit that my family is one of countless New England traditionalists who strongly believe that a chowder is best the day *after* it is made for no other reason than the meat indeed has become almost indistinguishable from the stock.

There you have the basic rules, and I encourage you to break them to suit your own personal tastes. Just keep in mind, though, the tastes of others you might want to please. If you can eat it, then feel free to cook it; otherwise, you'll have done nothing more than concoct a bucket of garbage.

Rules for Making Soops or Broths

HANNAH GLASSE

"First take great care the pots or saucepans and covers are very clean and free from all grease and sand, and that they be well tinned, for fear of giving the broths and soops any brassy taste. If you have time to stew as softly as you can, it will both have a finer flavour, and the meat will be tenderer. But then observe, when you make soops or broth for present use, if it is to be done softly, don't put much more water than you intend to have soop or broth; and if you have the convenience of an earthen pan or pipkin, and set it on wood embers till it boils, then skim it, and put in your seasoning; cover it cloase, and set it on the embers so that it may do very softly for some time, and both the meat and broths will be delicious. You must observe in all broths and soops that one thing does not taste more than another; but that the taste be equal, and it has a fine agreeable relish, according to what you design it for; and you must be sure, that all the greens and herbs you put in be cleaned, washed, and picked."

— *from* THE ART OF COOKERY

The Cooking Liquids

More than a few cookbooks and chefs use the terms *stock* and *broth* interchangeably. In this book, though, I like to make this distinction, however subtle it might seem. Whenever I use the word *broth*, I'm referring the liquid that results when you've cooked some fish in water or wine. For example, *broth* is made when you steam clams, mussels, or shrimp. When I use the word *stock*, though, I think of a process that involves the simmering in water of some aromatic herbs and vegetables, along with some otherwise dispensable part of a fish, such as a fish frame (the heads, bones, trimmings, and tails of a fish.) or some crustacean (shrimp, crabs, lobsters, etc.). And though this process is intentional, it is not at all complicated.

About the only other distinction you ought to watch for in following these recipes and procedures is the difference between *simmering* and *boiling*. Aside from the fact that the *simmer* takes place at a lower heat (190°F at sea level) than the *boil* (212°F), that range in temperature not only means an obvious difference in cooking times, but also an obvious difference in the final kettle of fish. While the languid movement of the *simmer* extracts the full flavor of the ingredients over that longer period of time, it does not break them down into a cloudy stock repleat with emulsified fat. The *boil*, on the other hand, serves to break the ingredients down, as well as to evaporate a good part of the liquid. And though it is sometimes necessary to reduce the liquid in a kettle of fish in order to develop a more intense flavor, this is often done after the *simmer* and after most of the solids have been removed and discarded.

So, now that I've made this personal distinction between *broth* and *stock*, as well as between the *simmer* and the *boil*, I encourage you to follow the relatively simple steps of making your own stock. And from there, you should have no difficulty in making any one of the progressions that can be called fine kettles of fish. Briefly, this is the distinction that I try to make among them:

Broth: The liquid that results when you've cooked some fish in water or wine.

Dashi: A simple and quick Japanese stock made from seaweed and dried bonito flakes.

Stock: The liquid which the French would call *bouillon*, which is produced from the slow simmering of aromatic herbs and vegetables in water or wine, along with some otherwise dispensable part of a fish, such as a fish frame or some crustacean shells.

Consommé: Though many will interchange the terms *broth, stock, bouillon,* and *consommé,* I use this last term to mean a more concentrated, as well as a clarified *stock.* The clarification is accomplished not only by defatting the stock, but also by simmering it with egg whites and egg shells before straining it through a fine cheesecloth.

Soup: A kettle of fish in which the stock is proportionately greater than the solid ingredients.

Gumbo: A soup/stew of Creole origin.

Stew: A kettle of fish in which the solid ingredients are proportionately greater than stock; often cooked more slowly.

Puréed soup: A soup strained so that particles of the fish itself help thicken the soup and enhance flavor.

Bisque: A rich soup that includes some kind of starchy binder (rice or bread crumbs) to help keep the particles of puréed fish in suspension

Cream soup: Any one of the above which includes milk or cream added as a final ingredient.

Chowder: Generally, cream soup with starchy ingredient such as potato or corn; however, some regional chowders do not include any milk or cream among their ingredients.

Making a Stock

You can get the essentials for making a stock for little or no cost from your fishmonger or from someone's fishing trip. More often than not, you'll find trimmings from a seafood meal in your own kitchen. Rather than throw any away, make a rich stock that you can freeze in portions. If you can learn to recognize the ingredients, develop foresight, and spend a little time, then you'll always be prepared to make a fine kettle of fish with little or no more effort.

Basic Fish Stock

Some cookbooks will call this a *fumet* or *fonds de poisson*, but it's nothing other than a basic stock made from the frames of round fish, such as cod, grouper, red snapper, or striped bass. In most instances, the frames from flat fish, such as flounder and halibut, have too many tiny bones. And in almost every instance, an oily fish, such as bluefish or shad, will yield a strong, cloudy stock.

None of this should be difficult to find. Though your local fish market or fisherman might be more than happy to give you the necessary frames, these *must* be from fish trimmed that very day. Remember, if they smell at all, don't use them! Finally, remove and discard any gills that might still be attached to the head.

IN YOUR KETTLE, melt the butter and stir in the pieces of fish frame. Cover and bring to the boil for 5 minutes.

Reduce the heat and add the onions, celery, leeks, parsley, salt, and lemon juice. Cover and simmer another 5 minutes.

Add the water and bring to the boil. Reduce the heat and stir in the clove, garlic, bay leaf, thyme, and peppercorns. Simmer uncovered for 45 minutes.

Remove the kettle from the heat and skim the top if necessary.

Allow the stock to rest for 30 minutes.

Strain the liquid through a sieve into a heatproof bowl. Discard all the solids.

Refrigerate, freeze, or use as required.

INGREDIENTS:
4 lbs. fish frames, rinsed & chopped in 3-inch pieces

2 T. butter
5 onions, chopped coarse
4 celery ribs (with tops), chopped coarse
3 leaks (with tops), chopped coarse
6 parsley sprigs
1 t. salt
1 t. lemon juice
5 qts. cold water
1 clove
1 garlic clove, minced
1 bay leaf, crumbled
1/4 t. thyme
1/2 t. whole black peppercorns

21

Basic Fish Stock with White Wine

INGREDIENTS:

4 lbs. fish frames, rinsed & chopped in 3-inch pieces

2 T. butter
5 onions, chopped coarse
4 celery ribs (with tops), chopped coarse
3 lemons, quartered
12 whole black peppercorns
4 qts. cold water
4 cups dry white wine
Bouquet garni

IN YOUR KETTLE, melt the butter and stir in the pieces of fish frame. Cover and bring to the boil for 5 minutes.

Reduce the heat and add the onion, celery, lemon, and peppercorns. Cover and simmer another 5 minutes.

Add the water and wine, then bring to the boil.

Add the *bouquet garni*, reduce the heat, and simmer for 20 minutes. As residue rises to the surface, skim and discard.

Remove the kettle from the heat and skim the top if necessary.

Allow the stock to rest for 30 minutes.

Strain the liquid through a sieve into a heatproof bowl. Discard all the solids.

Refrigerate, freeze, or use as required.

Bouquet Garni

The purpose of tying together fresh herbs or bundling dried herbs in cheesecloth is simply to make them easier to remove after their purpose has been served.

Until rather recently, fresh herbs were not as common in the United States as they long have been in Europe. Americans, then, have tended to rely upon the cheesecloth bundles, while European recipes have called for *faggots* of fresh herbs. Whatever your preference, a *bouquet garni* for 5 quarts of stock should include:

Fresh herbs tied with string:
10 thyme sprigs
1 parsley bunch
1 bay leaf
Using ordinary kitchen string, tie the bundle in several places.

Dried herbs bundled in cheesecloth:
2 t. thyme leaves, dried
1 parsley bunch, chopped
1 bay leaf, crushed
Using a 6-inch square of cheesecloth, be certain that all corners are tucked in and that none of the herbs can float freely in the stock.

Basic Crustacean Stock I

(LOBSTER, CRAB, CRAWFISH)

Making crustacean stocks provides you with your best opportunities to practice frugality. No matter how high the price might be of lobster or crab, this is your chance to extend the ingredients of your first-class meal into at least one more. Let your friends and family pick the bodies of these crustaceans as clean as they are able. In most cases, they will not eat the orange coral (roe) of the female lobster, the feathery gills, or the thin, milky layer of milt that lines the shell of the body; however, each of these provides a world of flavor.

INGREDIENTS:

Claw shells and bodies of 4 lbs. of lobsters and/or crabs, chopped in 2-inch pieces

2 T. butter
5 onions, chopped coarse
4 celery ribs (with tops), chopped coarse
3 lemons, quartered
5 qts. cold water
Bouquet garni

IN YOUR KETTLE, melt the butter. Add the crushed shells and bodies, cover, then cook over low heat for 5 minutes.

Add the onion, celery, and lemon. Stir. Cover and cook another 5 minutes.

Add the water, then bring to the boil.

Add the *bouquet garni*, reduce the heat, and simmer for 45 minutes. As residue rises to the surface, skim and discard.

Remove the kettle from the heat and skim the top if necessary.

Allow the stock to rest for 30 minutes.

Strain the liquid through a sieve into a heatproof bowl. Discard all the solids.

Refrigerate, freeze, or use as required.

Basic Crustacean Stock II

(Shrimp)

Though you might begin this stock with the broth from a kettle of steamed unpeeled shrimp, along with the shells from the same, you might want to consider peeling the shrimp before you steam them. If so, reserve these uncooked shells until you make this stock, even if that means freezing the uncooked shells until you've accumulated enough of them to make this recipe.

INGREDIENTS:

Reserved shells of 4 lbs. of shrimp, preferably uncooked

2 T. butter
5 onions, chopped coarse
4 celery ribs (with tops), chopped coarse
4 garlic cloves, minced
12 black peppercorns, whole
5 qts. cold water
Bouquet garni

IN YOUR KETTLE, melt the butter over medium heat. Add the shells, cover, and cook over low heat for 5 minutes.

Add the onion, celery, garlic, and pepper. Stir. Cover and cook another 5 minutes.

Add the water, then bring to the boil.

Add the *bouquet garni,* reduce the heat, and simmer for 20 minutes. As residue rises to the surface, skim and discard.

Remove the kettle from the heat and skim the top if necessary.

Allow the stock to rest for 30 minutes.

Strain the liquid through a sieve into a heatproof bowl. Discard all the solids.

Refrigerate, freeze, or use as required.

Dashi

JAPAN

Something more than a stock, but less than a consommé, *dashi* is used as the basis for Japanese soups. Though two of these three main ingredients — *konbu* (seaweed strips) and *hana-katsuo* (dried bonito flakes) — might have native names foreign to the average American cook, they are neither expensive, nor difficult to find in ethnic markets, gourmet shops, or through mail-order companies. But don't be suprised if the *konbu* is sold in an 18-inch strip that looks like moldy leather. The dark brown seawood is often covered with a coat of its natural sea salt, which will wash off. That said, be pleasantly surprised by a quick and easy recipe that's more like making tea than making stock.

IN YOUR KETTLE, place the folded piece of *konbu* and add the water. Bring to the simmer over low heat.

Once the water comes to the simmer, remove and reserve the *konbu*, then bring the water to the boil.

Stir in the *hana-katsuo*.

Remove the kettle from the heat and allow to stand for 1 minute.

Strain the *dashi* through a fine sieve and reserve the solids.

Refrigerate, freeze, or use as required.

The reserved *konbu* and *hana-katsuo* can be used to make a second batch of *dashi*, which will have a little stronger taste.

INGREDIENTS:

1 18-inch piece of *konbu*, whole & folded

5 cups cold water

4 cups *hana-katsuo*, packed

IN YOUR KETTLE, add the reserved *konbu* and *hana-katsuo* together with the water. Simmer for 20 minutes.

Add the fresh *hana-katsuo*, stir, and remove the kettle from the heat. Allow to stand for 1 minute.

Strain the *dashi* through a sieve into a heatproof bowl. Discard all the solids.

Refrigerate, freeze, or use as required.

INGREDIENTS:

4 cups cold water

1 18-inch piece of reserved *konbu*, whole & folded

4 cups of reserved *hana-katsuo*, packed

1¼ cup of fresh *hana-katsuo*, packed

Poaching Liquid

(LOBSTER, SHELLFISH, TROUT & SALMON)

INGREDIENTS:

8 cups cold water
1/2 cup malt vinegar
2 onions, sliced
2 carrots, peeled & sliced
12 black peppercorns, cracked
1 bay leaf
1 thyme sprig
3 parsley sprigs
1½ T. salt

IN YOUR KETTLE, combine the water and malt vinegar, then bring to the boil.

Add the onions, carrots, black peppercorns, bay leaf, thyme, parsley, and salt. Stir, reduce the heat, and simmer for 10 minutes.

Remove the kettle from the heat and strain the liquid through a sieve into a heatproof bowl. Discard all the solids.

Refrigerate, freeze, or use as required.

Beer Bouillon

This recipe makes a flavorful poaching liquid, as well as a delicious sauce for shellfish, especially shrimp, crab, and crawfish.

IN YOUR KETTLE, melt the butter and sauté the onion for 10 minutes.

Sprinkle the flour into the kettle, then stir to incorporate into the butter.

Gradually, stir in the beer.

Add the sugar and the bay leaf, then bring to the boil over medium heat.

INGREDIENTS:

4 T. butter
1 onion, diced
2 T. flour
2 cups beer, flat
1 T. sugar
1 bay leaf

Court Bouillon

This is probably the first — but most definitely *not* the last — time that you will be cautioned that this stock made from vegetables should not be confused with the legendary Louisiana Court Bouillon that is a true kettle of fish unto itself.

INGREDIENTS:

2 T. butter
1 onion, chopped
8 cups water
1 cup dry white wine
2 T. white wine vinegar
1 carrot, peeled & chopped
3 celery ribs, chopped
2 parsley sprigs
2 t. salt
6 whole black peppercorns
2 whole cloves
1 bay leaf

IN YOUR KETTLE, melt the butter, then sauté the onion for 3 minutes.

Add the water, white wine, vinegar, carrot, celery, parsley, salt, black peppercorns, cloves, and bay leaf.

Bring to the simmer for 1 hour.

Remove the kettle from the heat and strain the court bouillon through a sieve into a heatproof bowl. Discard all the solids.

Refrigerate, freeze, or use as required.

Cooking with Finfish

The ingredients for any kettle of fish ought to take into consideration the fact that that the simple word *fish* in the English language represents more than 22,000 known species worldwide, from the waters of world's highest lake in Peru's Lake Titicaca (some 12,500 feet above sea level) to those of the world's deepest oceans (a full 22,960 feet down). And though these fish can range in size from the half-inch goby to the 50-foot whale shark, not every one of them lends itself to the makings of a fine kettle of fish. So, we have to keep in mind some basics, and in this chapter we'll cook with finfish, those that have skins and fins rather than shells.

For the most part, we'll also assume that you can do business with a local fishmonger, most of whom will not only be more than willing to do any cutting and trimming for you, but also be willing to sell you so-called *chowder fish*, odd-sized pieces that are the by-product of some other filleted fish and whose only shortcoming is that they are not as pretty as a fillet or steak. Still, you should know something about buying a whole, fresh fish, and you ought to have some inkling about cutting the fresh fish itself.

The Freshness of a Fish

Because finfish and shellfish alike are cold-blooded animals from an aquatic environment that is altogether different from that of the warm-blooded animals and poultry that provide us with other kinds of meats for our recipes, the flesh of both types of fish is more tender and delicate than the others. Consquently, it must be handled

29

with care from the moment it comes out of the water. If not, the natural flavor and texture will not be preserved, and deterioration will encourage bacterial growth.

Health reasons aside, the purpose of determining the freshness of a fish is to be certain that the taste you get from a recipe comes from the natural state of a fish and not from any state of deterioration. And though a fish might not have been caught just hours before it appears in your fishmonger's display case, commercial fishermen understand how to handle a fish so that health and culinary concerns alike are of paramount importance.

For starters, try to view a whole fish whenever possible. Whether you then prepare it yourself or have your fishmonger do so for you, seeing the entire fish allows you to look for some important characteristics of freshness:

1. *Rigor mortis:* The fish should be flexible, not stiff; however, the flesh should be firm to the touch.

2. *Smell:* There really should be none; if anything, a fish should smell like the ocean, not the wharf!

3. *Clear eyes:* They should be shiny and bright.

4. *Bright gills:* These should be bright red, covered with clear mucous.

5. *Skin color:* Though some fading will begin once a fish comes out of the water, the natural colors should remain fairly bright.

Cuts of the Fish

As with any other type of meat prepared for cooking, finfish has its own terminology used by the fishmonger and cook alike:

Whole fish: Though the scales and the entrails are removed, the head, fins, and tails remain.

Half-round: The fish is split lengthwise, and the backbone remains in one of the halves.

Drawn: Also called *pan-dressed,* this generally applies to a smaller fish that have had the entrails and scales removed.

Steak: The cross-section of fish that has had the entrails and scales removed; the skin and a piece of backbone usually remain.

Fillet: Sometimes with the skin still attached, this is a piece of fish cut away from the backbone the length of one side of the body.

Chowder fish: These are usually the odds and ends, the trimmings that are too small or too roughly cut to be sold as a premium cut; however, they are also too valuable to toss away. They might also just be an underutilized species.

How to Dress a Whole Fish

It used to be said that "yesterday's news is only good for wrapping today's fish," and this remains true. Spread out a few layers of old newspapers before you begin this task. And when you're done, just wrap up the mess and dispose of it all.

1. If the fish has scales, these should be removed first. Having a scaling tool is great, but it's not a necessity. That old dull knife will do.

   Wet the fish so that the scales don't scatter too far. Hold the fish firmly by the tail, then scrape your scaling tool or dull knife along the body toward the head. Repeat this several times on each side of the fish until all the scales are removed. Plan on discarding the scales, then rinse the fish.

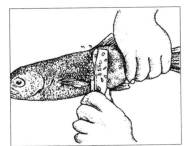

2. Locate the ventral fin just behind the gill. Insert the point of your knife in the belly of the fish just beneath the ventral fin, then cut the length of the belly to the pelvic fin.

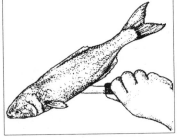
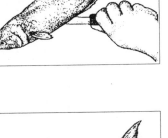

3. Make another incision at the gills and cross beneath the throat, then remove the entrails with your knife or fingers. Plan on discarding the entrails.

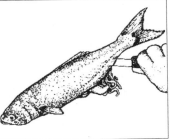

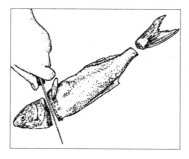

4. Remove the head by cutting across the body just behind the gills; then, cut through the body just before the tail. Depending upon the type of fish, the head(s) and tail(s) may be reserved or frozen for making stock.

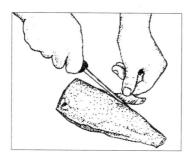

5. Use the point of your knife to cut away the ventral and pelvic fins; then, to cut along the top and around the dorsal fin to remove the backbone. Pull the dorsal fin forward from the body. Plan on discarding the fins. Depending upon the type of fish, the bone(s) may be reserved or frozen for making stock.

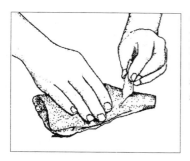

6. If you do not plan to cut steaks from the body, you may wish to peel away the skin by starting near the tail. Depending upon the fish, the skin may add or detract from the flavor. Similarly, the skin may be discarded or reserved for making stock.

How to Fillet a Whole Fish

1. Follow the first 2 steps for How to Dress a Whole Fish.

   Use the point of your knife to make an incision behind the gills and along the backbone of the fish.

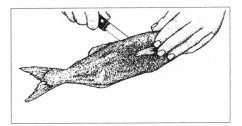

2. Run your knife along the rib cage of the fish to cut away a fillet strip.

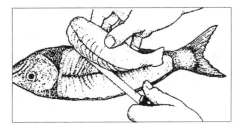

3. Remove any belly fat from each fillet.

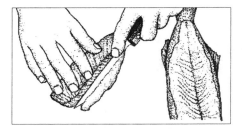

4. Hold the skin by the tail end, then slide the knife in a continuous motion between the skin and the flesh.

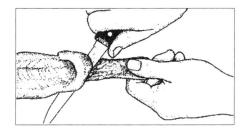

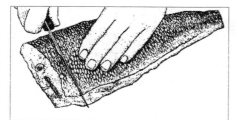

How to Cut Steaks from a Fish

1. Place the dressed body on a clean, cutting board, then cut one-inch sections across the width of the fish.

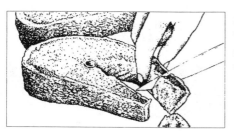

2. Depending upon the fish, you may wish to cut away the fatty tips of each steak. Similarly, the tips may be discarded or reserved for making stock.

Fish Chowder

HERMAN MELVILLE

It was quite late in the evening when the little *Moss* came snugly to anchor, and Queequeg and I went ashore; so we could attend to no business that day, at least none but a supper and a bed. The landlord of the Spouter-Inn had recommended us to his cousin Hosea Hussey of the Try Pots, whom he asserted to be the proprietor of one of the best kept hotels in all Nantucket, and moreover he had assured us that cousin Hosea, as he called him, was famous for his chowders. In short, he plainly hinted that we could not possibly do better than try pot-luck at the Try Pots.

But the directions he had given us about keeping a yellow warehouse on our starboard hand till we upon a white church to the larboard, and then keeping that on the larboard hand till we made a corner three points to the starboard, and that done, then ask the first man we met where the place was: these crooked directions of his very much puzzled us at first, especially as, at the outset, Queequeg insisted that the yellow warehouse — our first point of departure — must be left on the larboard hand, whereas I had understood Peter Coffin to say it was on the starboard. However, by dint of beating about a little in the dark, and now and then knocking up a peaceable inhabitant to inquire the way, we at last came to something which there was no mistaking.

Two enormous wooden pots, painted black and suspended by asses' ears, swung from the cross-trees of an old top-mast, planted in front of an old doorway. The horns of the cross-trees were sawed off on the other side, so that this old top-mast looked not a little like a gallows. Perhaps I was over sensitive to such impressions at the time, but I could not help staring at this gallows with a vague misgiving. A sort of crick was in my neck as I gazed up to the two remaining horns; yes, two of them, one for Queequeg; one for me.

"It's ominous," thinks I. "A Coffin my Innkeeper in my first whaling port; tombstones staring at me in the whalemen's chapel; and here a gallows! and a pair of prodigious black pots too! Are these last throwing out oblique hints touching Tophet?"

I was called from these reflections by the sight of a freckled woman with yellow hair and a yellow gown, standing in the porch of the inn, under a dull red lamp swinging there, that looked much like an injured eye, and carrying on a brisk scolding with a man in a purple woollen shirt.

"Get along," said she to the man, "or I'll be combing ye!"

35

"Come on, Queequeg," said I, "all right. There's Mrs. Hussey."

And so it turned out, Mr. Hosea Hussey being from home, but leaving Mrs. Hussey entirely competent to attend to all his affairs.

Upon making known our desires for a supper and a bed, Mrs. Hussey, postponing further scolding for the present, ushered us into a little room, and seating us at a table spread with relics of a recently concluded repast, turned round to us and said: "Clam or Cod?"

"What's that about Cods, ma'am?" said I, with much politeness.

"Clam or Cod?" she repeated.

"A clam for supper? A cold clam? Is that what you mean, Mrs. Hussey?" says I. "But that's a rather cold and clammy reception in the winter time, ain't it, Mrs Hussey?"

But being in a great hurry to resume scolding the man in the purple shirt, who was waiting for it in the entry, and seeming to hear nothing but the word "clam," Mrs. Hussey hurried towards an open door leading to the kitchen, and bawling out "clam for two," disappeared.

"Queequeg," said I, "do you think that we can make out a supper for us both on one clam?"

However, a warm savory steam from the kitchen served to belie the apparently cheerless prospect before us. But when that smoking chowder came in, the mystery was delightfully explained.

Oh, sweet friends! hearken to me. It was made of small juicy clams, scarcely bigger than hazel nuts, mixed with pounded ship biscuit, and salted pork cut up into little flakes; the whole enriched with butter, and plentifully seasoned with pepper and salt. Our appetites being sharpened by the frosty voyage, and in particular, Queequeg seeing his favorite fishing food before him, and the chowder being surpassingly excellent, we despatched it with great expedition.

When leaning back a moment and bethinking me of Mrs. Hussey's clam and cod announcement, I thought I would try a little experiment. Stepping to the kitchen door, I uttered the word "cod" with great emphasis, and resumed my seat. In a few moments the savory steam came forth again, but with a different flavor, and in good time a fine cod chowder was placed before us.

We resumed business; and while plying our spoons in the bowl, thinks I to myself, "I wonder now if this here has any effect on the head? What's that stultifying saying about chowder-headed people?"

"But look, Queequeg, ain't that a live eel in your bowl? Where's your harpoon?"

Fishiest of all fishy places was the Try Pots, which well deserved its name, for the pots there were always boiling chowders.

Chowder for breakfast, and chowder for dinner, and chowder for supper, till you began to look for fish-bones coming through your clothes. The area before the house was paved with clam-shells. Mrs. Hussey wore a polished necklace of codfish vertebra; and Hosea Hussey had his account books bound in superior old shark-skin.

There was a fishy flavor to the milk, too, which I could not at all account for, till one morning happening to take a stroll along the beach among some fishermen's boats, I saw Hosea's brindled cow feeding on fish remnants, and marching along the sand with each foot in a cod's decapitated head, looking very slip-shod, I assure ye.

Supper concluded, we received a lamp, and directions from Mrs. Hussey concerning the nearest way to bed; but, as Queequeg was about to precede me up the stairs, the lady reached forth her arm, and demanded his harpoon. She allowed no harpoon in her chambers.

"Why not?" said I. "Every true whaleman sleeps with his harpoon — but why not?"

"Because it's dangerous," says she. "Ever since young Stiggs coming from that unfort'nt v'y'ge of his, when he was gone four years and a half with only three barrels of ile, was found dead in my first floor back, with his harpoon in his side; ever since then I allow no boarders to take sich dangerous weepons in their rooms at night. So, Mr. Queequeg" (for she had learned his name), "I will just take this here iron, and keep it for you till morning. But the chowder; clam or cod to-morrow for breakfast, men?"

"Both," says I, "and let's have a couple of smoked herring by way of variety."

— *from* MOBY DICK

Fish Chowder

BASS RIVER, CAPE COD, MASSACHUSETTS

On the Massachusetts mainland shore, just along the western coastline of Cape Cod Bay, sits a handful of historic harbors offering safe haven to fishing boats of all sizes. It was from one of these harbors that my father took this child along on a fishing charter. And though I was too young to now recall the name of the port, I shall never forget the chowder.

What made it so special was the first fish caught was immediately dressed and taken below, where the mate of the vessel had already peeled his potatoes, chopped his onions, and prepared his kettle long before the fish had arrived. In retrospect, I suppose that this must have been viewed by the adults aboard as a sign of confidence; to me, it was nothing less than a wonderment.

Perhaps there were other fish caught that day. Perhaps there was sun or rain or fog. Quite frankly, I don't recall. All that I can remember about the rest of the trip is that we ate a fish chowder so delicious that it stands apart not only from all the other events of that day, but also from all the other kettles of fish in my life.

After that, I insisted that my father store the right provisions aboard his fishing boat so that we could make chowder of the first catch of each venture upon the waters around the Cape & Islands. From the coast of Cohasset (just south of Boston), to the shores of South Darmouth (just south of New Bedford), I practiced making kettles of fish out of our homeport of Bass River on Nantucket Sound. This is the kind of recipe that set me out on this course.

These ingredients might well stir a debate among devotées of this traditional New England dish; however, I truly believe that any argument simply stems from the fact that they usually depend upon what the cook has on hand. Aside from the fact that we always stored plenty of cans of evaporated milk in our galley, butter or bacon was often more readily available than salt pork. Similarly, proportions eventually became abitrary, because most cooks will make this kettle of fish by eye, not by measurement.

Keep in mind that there are well-meaning people who will begin with a roux or else later add flour or even mashed potatoes as a thickening agent. As for me, however, I remain one of those who enjoys my chowder the *next* day when all the pieces of fish have begun to break down with the cooked potatoes and milk.

In short, if there is any place to begin to experiment or to improvise, this is it. As you'll see in following recipes, leeks or shallots can be substituted for onions; sweet potatoes, for white potatoes; and salmon, for cod. So, let's get started!

IN YOUR KETTLE, melt the butter then sauté the onion.

Add potatoes and water, then bring to the simmer until the potatoes are fork tender.

Add the fish and evaporated milk, then cover and simmer until the fish begins to flake.

Stir, taste, and adjust the seasonings with salt & pepper.

Ladle into individual heated bowls.

Garnish each with a pat of butter.

Serve with pilot crackers. (*See* Finishing Touches.)

INGREDIENTS:

16 oz. whitefish fillets, in 1-inch pieces

2 T. butter
1 onion, diced
2 potatoes, peeled & diced
2 cups water
4 cups evaporated milk
Salt & pepper, to taste
4 t. butter, garnish

Fish Chowder

MARBLEHEAD, MASSACHUSETTS

In the 1871 edition of *The Young Housekeeper's Friend,* Mary Cornelius provided this recipe for "Marblehead Fish Chowder," which had not been in earlier editions. Though the historic sailing port itself lies between Boston and New Hampshire, this chowder lacks the one ingredient assumed by many to be essential to a true New England chowder of this sort; namely, milk or cream. In fact, she had noted in one recipe for the 1845 edition that: "Some people add a cup of milk just before it is served." Food historians point to the entry as the first reference of milk in a chowder. Until that time, the recipe had been thickened with crackers. (*See* Finishing Touches.)

INGREDIENTS:

24 oz. whitefish fillets, in 1-inch pieces

4 oz. salt pork, diced
12 pilot crackers
2 cups water
3 onions, sliced thin
1 t. salt
1 t. black pepper
4 cups boiling water

IN YOUR KETTLE, render the salt pork until crisp and brown.

Meanwhile, in a small bowl soak the pilot crackers in 2 cups of water.

Remove from the kettle and discard the browned pieces of salt pork.

Layer half of the soaked crackers along the bottom of the kettle, then layer half of sliced onion.

Layer the fillets along the top of the onions, the sprinkle with salt & pepper.

Layer the remaining crackers, then the remaining onion.

Add enough boiling water to the kettle to a level 1 inch above all the layers.

Bring the kettle to the boil, then reduce the heat, cover, and simmer for 1 hour.

Fish Chowder

SABLE ISLAND, NOVA SCOTIA

This recipe from the Canadian Maritimes does have the dairy ingredient believed to be so important to most New England recipes; however, it also has more spices and herbs than any downeaster would ever allow. Nonetheless, it is a fine kettle of fish that can be made with any one — or even combination — of a variety of whitefish, especially those of the cod family, including haddock, pollock, and hake.

INGREDIENTS:

16 oz. whitefish fillets, in 1-inch pieces

2 slices bacon
1/2 onion, diced
1/2 leek, diced
2 celery ribs, diced
1 garlic clove, minced
2 large potatoes, diced
1 1/2 cups water
3 cups stock
1 t. dry mustard
1 T. parsley, minced
1/2 t. thyme, crushed
1/4 t. black pepper
1/4 t. Tabasco sauce
2 bay leaves
1 t. Worcestershire sauce
2 cups milk
1 cup cream

IN YOUR KETTLE, render the bacon until crisp and brown.

Remove and reserve the bacon slices to a paper towel.

Remove and discard all but 2 T. of the drippings, then sauté the onions, leeks, and celery for 3 minutes.

Stir in the garlic and potatoes, then add the water and bring to the boil.

Add the stock, mustard, parsley, Tabasco, bay leaves, and Worcestershire sauce, then bring to the boil.

Reduce the heat, cover, and simmer for 15 minutes.

When the potatoes are fork tender, remove the kettle from the heat and add the fish. Allow to stand for 5 minutes.

Meanwhile, in a small saucepan warm the milk and cream together. Be careful not to scald or burn them. When they are warm, stir them into the kettle.

Remove and discard the bay leaf.

Ladle into individual heated bowls.

Garnish with crumbled bacon.

Salt Cod Chowder

MENEMSHA, MARTHA'S VINEYARD, MASSACHUSETTS

Thanks to the drying and preserving qualities of salt once harvested from the sea, fishermen were able to send their catch to markets far inland from their ports. In fact, for years the salt-makers on Cape Cod dotted the shoreline with windmills that pumped the water into the large troughs for evaporation. Though modern refrigeration and express transportation now make our local, fresh catch more readily available to distant places, salt cod and its recipes still remain popular in a great many households worldwide.

INGREDIENTS:

16 oz. salt codfish

6 cups hot water
4 potatoes, peeled & sliced
2 onions, sliced
Salt & pepper
6 cups hot milk
2 T. butter

IN YOUR KETTLE, shred the salted cod and cover with hot water. Allow to soak for 1 hour, then drain and discard the water.

Cover the salted cod with more hot water and soak for another hour. Once again, drain and discard the water.

Remove the soaked cod to a clean bowl.

Wipe clean the kettle and place a layer of potato upon the bottom.

Cover the layer of potato with a layer of fish, then a layer of sliced onion. Sprinkle with salt & pepper.

Repeat this layering until you have used all the potatoes, fish, and onion.

Add enough hot milk to cover all the layers.

Cover and bring the kettle to the simmer until the potatoes are fork tender.

Add the butter to the top of the chowder.

Ladle into individual heated bowls.

Codfish Stew

ÎLE d'OLÉRON, FRANCE

On this island just off the coast of France, they bring together the flavors of the Bay of Biscay — in the form of cod and pollock — with those of their summer gardens. Traditionally, the key to making a *ratatouille* is not so much the ingredients in the recipe, but more the cooking time for each. Though a ratatouille made without fish can be served either hot, or cold, this kettle of fish is best served-up hot. Still, it is important that each element here be cooked until just done and not let to stew beyond that.

As with any recipe the includes eggplant, you might wish to remove some of the vegetable's bitter juices by first placing the cubes of eggplant in a colander, sprinkling with salt, then allowing to drain for at least 30 minutes. Rinse off the dark juices and salt before adding the eggplant to the kettle.

IN YOUR KETTLE, heat the olive oil, then sauté the onions, garlic, green pepper, eggplant, and zucchini for 5 minutes.

Add the stock, tomatoes, basil, parsley, and thyme, then bring to the boil.

Reduce the heat and simmer 15 minutes.

Add the fish to the kettle, then cover and simmer for 5 minutes more.

Stir, taste, and adjust the seasonings with salt & pepper.

Remove the kettle from the heat and allow to stand for 5 minutes.

Ladle into individual heated bowls.

INGREDIENTS:
24 oz. whitefish fillets, in 2-inch pieces

2 T. olive oil
2 onions, sliced
2 garlic cloves, minced
1 green bell pepper, seeded & in 1-inch pieces
1 eggplant, in 1-inch cubes
1 zucchini, in 1-inch chunks
2 cups stock
4 tomatoes, peeled, seeded & diced
1/4 cup basil, chopped
1/4 cup parsley, chopped
1/4 t. thyme
Salt & pepper, to taste

Tuna Stew

CABO FISTERRA, PORTUGAL

The meat of the prized bluefin tuna is both light and dark; however, many people are surprised to see that a steak of fresh tuna is almost as dark and red as that of a steer. This is because tuna are actually a warm-blooded species that must constantly swim in order to move water through its gills and oxygen throughout its body. As a result of all this swimming, the meat (which is really muscle) is much thicker than that of most fish and the body heat does not as easily dissipate into the water; as a result of all this rich oxygen, the meat (muscle) is also much redder, as well as richer in carbohydrates.

In this recipe, though, the meat of preference is the lighter cut of the bluefin. In fact, this ingredient can be substituted with the lighter albacore tuna, with whitefish, or even shrimp.

All that said, the other important aspect of this recipe is the use of any one of the various spicy sausages made by the Portuguese.

INGREDIENTS:

12 oz. tuna steak, skin & dark meat removed, in 1-inch pieces

1/4 lb. chourice or linguica, sliced thin
1 T. olive oil
1 celery rib, diced
1/2 onion, diced
1/2 red bell pepper, diced
1 garlic clove, minced
5 cups stock
1 potato, in 1/2-inch cubes
2 tomatoes, peeled, seeded & diced
8 black olives
1 bay leaf
Juice of 1/2 lemon
1 cup kale, washed & torn
1 T. parsley, minced

IN YOUR KETTLE, render the sausage until crisp and brown.

Remove the browned pieces of sausage to a paper towel.

Remove and discard all but 2 T. of the drippings, then sauté the celery, onion, peppers, and garlic for 3 minutes.

Return the sausage to the kettle, along with the stock, potato, tomatoes, olives, bay leaf, and lemon juice, then bring to the boil.

Reduce the heat, cover, and simmer until the potatoes are fork tender.

Remove the kettle from the heat.

Stir in the fish, kale, and parsley, then allow to stand for 10 minutes.

Remove and discard the bay leaf.

Ladle into individual heated bowls.

Tuna Chowder

KONA, HAWAII

While a good many people quickly assume that recipes from our 50th state must include pineapple, this delightful kettle of fish more closely resembles a chowder from the opposite corner of the nation. There is a distinctively different taste, however, that comes not only from the fresh ginger that is a staple of the western Pacific, but also from the local yellowfin tuna. As with all species of tuna, the yellowfin is a member of the mackerel family.

IN YOUR KETTLE, render the salt pork until crisp and brown.

Remove and discard the pieces of salt pork, as well as all but 2 T. of the drippings.

Add the onion, along with the tuna, then sauté for 5 minutes.

Stir into the kettle the stock and potatoes, then cover and simmer for 30 minutes.

Add the cream and simmer 10 more minutes,

Stir, taste, and adjust the seasonings with salt, pepper & ginger.

Ladle into individual heated bowls.

INGREDIENTS:

16 oz. fresh tuna steak, skin removed and in 1-inch cubes

4 oz. salt pork, diced
1 onion, minced
2 potatoes, diced
4 cups stock
1½ cups cream
Salt & pepper, to taste
Fresh grated ginger, to taste

Cold Tuna Chowder

AVALON, SANTA CATALINA ISLAND, CALIFORNIA

Whenever they talk tuna in California, they mean the yellowfin tuna that doesn't stray very far north in the Pacific and is the mainstay of the state's commercial fishing fleet. While the yellowfin is readily distinguished by its coloring from the other four kinds of tuna in our waters, the color of its meat is just about in between. The meat of the albacore is whiter; that of the bluefin, darker.

INGREDIENTS:

8 oz. yellowtail tuna steak, in 1-inch pieces

3½ cups stock
8 oz. wide egg noodles
1 cup watercress, washed & chopped
1 T. parsley, chopped
1 scallion (white part only), chopped
1½ cups cream
Salt & pepper, to taste

IN YOUR KETTLE, bring the stock to the boil.

Add the noodles and cook for 5 minutes, stirring occasionally.

Reduce the heat and stir in the watercress, parsley, scallion, and tuna. Simmer for 15 minutes.

Remove the kettle from the heat, then add the cream.

Stir, taste and adjust the seasonings with salt & pepper.

When the kettle has cooled, pour the chowder into a clean bowl or tureen, then refigerate at least 1 hour.

Ladle into individual chilled bowls.

Fish Consommé

HYANNIS PORT, CAPE COD, MASSACHUSETTS

Though this sort of recipe is almost the antithesis of a rustic and hearty kettle of fish, now and then there comes an occasion that simply calls for a light dish. In this case, it's a consommé: basic stock further enriched with additional vegetables and sumptuous pieces of fish, then clarified with egg whites. The time and effort involved in preparing this recipe might seem more to you than it is worth, and you won't get any argument from me on that matter. Still, this might be something to keep in your repertoire or just to know why you haven't bothered to attempt it.

IN YOUR KETTLE, warm the stock.

Meanwhile, in a large bowl combine the fish, onion, carrot, celery, parsley, and egg whites. Use your hands to knead the ingredients together and make certain that the egg whites cover the fish and vegetables as much as possible.

Gradually add the fish and vegetables to to the kettle, then stir.

Bring the kettle to the simmer, then carefully move it to one side of the burner so that the heat is not directly beneath the center of the kettle. Stir and allow to simmer for 45 minutes.

Every 10 minutes or so, adjust the kettle around the burner so that the heat does not cook in the same place.

After this time, the cooked ingredients a thick froth will have risen to the top of the stock. Create an opening in the froth so that the stock can continue to simmer to the surface, then simmer another 10 minutes or so until only a few particles of vegetables, fish, and egg can be seen in the clear broth.

Place a fine sieve over a heatproof bowl. Being careful not to disturb the thickened layer of froth, ladle the consommé into the sieve.

Wipe clean your kettle, then add the consommé and bring to the simmer.

Ladle into individual heated bowls.

INGREDIENTS:

24 oz. whitefish fillets, in 1/2-inch pieces

8 cups stock
1 onion, chopped
1 carrot chopped
1 celery rib, chopped
1/4 cup parsley, chopped coarse
5 egg whites

47

Monkfish Soup

SEAL COVE, NEWFOUNDLAND

Long a favorite among Europeans, Scandinavians, and Newfoundlanders, this rather ugly looking species has remained underutilized in the United States. Sometimes called an *anglerfish* or a *goosefish*, it has developed a following among those who find its delicate taste and texture to be similar to that of lobster.

Though you can substitute any whitefish in this recipe, you really ought to try this with monkfish. As your fishmonger to let you know if there ever is any available, but you might tell him that you only want to look at the tail fillets, thank you.

INGREDIENTS:

12 oz. monkfish fillets, membrane removed, in 1-inch pieces

1 T. olive oil
1 onion, diced
1 carrot, diced
1 cup cabbage, shredded
1/4 t. black pepper
4 cups stock
1 potato, in 1/2-inch cubes
1 T. cider vinegar
1 T. parsley, minced
1/4 t. dried thyme

IN YOUR KETTLE, heat the oil, then sauté the onion, carrot and cabbage for 5 minutes.

Stir in the stock, potato, vinegar, parsley, thyme, and pepper.

Cover and bring to the simmer until the potatoes are fork tender.

Remove the kettle from the heat, then add the fish, stir, and allow to stand for 10 minutes.

Ladle into individual heated bowls.

Monkfish Soup
FINISTERRE, SPAIN

Though the monkfish on this side of the Atlantic is a different species from that of the western shores, they both have many characteristics in common. Their smooth, shark-like skin is one of those, and their flat, narrow tail section is another. Though the monkfish appears to be more mouth and stomach than anything else, the tapered portion behind it yields a white meat, firm and moist, that has only the backbone to remove. Because such a fish of 20 pounds yields only 5 pounds of meat, most fishermen cut off the tail and toss the rest of the large carcass overboard simply to save storage space.

INGREDIENTS:

16 oz. monkfish fillets, in 1/2-inch cube

6 cups stock
2 potatoes, peeled & sliced
1/4 t. saffron threads, crushed
3 tomatoes, peeled, seeded & diced
2 garlic cloves, minced
1 t. paprika
1/4 t. cumin, ground
Salt & pepper, to taste
1 T. olive oil
1 sweet red bell pepper, roasted & in thin strips

IN YOUR KETTLE, bring the stock to the boil.

Add the potatoes, reduce the heat, and simmer for 5 minutes.

Stir in the saffron, tomato, garlic, paprika, and cumin, then simmer until the potatoes are fork tender.

Remove the kettle from the heat, then strain the stock through a sieve into a heatproof bowl. Use a pestle to force the solids through the sieve.

Stir, taste and adjust the seasonings with salt & pepper.

Return the stock to the kettle, along with the olive oil, then bring to the boil.

Stir in the monkfish, reduce the heat, and simmer until the fish is just cooked.

Stir in the roasted pepper strips, then simmer for 3 more minutes.

Ladle into individual heated bowls.

Cold Salmon Bisque

SOGNDALSFJØRA, NORWAY

The fact that this particular kettle of fish is served cold has absolutely nothing to do with the fact that it comes from a rugged coastline still bound, in parts, by glaciers. While the Aaro River is a paradise for salmon fishermen, the Norwegians were pioneers in the farming of this fish, much of which they export to the rest of the world. Clearly, this is not a dish for a long winter's night, but a sultry summer's day in a lower latitude.

INGREDIENTS:

8 oz. salmon fillets, poached & chilled

1 T. butter
1/2 garlic clove
1 onion, diced
1/2 green pepper, chopped
1 cup milk
2 T. dill, chopped
2 T. dry sherry
Dash Tabasco
Dash pepper
1 cup cream
Dill sprigs, garnish

IN YOUR YOUR KETTLE, melt the butter, then sauté the garlic, onion, and green pepper for 5 minutes.

Flake the cold salmon and place in a blender.

Add the sautéed vegetables, milk, dill, sherry, Tabasco, and pepper, then cover and blend on high speed until smooth. Gradually add the cream.

Place the uncovered bowl in the refrigerator to chill for at least 1 hour.

Ladle into individual chilled bowls. Garnish each with fresh dill.

Cold Salmon & Cucumber Soup

CAPE DISAPPOINTMENT, WASHINGTON

There are some 6 species of Pacific salmon, and our nation's western continental coastline from Alaska down to San Diego is home to 5 of those: the chinook, the chum, the coho, the pink, and the sockeye. Unless you live along the coast, though, your earliest recollections of this fish were those dramatic pictures shown in Science class of salmon swimming upstream to spawn. The Pacific salmon reproduce but once; however, the Atlantic species can spawn 4 or 5 times.

The other image most of us tend to have of salmon is that of a fly-fisherman deftly luring his prey to the hook; however, the chinook of the Columbia River is caught in the shoreline waters of the ocean by fishermen trolling in boats.

IN YOUR KETTLE, bring the stock to the boil.

Add the onion and cucumbers, reduce the heat, and simmer for 5 minutes.

Remove the kettle from the heat, then stir in the dill and yogurt.

Strain the stock through a sieve into a heatproof bowl. Use a pestle to force through the solids.

Stir, taste, adjust the seasonings with salt & pepper.

Place the uncovered bowl in a refrigerator to chill for at least 1 hour.

Before serving, gently stir in the flaked salmon.

Ladle into individual chilled bowls.

Garnish each with a sprig of fresh dill.

INGREDIENTS:

24 oz. salmon fillets, steamed, chilled & flaked

4 cups stock

I onion, chopped

I ½ T. dill, chopped

3 cups yogurt

2 cucumbers, peeled, seeded & diced

Salt & pepper, to taste

Dill sprigs, for garnish

Salmon Soup

SPURN HEAD, ENGLAND

This is a practical kettle of fish that makes economical use of all the basic ingredients. In fact, if you have made and reserved stock in your freezer, this recipe can be brought together in very little time.

INGREDIENTS:

8 oz. salmon fillets, cooked & in 1-inch pieces
12 oz. salmon trimmings
8 oz. bones of sole

1 carrot, diced
1/2 cup turnip, diced
1 celery rib, chopped
1 onion, chopped
4 cups water
6 potatoes, peeled & diced
1 T. parsley, chopped fine
Salt & pepper, to taste
1/4 cup white breadcrumbs, garnish

IN YOUR KETTLE, combine the salmon trimmings together with the sole bones, carrots, turnip, celery, and onion. Cover with water and bring to the boil.

Skim the surface, then cover and simmer for 1 hour.

Remove the kettle from the heat, then strain the stock through a sieve into a heatproof bowl. Discard the solids and allow the stock to cool.

Meanwhile, in a small saucepan cook and mash the potatoes.

After the stock has cooled, skim any fat from the surface. Return the stock to the kettle and bring to the simmer.

Stir the mashed potatoes into the heated stock, then add the salmon fillets, along with the parsley, and simmer for 10 minutes.

Stir, taste, and correct the seasonings with salt & pepper.

Ladle the soup into individual bowls.

Garnish with breadcrumbs.

Salmon Soup
PORT RENFREW, VANCOUVER ISLAND, BRITISH COLUMBIA

With the exception of the Baltic salmon, which does not migrate and has a very light flesh, the meat of the other salmons of the world is readily recognized by a distinctive color ranging from pink to red. Though the meat of some farm-raised salmon might have been colored by an additive to their diet, that of the wild salmon is the result of its natural diet of crab and other crustaceans. More important than the coloring, though, is the rich flavor of the meat, which — along with its low fat content — has led many to proclaim the salmon as "the perfect fish." If you were unaware of any of that, this recipe from one of the world's most picturesque spots might well convince you, too.

INGREDIENTS:

Frame of 1 large salmon

1 onion, chopped
1 clove garlic, chopped
1/2 t. coriander seed
1 t. salt
1 t. butter
1 t. olive oil
Dash cayenne
6 cups water
Parsley, chopped for garnish

IN YOUR KETTLE, stir together the onion, garlic, coriander seed, salt, butter, olive oil, cayenne, and water, then bring to the boil.

Reduce the heat, cover, and simmer for 1½ hours.

Stir, taste and adjust the seasonings with salt & pepper.

Strain the stock through a colander into a heatproof bowl, then return the stock to kettle.

Ladle into individual heated bowls.

Garnish with parsley.

Golden Fish Soup

VYTEGRA, RUSSIA

Like their Scandinavian neighbors in Norway, the Russians have been farming salmon for many years and make this fish a staple of their diet. While some of the ingredients in recipe might at first appear to be rather rustic, their combined flavors are quite exquisite. And the garnish of salmon caviar raises an interesting point.

Though the roe of salmon, tuna, and lumpfish are often called caviar, they can only be called such in the United States if the term is preceded by the name of that fish, such as *salmon caviar*. Otherwise, the U.S. Food & Drug Administration recognizes only sturgeon roe as true *caviar*.

The word itself is the Anglicized form of the Turkish *havyar*, dating back through the centuries when the peoples of the Middle East and eastern Europe regularly ate the eggs of the sturgeon. By the end of the 19th century, American fisheries along the Delaware River on the east coast and the Columbia River on the west coast were made this nation the world's largest suppliers of caviar. Before 1900 ended, however, the supply of sturgeon had been depleted, and true Russian caviar was imported.

INGREDIENTS:

12 oz. salmon steak, in 1-inch chunks
3 lbs. fish frame, washed & chopped

2 T. butter
1 onion, diced
1 carrot, peeled & sliced
1 parsnip, peeled & sliced
1 celery rib, sliced
1 bay leaf
8 cups water
6 white peppercorns, whole
1/8 t. saffron threads, crushed
Salt, to taste
3 potatoes, peeled & in 1/2-inch cubes
1 lemon, peeled & sliced thin
2 T. parsley, chopped for garnish
4 T. salmon caviar, for garnish

IN YOUR KETTLE, melt the butter, then sauté the onion, carrot, parsnip, and celery rib for 3 minutes.

Add the water and bring to the boil.

Reduce the heat, then add the bay leaf, peppercorns, and saffron. Stir and simmer for 30 minutes.

Strain the stock through a sieve into a heatproof bowl, then discard the solids.

Return the stock to the kettle and bring to the boil until reduced to 6 cups.

Taste and adjust the seasonings with salt.

Reduce the heat, add the potatoes, and simmer until they are fork tender.

Stir in the salmon and simmer until the fish flakes easily.

Ladle into individual heat bowls.

Garnish each with a lemon slice dipped in parsley and floated on the soup. Place 1 T. of the caviar atop each slice.

Solianka

KHATYRKA, RUSSIA

Variations of this kettle of fish abound throughout Alaska, British
Columbia, Washington state and Oregon, where it is believed that
the recipe found its way along the China trade after the Russian
revolution. Devoid of any true vegetables, its ingredients generally
include salmon and dill, and quite often the latter is in the form of
dill pickles or pickle juice.

IN YOUR KETTLE, bring the stock to the boil.
Add the salmon and cook for 5 minutes.
Reduce the heat and simmer 15 minutes.
Remove the fish from the kettle and
reserve on a clean dish. Remove and discard any
bones, as well as the skin.

Taste the stock and adjust the seasonings
with the salt & cayenne pepper.

Stir the dill and wine into the kettle, then bring to the boil.
Add the fish, stir, and reduce the heat. Simmer for 5 minutes.
Ladle into individual heated bowls.
Garnish with lemon slices.

INGREDIENTS:

16 oz. salmon steak, 1-inch thick

2 cups fish stock
1½ T. dill, minced
Salt and cayenne pepper, to taste
3 cups sautérne
Lemon slices, garnish

Salmon Soup

NORTH BEND, OREGON

This kettle of fish is a variation of the Solianka. Though there are a few more ingredients, the preparation itself is less involved.

INGREDIENTS:

16 oz. salmon fillets, sliced in thin strips

2 T. butter
2 tomatoes, peeled, seeded & chopped
1 onion, chopped
2 dill pickles, chopped fine
1 t. capers
1 t. black olives, chopped
1 t. green olives, chopped
1 bay leaf
6 cups stock
Salt & pepper, to taste
4 T. butter, for garnish
2 T. dill, chopped for garnish
4 lemon slices, for garnish

IN YOUR KETTLE, melt the butter and simmer the tomatoes for 15 minutes.

Place the salmon atop the tomatoes, then add the onion, dill pickles, capers, and olives.

Carefully add the stock and the bay leaf, then bring to the simmer for 15 minutes.

Stir, taste and adjust the seasonings with salt & pepper.

Ladle into individual heated bowls.

Top each with 1 T. of butter, some dill, and a slice of lemon.

Fishcamp Soup
NEW TOWN, NORTH DAKOTA

Though many of the ingredients in this kettles of fish are the same as several of those popular throughout the Pacific Northwest, including the Solianka, the main difference is in the use of whitefish, rather than salmon.

That said, what endears me to this recipe even more than the taste is the name that conjurs up a woodside cottage with nothing other than the barest of essentials: a hand-pump for water, an oil lamp for light, and a cast-iron stove for cooking and warmth.

IN YOUR KETTLE, melt the butter, then gently sauté the garlic, onion, celery, pepper along with the sugar for 5 minutes.

Meanwhile, tie the fish frame & trimmings in cheesecloth and place in the kettle.

Stir in the lemon juice, dill pickle juice, and water, then bring to the boil.

Add the tomatoes and tomato juice. Stir, reduce the heat, and simmer for 20 minutes.

Stir in the rice and simmer until the rice is cooked.

Add the fish to the kettle.

Stir, taste, and adjust the seasonings with Tabasco, Worcestershire, salt & pepper, .

Simmer until the fish begins to flake.

Remove and discard the cheesecloth bag.

Ladle into individual heated bowls.

INGREDIENTS:

16 oz. whitefish fillets, cut in 1-inch cubes
fish frame & trimmings

2 T. butter
1 garlic clove, crushed
1 onion, chopped
1 celery rib, chopped
1 green pepper, chopped
1/2 t. sugar
1 t. lemon juice
2 T. dill pickle juice
8 cups water
1½ cup canned tomatoes, with juices
2 cups tomato juice
1/4 cup uncooked quick rice
Dash Tabasco
Worcestershire sauce, to taste
Salt & pepper, to taste

Haddock Soup

CROMARTY, SCOTLAND

This is the sort of soup that contributes to the image of a Scotsman's thrift, for it makes use of the sort of fish parts that others might discard. As you well know from reading this book, however, these are the choice ingredients for a rich stock.

On the other hand, you might not be familiar with the other key ingredient: *mushroom ketchup*. (*See* Finishing Touches.)

INGREDIENTS:

8 fresh haddock heads, cleaned & washed

2 cups water
2 carrots, sliced
1 cup turnip, chopped
2 celery ribs, chopped
1 onion, chopped
4 sprigs parsley
2 T. flour
2 T. butter
2 cups milk
Pinch of thyme
3 T. mushroom ketchup (optional)
1 egg yolk
3 oz. cream
Salt & pepper, to taste
Parsley, for garnish

IN YOUR KETTLE, make a fresh stock with the haddock heads and water. Cover and bring to the boil.

Skim the surface of the water, then add the carrots, turnip, celery, onions, and sprigs of parsley. Cover and simmer for 20 minutes.

Strain the stock through a colander into a heatproof bowl. Discard the fish heads and vegetables.

Return the stock to the kettle and allow to simmer.

Meanwhile, in a small saucepan make a white roux from the flour and butter.

Gradually stir the roux into the kettle until all has been added. Cover and bring to the boil.

Reduce the heat, then add the milk, thyme, chopped parsley and mushroom ketchup. Allow to simmer.

In a small bowl, make a liaison with the egg yolk and cream. Blend this into the soup, but do not allow it return to the boil.

Stir, taste and adjust the seasonings with salt & pepper.

Ladle into individual heated bowls.

Garnish with chopped parsley.

Cullen Skink

STONEHAVEN, SCOTLAND

For more than 300 years, the villagers of Findon and Boddam along Scotland's Aberdeenshire coast have preserved their meats by drying them in the smoke of their highland peat. Thus was developed the lightly smoked haddock that's known as *Finnan Haddie*. *Skink*, on the other hand, is a word that the old Scots called their broth. This is one kettle of fish which will not accept substitute ingredients well.

INGREDIENTS:
1 Finnan haddock, skinned

4 cups boiling water
1 onion, chopped fine
1 cup milk
1/4 cup mashed potato
1/4 cup cream
1 T. butter
Salt & pepper, to taste
Parsley, garnish

IN YOUR KETTLE, cover the haddock with boiling water, then bring to the boil.

Add the onion, cover, and simmer until the fish is softened.

Remove the haddock to a clean plate and remove all bones.

Return the bones to the kettle and simmer for 1 hour.

Meanwhile, flake the haddock.

When the hour is up, strain the stock through a sieve into a heatproof bowl. Discard the solids.

Return the stock to the kettle, cover, and bring to the boil.

Meanwhile, in a separate saucepan carefully bring the milk to the boil.

Add the flaked fish and heated milk to the kettle, along with the mashed potato, cream, and butter.

Stir, taste, and adjust the seasonings with salt & pepper.

Simmer until heated through.

Ladle into individual heated bowls.

Garnish with parsley.

Cream of Herring Soup
KIRKCUDBRIGHT, SCOTLAND

More often than not, most people think of this fish as one that is only pickled or smoked. Because of the high fat content among some species, herring do lend themselves well to those processes, and smaller herring are often marketed as sardines. Fresh herring, on the other hand, do have a very delicate flavor that works well in a kettle of fish.

INGREDIENTS:

12 oz. herring fillets

1 onion, sliced fine
2 T. oil
2 T. oatmeal
2 1/2 cups stock
2 bay leaves
Salt & pepper
2/3 cup light cream

IN YOUR KETTLE, heat the oil, then sauté the onion for 4 minutes.

Add the oats and stir well.

Add the stock, bay leaves, and herring, then bring to the boil. Reduce the heat and simmer for 30 minutes.

Ladle the soup into a blender and purée in batches until thick and smooth. Stop the blender and stir each batch to be certain that there are no bones that have not been adequately blended in the process.

Return the blended soup to the kettle, then add the cream and bring to the simmer.

Stir, taste, and adjust the seasonings with salt & pepper.

Ladle into individual heated bowls.

Kipper Soup
LYME REGIS, ENGLAND

A favorite breakfast dish in England, kippers are generally herring smoked to a golden brown from the wood carefully chosen for the curing; however, it is possible to *kipper* other fish, such as halibut, salmon, or trout. The process involves dressing, salting, drying and smoking the fish. If the fish is heavily smoked, then it may need to be *jugged* (soaked in boiling water for a few minutes) before it is cooked in a recipe.

IN YOUR KETTLE, bring the water to the boil.

Remove the kettle from the heat, then add the kippers and jug them for 5 minutes.

Remove and reserve the kippers on a paper towel. Drain and discard all but 2 cups of the broth.

Return the reserved broth to the kettle, along with the skim milk, and bring to the simmer.

Meanwhile, skin the kippers and flake them, then place them in a blender. Add the tomatoes, garlic, and tomato paste, then blend until smooth.

Stir the blended mixture of kippers, garlic, and tomatoes into the kettle, then simmer for 5 minutes.

Stir, taste, and adjust the seasonings with black pepper.

Ladle into individual heated bowls.

Garnish each with a swirl of yogurt.

INGREDIENTS:

12 oz. kipper fillets

4 cups stock
2½ cups canned tomatoes, with juices
1 garlic clove, crushed
2 T. tomato paste
1 cup skim milk
Black pepper, to taste
1/2 cup yogurt, for garnish

Fish Chowder

YAIZU, JAPAN

This *Shiromi-zakana no Shiru* is closer to an occidental consommé than to a soup, but its rich taste belies the simplicity of its ingredients.

If nothing else, this provides you with a good excuse to invest in a mortar & pestle. Inexpensive as they are, these timeless kitchen utensils have been forsaken by many in favor of food processors and blenders. In cases such as this, though, you'll discover that using anything other than a mortar & pestle (or a Japanese *suribachi* and *surikogi*) will produce a gummier texture than you want.

INGREDIENTS:
4 oz. whitefish fillets

5 cups stock
1 egg white
1 t. light soy sauce
1/2 t. salt
2 cups *bok choy* leaves, washed & minced

IN YOUR KETTLE, bring the stock to the boil.

Use a mortar & pestle to pulverize the fish. When the fish is nearly powdered, stir in the egg white, then add 2/3 cup of the soup stock. Season with salt and soy sauce.

Stir the fish mixture into the boiling kettle, then add the *bok choy*.

Allow to boil 1 more minute.

Ladle into individual heated bowls.

Fresh Sardine Soup

KITHIRA, GREECE

What a shame it is that many associate this fish with that flat little rectangular can that must be opened with a key, for Mediterranean gourmets have long made the most of sardines fresh from the sea. In the Provence of France, in fact, they have long remained an essential ingredient to a *bouillabaisse*, which had its own origins in the Greek *kakavia*. (*See* Cooking with a Variety of Seafood.)

This species takes its name from the Mediterranean island of Sardinia, off the west coast of Italy, where centuries of fishermen have brought them ashore by the tons. If your own fish market cannot provide you with fresh sardines, you could substitute small herring or smelt.

IN YOUR KETTLE, heat the oil and sauté the onion for 3 minutes.

Stir in the tomatoes and water, then cook another minute or so.

Cover and simmer for 30 minutes.

Meanwhile, wash the sardines and allow to drain.

After the kettle has simmered, add the fish and simmer until the sardines have cooked to a pulp.

Strain the soup through a sieve into a heatproof bowl. Use the back of a ladle to force the pulp through. Return the soup to the kettle.

Stir, taste, and adjust the seasonings with salt & pepper.

Simmer another 5 minutes.

Ladle into individual heated bowls.

Garnish with croutons.

INGREDIENTS:

16 oz. small sardines, dressed

1/4 cup olive oil
1 onion, chopped
1 cup canned tomatoes, with juices
Salt & pepper, to taste
4 cups water
Croutons, for garnish

Aunt Cilla's Boatmen's Stew

ONSET ISLAND, MASSACHUSETTS

At the head of Buzzards Bay, just east of the Cape Cod Canal, sits tiny Onset Island with its colony of summer cottages. Accessible only by boat, the island still holds fast to the best of traditions. Among those is a reliance upon the finfish and shellfish from the surrounding waters. This recipe reflects the bounty of the bay.

INGREDIENTS:

24 oz. whitefish fillets, in 1-inch pieces

1/3 cup olive oil
2 large onions, chopped
1/3 cup parsley
4 fresh tomatoes, peeled, seeded & chopped
1 t. red pepper flakes, crushed
1/2 t. salt
1 cup water
1/2 cup dry white wine

IN YOUR KETTLE, heat the olive oil, then sauté the onion for 5 minutes.

Add the parsley, tomatoes, red pepper flakes, water, and wine, then bring to the simmer for 30 minutes.

Stir, taste, and adjust the seasonings with salt.

Add the fish to the kettle and simmer until fish begins to flake..

Ladle into individual heated bowls.

Fish Chowder

KODIAK, ALASKA

When this recipe was passed along to me, it came with the expressed explanation that this recipe from Alaska was not a dish of native Eskimos. Though the elbow macaroni among the ingredients was an immediate indication of that, I had to be reminded (if not taught) that the climate of Alaska's indigenous peoples was far too cold for any edible vegetation. And though we might not recognize it as a *chowder*, this is most certainly a kettle of fish.

IN YOUR KETTLE, render the bacon until crisp and brown.

Add the onion and sauté for 10 minutes.

Add 1 cup of water and bring to the boil.

Reduce the heat, then add the fish and the macaroni.

Stir, taste, and adjust seasonings with salt.

Simmer until the macaroni is cooked.

Add remaining water and bring to the boil.

Ladle into individual heated bowls.

INGREDIENTS:

16 oz. whitefish fillets, in 1-inch pieces

4 strips bacon, diced
1 onion, diced
1/2 cup elbow macaroni
4 cups water
Salt to taste

Easter Stew

OMETEPEC, MEXICO

On the one hand, this kettle of fish is much like the "Marblehead Fish Chowder" in that it is made and cooked in layers. On the other, however, it has distinct religious roots.

Given the predominance of the Catholic religion in Mexican cities, Lent has long been observed by a strict abstinence from the eating of meat. In the outlying farming villages, though, the Christian holiday closely coincides with the start of the rainy season each spring, when many pagan rituals are still kept in mind. Among them is a belief that the rain gods might be pleased if the people served foods associated with water, such as fish. Thus, this Easter Stew has attained a national popularity.

INGREDIENTS:

4 whitefish fillets

1 onion, sliced in rings
1 green pepper, cut in strips
2 tomatoes, peeled, seeded, & sliced in circles
1/4 t. cinnamon
1/4 t. thyme, crushed
1/4 t. oregano, crsuhed
1/4 t. cumin seeds, crushed
1/4 t. rosemary, crushed
1/4 t. chili powder
Salt & pepper, to taste
1 cup olive oil
1 cup dry white wine
3 cups stock
Juice of 1/2 lemon
Pickled chili peppers, chopped for garnish
Green olives, sliced for garnish

IN YOUR KETTLE, arrange the fish fillets along the bottom. Cover them with the onion, green peppers, and tomatoes.

Mix together the cinnamon, thyme, oregano, cumin seeds, rosemary, and chili powder with the olive oil, wine, lemon juice, and 1 cup of the stock. Pour this spice mixture over the layers.

Bring to the boil and simmer for 1 hour. Do not stir, but add 1 cup of stock at 15 minute intervals.

Ladle into individual heated bowls.

Garnish with pickled chili peppers and green olives.

Grouper Stew
ANDROS TOWN, ANDROS ISLAND, THE BAHAMAS

Much like the spice mixture that covers the Easter Stew of Mexico, there is a spicy sauce that covers the layers of this stew from the largest island in the Bahamas.

To make the sauce:

IN YOUR KETTLE, render the salt pork until crisp and brown.

Remove and discard the browned salt pork, as well as all but 2 T. of the drippings.

Add the onion and sauté 10 minutes.

Stir in the tomatoes, tomato paste, ketchup, chili sauce, Worcestershire, Tabasco, thyme, bay leaf and lime juice., then simmer 10 minutes.

Stir, taste, and adjust the seasonings with salt & pepper.

To make the kettle of fish:

IN YOUR KETTLE, place a layer of fish, a layer of potato slices, a layer of peppers, a layer of crackers, then a layer of the sauce.

Add enough stock so that it covers about an inch above the layers of ingredients. More will be added as the chowder cooks.

Cover and bring to the simmer for 2 hours. Do not stir, but check frequently to maintain the stock level.

During the final 15 minutes, add the white wine.

Ladle into individual bowls.

INGREDIENTS:

24 oz. grouper, sea bass, red snapper, in 1-inch pieces

The Sauce:

6 oz. salt pork, in 1/4-inch cubes
1 onion, diced
1 potato, sliced thin
3 tomatoes, peeled, seeded & chopped
3 t. tomato paste
1/3 cup ketchup
1/3 cup chili sauce
1½ t. Worcestershire sauce
1/4 t. Tabasco sauce
1/2 t. thyme
1 bay leaf
Juice of 1/2 lime
Salt & pepper, to taste

The Kettle of Fish:

6 potatoes, peeled & sliced thin
2 green bell peppers, sliced in rings
6 oz. unsalted crackers
4 cups stock
3/4 cup dry white wine

Walleye Chowder
IROQUOIS FALLS, QUEBEC

A member of the perch family, the largest of this species is the walleye, which can weigh upwards to 20 pounds. The perch itself has long been called the finest of freshwater fish, and the savory *John Dory*, as well as the *St. Pierre*, are held in high esteem among Europeans. In this province, those feelings are reserved for the walleye.

INGREDIENTS:

24 oz. walleye fillets, skinned & in
  1-inch cubes
Fish frame & trimmings

2 oz. salt pork
1 onion, chopped
2 potatoes, peeled & chopped
1 celery rib, chopped
2 carrots, peeled & chopped
1/2 green pepper, chopped
1 bay leaf
8 cups stock
1 cup evaporated milk
Salt & pepper, to taste

IN YOUR KETTLE, render the salt pork until crisp and brown.

Remove and discard the brown pieces.

Add the onion and sauté 5 minutes.

Stir in the potatoes, celery, carrots, green pepper, and bay leaf, then bring to the simmer for 3 minutes.

Meanwhile, tie the frame & trimmings in cheesecloth and place in the kettle.

Add the stock and bring to the boil.

Reduce the heat and simmer for 20 minutes.

Stir in the fish, then simmer until the fish will flake with a fork.

Remove and discard the fish frame & trimmings.

Stir in the evaporated milk and simmer for 5 minutes.

Ladle into individual heated bowls.

Brown Trout Stew

GREAT FALLS, MONTANA

Until the later 1880s, this species of fish remained a native trout of European streams, as well as colder waters as far north as Norway and Siberia. At that time, though they were brought to the United States, where they now thrive in the larger lakes across the upper part of the nation. Later they were introduced to the waters of Africa, New Zealand, and South America. And while most non-fishing cooks think that freshwater fish are only cooked over an open campfire, they will be pleased to find that they also make a fine kettle of fish.

IN YOUR KETTLE, render the bacon until brown and crisp.

Remove the browned slices to a paper towel. Remove and discard all but 2 T. of the drippings, then sauté the onions, celery, green pepper, and leeks about 3 minutes.

Add the garlic and sauté 2 minutes more.

Stir in the potatoes, stock, parsley, thyme, pepper, bay leaf, Worcestershire, mustard, and tomatoes, then bring to the simmer for 15 minutes.

When the potatoes are fork tender, remove the kettle from the heat and add the fish. Allow to stand for 5 minutes.

Remove the bay leaf.

Ladle into individual heated bowls.

INGREDIENTS:
12 oz. trout fillets, in 1-inch pieces

2 slices bacon
1/2 onion, diced
2 celery ribs, diced
1/2 green pepper, chopped
1/2 leek, sliced
1 garlic clove, minced
1 large potato, diced
4 cups, fish stock
1 t. thyme, crushed
1/4 t. black pepper
1 bay leaf
1 t. Worcestershire sauce
1 t. dry mustard
2 tomatoes, peeled, seeded & diced
1 T. parsley, chopped

Burbot Stew

GLEN LYON, PENNSYLVANIA

Though you might know nothing about the freshwater cod known as *burbot, ling,* or *cusk,* this recipe provides the perfect opportunity for you to use this or any other underutilized fish. More often than not, your fishmonger has something similar on hand, or else there might be a tray of trimmed chowder fish in the display case.

If you know nothing else of this or the other obscure species, you'll soon discover that they complement the other distinct flavors in this recipe.

INGREDIENTS:

16 oz. chowder fish, in 1-inch pieces

2 T. olive oil
1 red onion, chopped coarse
1 garlic clove, minced
4 plum tomatoes, peeled, seeded & chopped
8 red potatoes, in cubes
6 cups stock
8 oz. fresh green beans, in 1/4-inch pieces
4 T. oregano leaves, chopped
Salt & pepper, to taste

IN YOUR KETTLE, heat the oil, then sauté the red onion for 5 minutes.

Stir in the garlic and tomatoes, then simmer for 1 minute.

Add the potatoes, green beans, and stock, then bring to a boil.

Reduce the heat and simmer until the potatoes are fork tender.

Stir in the fish, then simmer 5 minutes.

Add the oregano to the kettle.

Stir, taste, and adjust the seasonings with salt & pepper.

Ladle into individual heated bowls.

Rockfish Muddle

MURFREESBORO, NORTH CAROLINA

While the Pacific rockfish that run from Alaska down to the Baja Peninsula have mild flesh that is often mistaken for cod, it is *not at all* the same as the fish that goes by this name in the Atlantic. In fact, those of us north of New Jersey know this prized catch as the striped bass. In recent years, stripers have been overfished in these waters and strict size limits have been imposed upon each catch. Many a spring morning has been spent along the revetments of the Cape Cod Canal awaiting the slack tide of dawn or dusk in hopes of catching a "keeper." Still, it remains a trophy that has eluded us, at times for want of another half-inch or so in length.

That frustration aside, I just love any kettle of fish that's called a *muddle*, because I know that the recipe has been concocted from the heart and soul of a region, rather than from some fancy kitchen.

INGREDIENTS:

32 oz. rockfish, dressed

6 cups water
12 oz. salt pork, 1/2 cubes
3 onions, chopped
2 cups canned tomatoes, with juices
8 oz. crackers, crumbled
14 eggs, beaten well
6 T. butter
Salt & black pepper, to taste
Red pepper flakes, crushed

IN YOUR KETTLE, place the dressed fish in water, then cover and bring to the boil until the fish begins to flake.

Remove the kettle from the heat and strain the broth through a sieve into a heatproof bowl.

Remove and discard the bones and reserve the meat.

Wipe clean your kettle and render the salt pork until crisp and brown.

Remove and reserve the cracklings, then discard all but 2 T. of the drippings.

Add the onions to the kettle and sauté for 3 minutes.

Return the fish, cracklings, and reserved broth to the kettle , along with the tomatoes and their juices, then simmer 30 minutes.

Stir, taste, and adjust the seasonings with salt & pepper.

Meanwhile, in a large bowl beat together the eggs, then stir them into the kettle, along with the crumbled crackers.

Simmer for 5 minutes.

Stir in the butter and simmer until completely melted.

Stir, taste, and adjust the seasonings with red pepper.

Ladle into individual heated bowls.

Fish Chowder

FUNCHAL, MADEIRA ISLAND, PORTUGAL

A rustic kettle of fish from the Portuguese archipelago due west of Casablanca, this recipe is ideal for using fresh bits of chowder fish from your fishmonger's case, or even whatever variety of trimmings you might have saved in your freezer. If possible, try to mix meats of different moistness and texture. An essential ingredient, though, is the hearty wine from this area that bears the same name.

INGREDIENTS:

8 oz. white fish fillets
8 oz. dark fish fillets

3 t. butter
3 t. olive oil
2 yellow onions, sliced thin
2 garlic cloves, minced
1 bay leaf
1/4 cup dry Madeira wine
2 tomatoes, peeled, seeded & diced
2 potatoes, peeled & cut 1/4-inch cubes
1 T. parsley, minced
2 cloves
Dash cayenne pepper
6 cups water
Salt, to taste

IN YOUR KETTLE, heat the butter and olive oil, then sauté the onions and garlic for 15 minutes.

Stir in the bay leaf, wine, tomatoes, potatoes, parsley, cloves, cayenne, and water, then cover and simmer for 1 hour.

Remove the cover, stir, and simmer about 2 more hours until the stock has reduced about 1/3.

Stir the fish into the kettle and simmer 5 more minutes.

Remove and discard the bay leaf.

Stir, taste, and adjust the seasonings with salt & cayenne pepper.

Ladle into individual heated bowls.

Louisiana Court Bouillon

LAKE CHARLES, LOUISIANA

Time and time again, you'll come across a similar cautionary note in most cookbooks about seafood or soups: this Creole kettle of fish should not be confused with the vegetable broth of a similar name, *court bouillon*. (*See* Cooking Liquids.)

Though the latter is often used as a poaching liquid for fish, this rich stew made with true red snapper is a national treasure. In fact, the meat from the throat section of this fish has a flavor so rich and delicate that it is often prized over that of the rest of the body. Because several species of fish, however, are marketed as "red snapper," the only way to guarantee its true identity is to view the fish as a whole. And purchase it whole if you are able. Should you only use the fillet in this kettle of fish, remember to use the head (with its precious throat pieces) to prepare a rich stock.

IN YOUR KETTLE, make a light roux by combining the flour and oil over medium heat. Stir constantly to prevent burning. The longer you allow this to cook, the darker it will become.

Add the butter to the kettle and stir until it is incorporated into the roux.

Stir in the onions, celery, garlic, and red pepper, then add the tomato paste.

Slowly stir in the water to avoid lumps.

Add the wine, Worcestershire sauce, sliced lemon, parsley, and bay leaf.

Stir, taste, and adjust the seasonings with salt & pepper.

Simmer uncovered for 30 minutes.

Add the fish and cook until the fish flakes at the touch of a fork.

Ladle into individual heated bowls.

INGREDIENTS:

16 oz. red snapper fillets, in 1-inch pieces

1/2 cup flour
1/4 cup olive oil
1/4 cup butter
4 onions, chopped
2 celery ribs, chopped
2 garlic cloves, chopped
1 sweet red pepper, seeded & chopped
6 oz. tomato paste
3 cups boiling water
1 cup red wine
2 t. Worcestershire
1/2 lemon, sliced
4 parsley sprigs
1 bay leaf
Salt & pepper, to taste

Pike Soup
KANAZAWA, JAPAN

Though the northern pike is a freshwater favorite of many throughout the northern United States and Canada, the firm, dry meat of the black spotted pike found in Asia is the one of choice for this kettle of fish. Also known as the Amur, the species was introduced to the waters of Pennsylvania in the 1960s, but there was not much success in its breeding. Consequently, you'll probably be using a North American pike or pickerel.

Meanwhile, two versions of this kettle of fish follow. The first is a delightful sweet and sour recipe made with pickled mustard greens; the second, a less spicy recipe made with lettuce.

Seun Choy Yee Tong

INGREDIENTS:
8 oz. pike fillets, sliced thin

6 cups stock
Salt, to taste
24 oz. pickled mustard greens (*seun gai choy*), rinsed & shredded
2 T. sugar
1/2 t. sesame oil

IN YOUR KETTLE, add the stock and bring to the boil.

Stir, taste, and adjust the seasonings with salt.

Add the sesame oil and mustard greens. Stir until the leaves of the greens separate.

Remove the kettle from the heat.

Add the fish, stir, and cover.

Allow this to stand for 3 minutes.

Ladle into individual bowls.

Shaang Choy Yee P'in Tong

INGREDIENTS:
8 oz. pike fillets, sliced thin

6 cups stock
Salt, to taste
1 head iceburg lettuce, cored & quartered
3-4 drops sesame oil

IN YOUR KETTLE, add the stock and bring to the boil.

Stir, taste, and adjust the seasonings with salt.

Add the sesame oil and lettuce. Stir until the leaves of the lettuce separate.

Remove the kettle from the heat.

Add the fish, stir, and cover.

Allow this to stand for 3 minutes.

Ladle into individual bowls.

Fish Stew

HONG KONG, CHINA

All too often, people quickly associate garlic with Italian cuisine; however, if given a moment more to think, they'll remember that it is tasted in Mediterranean dishes, as well as those from Europe, the United States, and even southern China. In fact, the garlic used in many Chinese recipes has an added pungency from the smoking used to preserve the heads.

Before beginning the stew, prepare a marinade in a large bowl by combining the light soy, rice wine, ginger, and cornstarch. Place the pieces of fish in the bowl and cover thoroughly with the marinade. Allow this to stand for 30 minutes.

IN YOUR KETTLE, heat the oil over high heat, then carefully add the pieces of fish. Fry until crisp and brown on each side.

Remove the fish and reserve on a paper towel.

Drain and discard all but 2 T. of the oil from the kettle.

Return the kettle to medium heat, then sauté the garlic, shallots, black beans, rice wine, and scallions for 2 minutes.

Stir in the soy sauce, stock, and sugar, then cover and bring to the boil.

Add the pieces of fish to the kettle and gradually stir.

Reduce the heat, cover, and simmer for 3 minutes.

Ladle into individual bowls.

INGREDIENTS:

16 oz. whitefish fillets, in 1-inch pieces

The Marinade:
2 t. light soy sauce
2 t. rice wine
1 T. ginger, minced
1 ½ T. cornstarch

The Kettle of Fish:
1/2 cup peanut oil
8 garlic cloves, peeled & chopped
8 shallots, peeled & chopped
2 T. fermented black beans
2 T. rice wine
4 scallions (whole), chopped
2 T. dark soy sauce
4 cups stock
2 t. sugar

Catfish Chowder

PASCAGOULA, MISSISSIPPI

Most of the catfish found these days in fish markets is farm-raised, and much of that from more than 100,000 acres of Mississippi devoted to catfish aquaculture alone. But it might surprise you to learn that the family of catfish not only has both freshwater and saltwater species, but is found in waters from the Great Lakes to the Gulf of Mexico. In fact, there are more species in South America (not to be confused with the North American "South") than anyplace else in the world.

If you have never tasted this southern staple, you'll be delighted to find the firm, moist flesh of this freshwater fish is just a little stronger than that of the saltwater flounder, but much more delicate than a saltwater bass. Just keep in mind that some catfish do have a meat that is darker than others.

INGREDIENTS:

24 oz. catfish fillets, in 1½-inch pieces

4 cups stock
1 onion, minced
2 potatoes, peeled & diced
1½ cups canned tomatoes, with juices
1 T. tomato paste
1 cup cream
Salt & pepper, to taste
1 T. lemon juice
2 T. chopped parsley, for garnish

IN YOUR KETTLE, add the stock and bring to the boil.

Add the onion, potatoes, tomatoes, and tomato paste, then simmer until the potatoes are fork tender.

Add the fish and simmer for another 5 minutes.

Stir in the cream, taste, and adjust the seasonings with salt & pepper.

Simmer for 3 more minutes, then remove from heat and add the lemon juice.

Ladle into individual heated bowls.

Garnish with parsley.

Catfish Stew

KINGSTREE, SOUTH CAROLINA

If you've kept some stock in your freezer, this kettle of fish will prove to be one of the easiest and quickest to bring together. Though it is made here with one of the South's most treasured natural resources, the recipe can utilize any chowder fish you prefer.

IN YOUR KETTLE, render the bacon until crisp and brown.

Drain and discard all but 2 T. of the fat, then sauté the onions for 5 minutes.

Stir in the condensed soup and stock, then bring to the boil.

Add the catfish to the kettle, reduce the heat, and simmer for 15 minutes.

Add the catsup.

Stir, taste, and adjust the seasonings with salt & pepper.

Simmer 5 more minutes.

Ladle into individual heated bowls.

INGREDIENTS:
24 oz. catfish fillets, in 1-inch pieces

6 oz. bacon, diced
3 onions, chopped
1 can cream of tomato soup, condensed
4 cups stock
1 cup catsup
Salt & pepper, to taste

Catfish Stew

HICKORY, NORTH CAROLINA

This recipe has a different twist for thickening the stock: eggs. Before you begin to think twice about that, give it a try.

INGREDIENTS:

24 oz. catfish fillets, in 1-inch pieces

4 oz. salt pork, cubed
1 cup flour
1 T. salt
1 T. black pepper
2 potatoes, peeled & cubed
2 cups stock
1 onion, chopped
3 eggs
1 cup evaporated milk
1 cup cream
Salt & pepper, to taste

IN YOUR KETTLE, render the salt pork until crisp and brown.

Remove and reserve the pork cracklings, then discard all by 2 T. of the drippings.

Meanwhile, on a clean plate mix together the flour, salt & pepper. Dredge the catfish pieces in the seasoned flour, then brown the fish in the bacon drippings.

Add the potatoes, stock, and onion, then bring to the boil.

Reduce the heat and simmer until potatoes are fork tender. Stir often.

Meanwhile, in a small bowl beat together the eggs, milk, and cream.

When the potatoes are fork tender, stir the beaten egg mixture into the kettle and blend well.

Ladle into individual heated bowls.

Garnish with the cracklings.

Catfish Stew

MOREAU CITY, LOUISIANA

The variable in this kettle of fish is not so much the fish, but the smoked meat you select for the other ingredient. Anything from bacon to scrapple to andouille sausage is possible, but don't forget that some smoked meats can overwhelm the flavor of the kettle. With that in mind, you might wish to adjust the amount of meat.

IN YOUR KETTLE, add the fish fillets, stock and onions, then cover and bring to the simmer for 10 minutes.

Meanwhile, in a small skillet render the meat until crisp and brown.

Drain the rendered fat from the skillet into the kettle and mix together with the fish and onions.

Stir in the chopped eggs and the butter, then simmer for 5 minutes.

Add the evaporated milk.

Stir, taste, and adjust the seasonings with salt & pepper.

Simmer another 5 minutes.

Ladle into individual heated bowls.

Garnish with browned side meat.

INGREDIENTS:

24 oz. catfish fillets

6 cups stock
4 onions, chopped
8 oz. smoked meat, in 1/2-inch cubes
6 hardboiled eggs, chopped
4 T. butter
1 cup evaporated milk
Salt & pepper, to taste

Bourride

SÈTE, FRANCE

A kettle of fish more closely associated with the Provence than other regions, this much like a fabled *bouillabaise* made with a single type of fish. Usually that fish is a smaller member of the flounder family; however, it can be made with the larger *plaice* found in the waters off northern Europe. Regardless of the species you select, keep in mind that the fillets of these flatfish are not only white, but also delicate, and they should not be overcooked.

INGREDIENTS:
8 oz. whitefish fillets

8 cups stock
1 cup dry white wine
2 leeks (white only), washed & sliced
1 onion, sliced
1 carrot, peeled & sliced
1 fennel bulb, sliced
1 thyme sprig, in cheesecloth
2 T. orange zest, in cheesecloth
Salt & pepper, to taste
2 t. *aïoli*
1 egg yolk
1 T. heavy cream
4 croutons
4 T. *aïoli*, for garnish

IN YOUR KETTLE, combine the stock and wine with the leeks, onion, carrot, and the fennel, along with thyme and orange zest tied in cheesecloth. Bring to the boil, then reduce the heat and simmer for 15 minutes.

Remove the kettle from the heat, then strain the stock through a sieve into a heatproof bowl and reserve.

Remove and discard the sachet of thyme and orange zest, but reserve the vegetables on a clean plate.

Return the stock to the kettle and bring to the simmer.

Add the fish fillets and poach until opaque. Remove the kettle from the heat.

Place a crouton in the bottom of each heated bowl, then remove and divide the fish among them.

Meanwhile, in a small bowl whisk together the *aïoli*, egg yolk, and cream, then add slowly to the kettle.

Return the kettle to the heat and stir until the stock comes to the low simmer and thickens to coat the spoon.

Divide the reserved vegetables among the bowls, then ladle the thickened stock upon them.

Garnish with *aïoli*. *(See* Finishing Touches.)

Bourride

GRUISSON, FRANCE

For those who think that wide-ranging variations of a recipe with the same name are simply a quirk of American thinking, compare this recipe from the Provence with that on the opposite page.

INGREDIENTS:

24 oz. whitefish fillets, skinned

4 cups water

16 oz. fresh spinach, cleaned, stemmed & torn

Salt

8 cups stock

2 T. olive oil

2 leeks (white & pale green), washed & chopped fine

2 cups *aïoli*

IN YOUR KETTLE, bring the water to the boil. Add the salt and spinach, then blanch for 2 minutes.

Drain the blanched spinach into a colander and discard the water. Squeeze any water from the spinach leaves and set them on a paper towel to further drain.

Wipe clean the kettle, then add the stock and bring to the simmer. Poach the fish for 10 minutes.

Meanwhile, in a small skillet heat the olive oil and sauté the leeks for 5 minutes.

Add the drained spinach to the skillet and sauté for 2 minutes.

Remove and distribute the leeks and spinach among individual heated bowls, then top with fish.

In a small bowl, whisk together 1 cup of the *aïoli* with 2 cups of the simmering stock. Return this mixture to the kettle and stir.

Ladle the stock among the individual heated bowls.

Garnish each with *aïoli*. *(See* Finishing Touches.*)*

Flounder Soup

VILLER-SUR-MER, FRANCE

The fillet of the flounder is also utilized in this kettle of fish; however, it does not require the gentle care that comes with maintaining each as a whole. In addition, the delicate flavor of the whitefish blends well with those brought forth in the spices.

INGREDIENTS:

12 oz. flounder fillets, in 1-inch pieces

1½ T. olive oil
1 t. garlic, minced
1 onion, minced
1 t. saffron, crumbled
1/2 t. thyme, chopped
2 dashes Tabasco
Salt & pepper, to taste
1/2 cup dry white wine
4 cups stock
2 T. tomato purée
1/2 t. fennel seed, crushed
2 T. Cognac
1 cup heavy cream

IN YOUR KETTLE, heat the oil, then sauté the garlic and onion for 3 minutes.

Stir in the saffron and thyme.

Add the flounder to the kettle, along with the Tabasco.

Stir, taste, and adjust the seasoning with salt & pepper.

Cook until the fish flakes at the touch of a fork.

Stir in the wine, stock, tomato purée, and fennel seed, then bring to the simmer for 15 minutes.

Add the Cognac and cream, stir, and simmer for another 10 minutes.

Ladle into individual heated bowls.

Porgy Chowder
IWAMI, JAPAN

Those of us who live along the northern corner of our Atlantic seaboard know this fish as a *scup*. Other parts of this coast, though, are very much familiar with a whole range porgies, including the firm and moist white flesh of the *jolthead*, which can be found in waters from Rhode Island down to Brazil.

The recipe for this kettle of fish, however, comes from a coastal town half a world away on the southern edge of the Sea of Japan.

IN YOUR KETTLE, cover the frame & trimmings with the *dashi* and bring to the simmer for 10 minutes.

Remove the kettle from the heat, then strain the *dashi* through a sieve into a heatproof bowl. Discard the solids and return the *dashi* to the kettle.

Add the fish, mushrooms, and tofu, then bring the kettle again to the boil.

Reduce the heat, add the lemon juice, and simmer for 10 minutes.

Stir in the vinegar, soy, and leek, then simmer 3 more minutes.

Ladle into individual heated bowls.

INGREDIENTS:

16 oz. porgies, dressed & in 1-inch pieces
Reserved frame & trimmings

4 cups *dashi*
4 mushrooms, sliced
12 oz. tofu, diced
Juice of 1/2 lemon
2 T. white vinegar
2 T. soy sauce
1 leek, sliced thin

Marlin Stew

COJÍMAR, CUBA

This tiny Cuban fishing village is the home of Gregorio Fuentes, the fisherman upon whom Hemingway based his protagonist in *The Old Man and the Sea*. And though I am not certain whether or not he ever enjoyed this particular kettle of fish, I do believe his tales of encounters with marlin "so big they dined on sailfish."

Of the various species of marlin that are found in the various warm and temperate waters of the world, only the blue marlin can be found in all of them. That includes the stream that flows from Cuba up past Cape Cod. The marlin's spactacular image as a fighting gamefish is something to behold, and I'd prefer that the marlin be kept in that sportsmen's category of catch-and-release: take the picture, then *let it go!* As a realist, though, I understand that there folks, such as Gregorio, whose own survival depends upon landing such a fish.

INGREDIENTS:
16 oz. marlin fillets, in 1-inch cubes

2 oz. bacon, cubed
1 onion, chopped
1 celery rib, chopped
1/2 green pepper, chopped
1 potato, cubed
3 tomatoes, peeled, seeded & diced
1 cup stock
1/2 cup rice, uncooked
Dash Worcestershire
Dash Tabasco
Salt & pepper, to taste
1 cup evaporated milk

IN YOUR KETTLE, render the bacon until crisp and brown.

Add the onion, then sauté for 5 minutes.

Add to the kettle the marlin, celery, green pepper, potato, tomatoes, stock, and rice, then bring to the simmer.

Stir, taste, and adjust the seasonings with Worcestershire, Tabasco, salt & pepper.

Simmer for 1½ hours.

Add the evaporated milk and stir.

Ladle into individual heated bowls.

Pompano Soup
TIMBIQUI, COLOMBIA

From the waters of Massachusetts down through the West Indies and onto Brazil, the warmer waters of the western Atlantic nurture the rich flavor of this tender whitefish that is also known as a *permit*. In truth, though, I don't personally know of anyone who has ever seen one in these parts, let alone *caught* one, and we tend to think of them more as a fish from southern waters. Off the coast of Colombia, they can catch them in the Caribbean and the Pacific.

This recipe comes from the western coastline, not far north of Ecuador. Unlike most others in this book, this calls for some cooking of the delicate fish outside of the kettle itself.

IN YOUR KETTLE, mix the garlic, pepper, onion, tomato, and spices into the stock, then bring to the boil.

Reduce the heat and simmer 15 minutes.

Meanwhile, in a small saucepan combine the lemon juice and water, then bring to the boil. Add the okra, reduce the heat, and simmer until tender.

Drain the okra and add to the kettle, along with the plantains and yams, then simmer for 1 hour.

Meanwhile, in a skillet melt the butter and sauté the pompano fillets. When they have become golden on each side, remove the fillets to a plate and cut them into pieces similar in size to those of the yams.

After the kettle has simmered for 1 hour, add the fish, tomato paste, and Worcestershire sauce.

Stir, taste, and adjust the seasonings with salt & pepper.

Simmer for another 30 minutes.

Ladle into individual heated bowls.

INGREDIENTS:

8 oz. pompano fillets

2 cloves garlic, chopped
1 hot pepper, seeded & chopped
1/8 t. cumin seed
1/8 t. allspice, ground
1 onion, minced
1 tomato, peeled, seeded & chopped
6 cups fish stock
Juice of 1/2 lemon
2 cups water
1½ cups okra, quartered
2 ripe plantains, peeled & diced
1/2 lb. yams, peeled & in 1-inch pieces
2 T. butter
3 t. tomato paste
1 t. Worcestershire sauce
Salt & pepper, to taste

85

Carp Roe Soup

EBENSEE, AUSTRIA

The unfertilized eggs of a fish, roe from some species is nothing less than a delicacy when it is presented as caviar. In others, though, it remains known as simply *roe*. Though this recipe calls for roe sets from the freshwater carp, it can also be used for the roe from the saltwater shad, bluefish, flounder, or mullet.

INGREDIENTS:

4 oz. carp roe

4 T. butter
2 cups celery, chopped
2 cups onion, chopped
2 cups carrot, chopped
2 T. flour
4 cups stock
I cup water
1/2 t. lemon juice
1/2 cup red wine
Salt, to taste
4 T. sour cream, garnish

IN YOUR KETTLE, melt 2 T. of the butter, then sauté the celery, onion, and carrot. When they have browned, remove and reserve on a clean plate.

Next, make a light brown roux by adding the remaining butter to the kettle, along with the flour. Stir constantly so that the flour cooks, but does not burn.

When the roux has become the color of peanut butter, add the vegetables and stir.

Slowly add the stock and continue to stir.

Allow this to simmer for 40 minutes.

Meanwhile, add the water to a small saucepan and simmer the roe for 20 minutes.

Using a slotted spoon, remove the roe and drain on paper towel. After it is dry, chop the roe into fine pieces.

Meanwhike, purée the stock and vegetables in a blender, then return them to the kettle and bring to the simmer.

Add the wine and chopped roe.

Stir, taste, and adjust the seasonings with salt.

Ladle into individual heated bowls.

Garnish each with a dollop of sour cream.

Bluefish Chowder
SOUTH YARMOUTH, CAPE COD, MASSACHUSETTS

Once the spring migration has brought the bluefish north in pursuit of the squid around Cape Cod, Nantucket & Martha's Vineyard, the fishing fun really begins. Some of my most enjoyable moments have been along the breakwater at the mouth of Bass River with a light rod and tackle. Generally, it's just catch-and-release, for I don't think that bluefish are the tastiest fish in the world. They must be dressed and washed immediately upon catching, otherwise they have a rather heavy taste to them. If, however, you are fortunate to be near a fishmonger who smokes the fresh catch, then you'll suddenly have a whole new taste before you.

Not quite a Cape & Islands version of Scotland's Cullen Skink, this is a kettle of fish that I've found to be making the bluefish an even worthier pursuit.

IN YOUR KETTLE, render the smoked bacon until crsip and brown.

Remove and reserve the bacon on a plate, then discard all but 2 T. of the drippings.

Add the onion to the kettle, then sauté for 5 minutes.

Add the potatoes and stock, then bring to the simmer until the potatoes are fork tender.

Add to the kettle the bluefish, corn, and parsley.

Stir, taste, and adjust the seasonings with salt & pepper.

Simmer for 10 minutes more.

Ladle into individual heated bowls.

Garnish each with reserved bacon.

INGREDIENTS:

8 oz. smoked bluefish, flaked

2 oz. smoked bacon, in 1/4-inch cubes
1 onion, diced fine
4 cups stock
2 potatoes, cubed
Salt & pepper, to taste
2 cups kernel corn
1/4 cup parsley, chopped

Eels

Contrary to popular opinion, an eel is *not* a snake. The former is a finfish; the latter, a reptile. In fact, eels have a spawning cycle that is even more fascinating than that of salmon or herring; however, I won't go into that here. Suffice it to say that the American eel is a catch of the western Atlantic from the St. Lawrence to the Chesapeake, and the European eel obviously comes from the eastern side of the ocean. Curious enough, neither species ever crosses the Atlantic to spawn in the waters of the other continent. Savored among Old World cooks, the eel has long been a Christmas dish, and its demand — even in the United States — is especially high during the holiday season.

The next (of even *first*) time that you find an opportunity to look at an eel, notice that it definitely has the head of a fish, as well as the fins.

How to Skin & Dress an Eel

Most folks that I know make a simple device for use in cleaning eels. It is nothing less that a 4-foot plank with a nail driven halfway into the board at one end. This provides a tying point, as well as a cutting board for the process.

1. Tightly tie a piece of string around the head of the eel, then tie the string to the nail.

2. Just behind the head, cut the skin around the body. Use a pair of pliers to grip the skin and strip it off much as you would a glove.

3. Cut off the head and slice open the length of the belly. Clean out the intestines and cut off the fins. Rinse thoroughly.

4. If you wish, you may cut fillets from either side of the back bone, or cut the meat into pieces.

Eel Stifle

EDGARTOWN, MARTHA'S VINEYARD, MASSACHUSETTS

The term *stifle* — which sometimes appears as *stiffle* — has been said to come from the concept of "smothering" the ingredients in this kettle of fish. In other places in this book, you'll see that the process is simply an earlier method of making a chowder.

Meanwhile, this very recipe has been related as a popular one on the Vineyard; however, it seems to have gone out of fashion in my own lifetime.

IN YOUR KETTLE, melt the butter over low heat.

Remove the kettle from the heat, then create a layer of potato slices along the bottom. Create a layer of onion slices, then a layer of eel.

Sprinkle flour and pepper atop the layer of eel, then a layer of salt pork.

Repeat the same layering process, then add enough stock to just cover all the layers.

Bring the kettle to the boil, then reduce the heat, cover, and simmer for until the potatoes are fork tender.

Ladle into individual heated bowls.

INGREDIENTS:

6 eels, skinned, dressed & in 3-inch pieces

6 potatoes, peeled & sliced
4 onions, sliced
4 T. Butter
I cup flour
Black pepper
8 oz. salt pork, diced
8 cups stock

Eel Soup

LOOE, ENGLAND

Originally a recipe from Olde England, this kettle of fish was also a seasonal standard in colonial New England, where it is said that the autumn run of eels was anticipated as eagerly as the apple harvest.

INGREDIENTS:
4 eels, skinned & dressed

3 T. butter
3 T. flour
5 cups stock
Bouquet garni
1 onion, sliced
8 peppercorns
1 blade of mace
Salt, to taste
1/2 cup cream

IN YOUR KETTLE, melt the butter, then sauté the eels. Cover and cook for 10 minutes, being careful not to let them brown. Remove the eels and keep them warm.

Gradually stir the flour into the kettle to make a roux.

Add the stock, *bouquet garni,* onion, peppercorns, and mace, then cover and bring to the simmer for 30 minutes.

Meanwhile, flake the eel meat off its bones and reserve on a clean plate.

Remove the kettle from the heat, then strain the stock through a sieve into a heatproof bowl. Discard the solids.

Return to the kettle the strained stock, along with the flaked eel meat and the cream, then bring to the simmer.

Stir, taste, and adjust the seasonings.

Simmer another 5 minutes.

Ladle into individual heated bowls.

Cooking with Shellfish

If you didn't have any difficulty understanding the term *finfish*, then I think that you'll understand *shellfish*. Very simply put, these fish have no backbone stucture, and so their body support comes from their shells. And much like the way that finfish can be simply divided into sub-categories of *roundfish* and *flatfish*, or *lean* fish and *oily* fish, shellfish can be quickly categorized into *mollusks*, *cephalopods*, and *crustaceans*.

The first of these groups of saltwater shellfish has two symmetrical shells, such as with clams, mussels, cockles, scallops, and oysters. The second group is a higher level of mollusks that has a head and eyes, as well as legs or tentacles, such as periwinkles, conch, squid, and octopus. The last group has a segmented body shell, as well as legs (and sometimes claws), that includes crabs, crawfish, shrimp, and lobsters.

In an attempt to keep things simple, recipes in this chapter will deal with ingredients that include the mollusks and cephalopods, then the next will be devoted to fine kettles of crustaceans.

Clams

There are very few people I know who don't use the word *clam* unless it is paired with the word *chowder*. And though there are species that range in size from the tiny bean clam, found along the intertidal zone, to the 500-pound *Tridacna gigas* that lives in the depths of the ocean, those of us who relish the clam think of it as either *softshell* (which has a "neck," as well as a "belly") or *hardshell* (which appears to have a "foot"). We steam the *softshell* variety and eat them with melted butter, but we devour the *hardshells* raw or else cook them in chowder. All that having been quickly noted, keep in mind that these recipes generally call for hardshell clams.

Throughout New England, you'll find us calling this clam by its American name of *quahog* (which is pronounced KO-hog and sometimes speall *quahaug*), but it can also be called other names, depending upon its size. The smallest ones are called *littlenecks;* the medium-sized, *cherrystones;* and the largest, *chowder* clams.

For the most part, recipes that call for hardshell clams will have them either cooked in their shells along with the the other ingredients, or else steamed open separately and chopped. In either case, the clams ought to have the outsides of their shells scrubbed well with fresh, running water to remove any sand, mud, or debris.

Occasionally, though, a recipe will call for *shucked* clams with their liquor reserved. The *liquor* is the succulent natural juice from inside the shellfish, as opposed to any liquid that results from cooking. In fact, whenever you do cook the shellfish directly with the other ingredients, this liquor automatically becomes part of the stock. In most instances, the reserved liquor is eventually added to the kettle anyway.

As for shucking a hardshell clam, this is a talent that is a bit easier than shucking the rough and reluctant oyster. There are 4 key aspects to this procedure: a strong clam knife, which is available in most culinary stores; a clean bowl in which to catch the liquor; a glove that can provide a good grip of the shell, as well as protect your hand from the knife; and a tray of crushed ice. If you place the hardshell clams undisturbed on the ice for a few minutes, they will relax a bit and provide just enough more of an opening between shells to make it easier to insert your knife.

How to Shuck a Clam

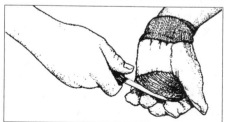
1. Keeping in mind that you don't want to startle the clam into closing its shell any tighter, take the clam in the palm of your gloved hand so that the hinge of its 2 shells fits snugly against the base of your thumb.

Insert the sharp edge of your knife into the groove between the 2 shells, then wrap the fingers of your gloved hand around the dull edge of the blade.

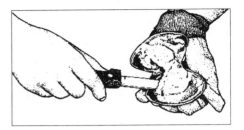

2. Carefully apply firm pressure with your gloved fingers to force the sharp edge of your knife through the groove and into the clam's shells.

Once the knife is inside, run the blade deeper around the perimeter to cut the muscles that hold the two shells together. If the clam should try to clamp down on your blade, a simple twist of the knife should be sufficient to open up the clam wide enough to see the muscles inside.

Remove the clam meat with the point of the knife or a fork.

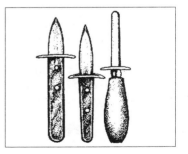

Clams and Quahaugs

JOSEPH C. LINCOLN

A New Yorker will tell you that there are two kinds of clams — hard and soft. The variety with the long, thin shell is a soft clam and that with the round, thick shell is a hard clam. The Cape Codder, however, will tell you nothing of the kind.

To him a clam is a clam and a quahaug is a quahaug. They are both shellfish — yes; but that does not prove anything. A hen and a canary are both feathered, but if you expect a hen to sing like a canary, you will be disappointed. And if you expect a quahaug soup with tomatoes in it to taste like a Cape Cod clam chowder, you will be even more so. Each of them may be good of its kind, but they are different kinds, that's all. You may call a clam a "sedge" or a "sea clam" or a "rundown," but he is a clam, just the same. And calling a quahaug a "Little Neck" or a "cherrystone" does not make him any the less a quahaug.

Yes, and there are other differences. For example, you dig clams and you rake quahaugs.

The distinction between the two is something that the Cape Cod child learns at his mother's knee — or at her table. He knows and therefore to him the carelessness of the outlander is surprising. Even more surprising is the indisputable fact that, in this world of ours, there are people who never saw a clam — would not recognize one if they met him on the flat at low tide.

In the course of years of story-telling I have occasionally — or semi-occasionally, anyhow — mentioned both clams and quahaugs. And, at various times, I have received letters from eager seekers for information. "Just what is the Cape Cod clam?" they want to know. "What does he look like? Does he really taste as good as you say he does?"

A correspondent from Australia sent a two-page letter not so long ago. He was really interested in clams, that Melbourne correspondent — "clam conscious" I suppose our Freudian friends might call him. They had shellfish in his part of the world that were sometimes called clams, but he was pretty certain that they were not our kind of clams.

He was right, they were not. He had drawn a picture of the Australian clam and the resemblance between it and our home-grown variety was faint. As I remember, judging by that picture, the clam who had posed for its portrait in the Antipodes was almost circular — not plumply round like a quahaug, either — but thinner, more anemic, if you know what I mean. And, too, if I remember correctly, the clam on our own Pacific coast is tiny, — about as big as a silver quarter. Delicious, though, if prepared by Monsieur Pierre in the little San Francisco restaurant where we made his acquaintance. It seems to me that he was not called a clam on the menu card; he had a more aristocratic name and his cost was more aristocratic also.

The dictionary — we infer that it was not compiled by a Cape Codder — says there are countless varieties of clams. It even mentions the "razor clam" among them. Now, every boy of our generation in our town knew that a "razor fish" was not a clam at all. He was not shaped like a clam. He was long and thin — he did have the look something like an old-fashioned razor with the blade closed into the handle — and he lived buried in the wet sand on the flats, a quarter of a mile or more from high-tide mark. He marked his home by the tiny ring, with a hole in the middle of it, in the sand above his head. He had made that ring by squirting water up through the hole. In that.respect he was like a clam, for clams squirt too — real clams, we mean, not quahaugs.

The Cape Cod boy's procedure with a razor fish was, and perliaps still is, simple and primitive. Having located him, he thrust his fingers into the sand and dug as rapidly as possible. Rapidity was essential for, unless one was very quick, the razor fish slid out from between his shells and downward; in which case, when the two shells were resurrected, their former occupant was no longer at home; he was at large and seeking lower levels.

But, if we were quick enough, we got him while at least a third of him was still in residence. After that, well, if you don't mind, we won't go into details.

I have known people who said that razor fish made a wonderful stew, as sweet and flavorsome as a scallop stew. I never tasted a stew made from the razor fish, but I do remember what he used to taste like. And, after all, everyone eats oysters and Little Necks *au natural*.

Our wide stretches of flats were habited by clams, thousands and thousands of them. At the inner edge, bordering the clumps of coarse beach grass, were the "sedge clams," the little fellows, tender and just right for a bake or a boil. Farther out were the "rundowns," the big chaps with their shells snowy white. Rundowns were best in a chowder. And, away out, along the outer bar, almost two miles from shore and only get-at-able when the tide was at full ebb, were the large "sea clams." Sea clams made the best clam pie.

To dig clams, as they should be dug, a clam hoe and a "dreener" are the proper equipment. The clam hoe, as of course almost everyone knows, differs from the garden hoe. To dig clams with a garden hoe is a rash and unprofitable adventure. The sharp edge of the blade cuts through the tender shells and, although you may get your clam, you are all too likely to get him in sections. I remember a neighborhood clam bake, presided over and superintended by a veteran Codder, where one of the guests, a city visitor, insisted on digging his own share and, as the clam hoes were all in use, he dug with an ordinary hoe. When he brought in his spoil, the veteran looked into the half-filled pail and sniffed.

"Say, Mr. Jones," he observed sadly, "it's too bad, but you've made a mistake in your figurin'. We wasn't cal'latin' for clam hash."

The Cape Cod clam hoe has three or four narrow and deep prongs instead of one shallow blade. Its handle, too, is short, not more than two or three feet long. You set the prongs into the sand at their full depth and then pull. The wet sand is heaped between your feet as you dig and, between hoefuls, you stoop and pick up the clams you have uncovered. By "stoop" I mean, of course, stoop lower, for you have been stooping all the time. Clam digging is a back-breaking business — for a greenhorn. An hour of it is enough to take the starch out of the most dignified backbone, and helps to add to a pious vocabulary.

The "dreener" is a sort of lath crate with a handle to carry it by. The clams, as they are dug, are deposited in it and, after digging, are washed by dipping the dreener and its contents into a pool of clean water. Moving the dreener up and down in the water rinses away the sand, or is supposed to.

The dreener was a drainer once, probably, but it has not been one for more than a century down on the Cape. It is a dreener, just as a Cape fisherman's barrel is a — a — I declare I don't know exactly how to tell you what it is. Something between a barrel and a "beerill" and a "burrill," but not precisely either. I could pronounce it for you but to save my life I cannot spell it adequately. There is a b-r-r-r in the middle of it that defies orthography.

Digging the rundowns is like digging for sedge clams, except that the digger works faster. And he gets fewer clams at a time. The results are worth the effort, however, for they — the clams — are often from three to four inches in length, fat — and, oh, so white and clean.

There is little real digging in a sea-clam hunt. These big, three-cornered fellows lie with their backs exposed or just beneath a clearly visible mound of sand. I never heard that sea clams were good for anything, as an edible, except, as stated before, in a clam pie. They are tough. The fish like them and they are gathered principally for bait.

The professional clam digger is usually an interesting chap. He knows his job; he doesn't make hash of his clams. I knew one old fellow who had dug and sold clams for forty years and, when he died at eighty-six, had dug his regular allotment only the week before. He was a tough old boy, physically strong and hard as nails, and proud of the fact. Proud of his digestion, too. The last time I met him he was boasting of the latter.

"There was a doctor fellow down here last summer," he said, "and he come into the shanty to see me. Wanted to know how old I was. When I told him he says, 'They tell me you can eat a piece of mince pie any time of night. Is that so?'

"'I can,' says 1, 'and when I feel like it, I do.'

"'And it don't bother you none afterwards?'

"'Neither afterwards nor then.' "He shook his head. 'I'm what they call a sort of specialist along eatin' lines,' he says, 'and you interest me. Would you mind if I sort of looked you over?'

"'Nary a mite,' says I, 'if you don't charge nothin' for doin' it. Heave aboard and look.'

"So he done it. Pawed me around and punched me alow and aloft and asked more 'n a million questions. When he got through he shook his head again.

"'Cal'late you've got the answer, do you?' I wanted to know.

"'Guess I've got the only one there is,' he says. 'I don't believe you've got any stomach. What you've got is a gizzard.'"

This old clam digger and his wife used to make and sell clam chowder to summer people. They provided chowder in any quantity on short notice for home consumption or for beach picnics. The wife died, several years before he did and, naturally, his former customers presumed that put an end to the chowder supply. But not a bit of it.

"Why, yes," he admitted dolefully, "she's gone . . . But," perking up, "that ain't no reason why you can't have your chowder. I can cook clams yet — I hope."

On the occasion when he told me the "gizzard" story, he finished the conversation with a laugh and a shrug.

"Oh, yes," he said, "they tell me I'm gettin' old and I presume likely I be. But," squaring his shoulders, "by gorry, I don't *feel* old."

And I think he was telling the truth. Forty years of clam digging and he still felt young! Why, one hour of it will make the average man feel that he is at least a hundred. I know that from personal experience.

The quahaug — please give him the local pronunciation *Ko-hog* — is not brought to the surface with a clam hoe. He must be raked for. If you are a casual, an amateur, quahauger, you may use a garden rake and go after him at low tide. He lies on the bottom, usually under a layer of seaweed and in at least a few inches of water. You rake the seaweed just as you would rake a lawn, lifting the rake after each stroke to pick the quahaugs from between its teeth. Then you put them into a bucket or dreener. Raking for quahaugs in this way is not as hard work as clam digging.

But if you are a professional — if you "go quahauging" regularly, to earn a living — you do work hard. Indeed you do. You may do it in two ways, the first a trifle easier than the second. The first way is to put on fisherman's boots, high rubber boots reaching above the hips and secured to your belt, and wade the submerged flats at the edges of the channels, raking as you go. And you use a regulation quahaug rake. Its teeth are much longer than those of an ordinary rake and are turned up at the ends, making the implement a sort of scoop. And, because a dreener would be a hindrance rather than an aid to this sort of work, you fasten a canvas or burlap bag, open end up, to your belt, and put your quahaugs into that. The bag is heavy and growing heavier all the time, the boots arc heavy, the rake anything but light, and the wading through the seaweed not easy. Does sound like hard work, doesn't it? Yes, but wait a moment. You have not been "deep quahauging" yet.

Deep quahauging is a comparatively recent innovation on the Cape — at least, I believe it is. Cape Codders have always raked quahaugs; no doubt the first settlers raked for them along the flats. But when we were youngsters, we never heard of anyone seeking them in deep water. To go quahauging in a boat would have been a town joke in our youth. But scores do that very thing now and do it daily.

There is a yarn to the effect that the idea originated like this: Someone was out in the bay — we were never told which bay — dredging for flounders. And, at one spot, the dredges brought up hundreds and hundreds of quahaugs, big ones. Flounders were scarce at the time and there was always a market for quahaugs. So this particular dredger marked the spot and returned to it next day and the days succeeding. Others, of course, followed his example and "deep quahauging" became a regular and profitable profession.

The deep quahauger goes out to the grounds in a motor-boat or skiff. There he anchors and begins to work. His rake is a toothed scoop, somewhat like that used by the wader, but bigger and heavier; sometimes it is weighted to make it heavier still. Its wooden handle is forty feet long and flexible. He throws the scooped end as far from the boat as he can, lets it sink to the bottom, and then draws it toward him and up to the boat, working the long handle backward over his shoulder in a series of jerks. When he gets it into the boat, he paws over the half bushel or so of mud and sand and seaweed, picks out his quahaugs, dumps the trash — "culch" he would call it — over the side and makes another cast. And he keeps on casting and jerking and sorting and dumping all day long, with a brief rest while he eats his lunch. He makes, so they say, a pretty fair wage, and I think he earns it.

If, in the summer, you are motoring by — well, let us say the upper end of Pleasant Bay, between Orleans and Chatham — and look out over the water toward the east, you will see a dozen or more boats anchored a mile or so out. The occupants of those boats are quahaugers, every one of them.

Seen from the shore, or even from a passing boat, one might consider deep quahauging in Pleasant Bay about as safe a semi-marine occupation as could be found. Ordinarily it is. The Bay is seldom very rough, land is not far distant, and the deep quahauger knows how to handle a boat. Hard work, very hard work, but perfectly safe.

And yet, a year or two ago, one of the occupants of those boats died while working, and it was because he was working that death came to him. He was a man in the thirties, married and the father of a good-sized family of young children.

His was one of a group of a dozen quahaug boats that summer afternoon. The forenoon had been clear and calm, but, about two o'clock, heavy clouds began rolling up from the western horizon. The quahaugers, weatherwise Capers all of them, knew what was coming — a thunderstorm, a "tempest," as we in Barnstable County term it. One by one they pulled in their rakes, hauled up their anchors and prepared to row to the beach. But "Bill" made no move. He kept on tossing out his rake and pulling it in again.

"Come on, Bill!" they shouted. "Can't you see we're goin' to have a tempest? Want to get soaked through, do you?"

Bill looked over his shoulder at them. "Nothin' but a shower," he said. "Be all over in half an hour. What's the matter with you fellows? Made of sugar and salt, are you? Little fresh water might do some of you good. Better stay on the job, I'd say."

They tried to persuade him to leave with them, but he was resolute.

"I've got a wife and five children to look out for," he declared. "I'm goin' to work for 'em while the workin's good."

So they rowed away and left him. On the shore, from the windows and door of one of the shanties, they watched the clouds spread across the sky, saw the flashes of lightning leap from cloud to cloud, and heard the thunder boom and rattle. The rain poured down. Out on the bay, in the midst of the deluge, they could see Bill working away, apparently not in the least disturbed by the "tempest."

And then came a blinding lightning flash and a thunderclap which seemed to burst at their very ears. They turned to look at each other and then they looked out over the Bay.

"Wonder how Bill liked that one?" asked somebody.

But Bill was not standing up in his boat. The boat was there, but he, apparently, was not. They ran to their own boats and rowed out. Bill was lying across the heap of quahaugs on the bottom of his skiff. He was dead. The lightning had struck the upper end of his long rake, as he held it over his shoulder, and had passed through his body. The self-sacrifice which had led him to brave a soaking for the sake of his wife and five children had brought death upon him.

In re-reading all this about clams and clam digging and quahaugs and quahaug raking — it does seem, I admit, to be unnecessary and superfluous. Everyone who lives on or habitually visits Cape Cod knows as much as I do about these things. But the publisher friend reminds me that there may be readers who have never dug a clam or raked a quahaug, have never even witnessed either process. This, to a 'longshore mind, does not seem possible, but it may be so. For their benefit, therefore, it shall stand and the sophisticated are at liberty to skip as much as they like.

At any rate there will be no more about gathering clams and quahaugs. I shall pass on to what, at my age, are far more attractive subjects — that is, cooking and eating them.

Let us not waste time with the young quahaug — the Little Neck or the "cherrystone." Everyone knows that he should be eaten raw and almost everyone must have so eaten him. The mature specimen, however, the hardened old veteran, is a different proposition. The only creatures that eat him raw and appear to enjoy the process are fish and seagulls. But a codfish will swallow a good-sized section of a "wrinkle" and come back for more. A "wrinkle" is the fisherman's name for a form of hardshelled conch, the flesh of which is about the consistency of the heel of a rubber boot. As for a gull, he will eat anything he can swallow, including a sculpin, or a hardshelled crab, or an oyster that died the previous winter, or a foot-long eel. He will try anything once — or, if necessary, twice.

A gull's procedure with a middle-aged quahaug is interesting. Even his iron beak cannot break throuch that armor-plate shell and he knows it. So, having secured his prey, he flies with it until he is over a rock or the planks of a wharf or the deck of an anchored boat — over something which, he figures, has the necessary power of resistance. Then he drops the quahaug and hovers, waiting hopefully for the smash. If the shell does not break the first time, he swoops, recaptures his victim, flies higher, and tries again. In the end he wins. Then he settles down to pick up his dinner from the ruins.

The full-grown quahaug, like the ancient clam digger before mentioned, toughens with age. After he has been put through a meat grinder, he does very well in a chowder, he is good in a stew and he makes a fair pie — if, in these degenerate days, you can still find the right person to make that kind of pie. But, even then — and certainly fellow Capers will agree with me — he is not one-two-three with the Cape Cod clam.

For a Cape Cod clam — the sea clam excepted — is sweet and tender. His flavor is more delicate than that of the quahaug. His shell is thin. He does not live in the mud — on the Cape he doesn't — but in clean sand and washed over by pure, clean water. And when you use him, as the basis of a chowder, or a bake, or steamed, as the beginning of a shore dinner, you have something worth gloating over.

I referred to letters from readers of my Cape Cod stories asking for information concerning clams. There have been many of them, but not nearly as many as there have been from anxious inquirers who ask to be told how to make a "genuine" Cape Cod clam chowder. Giving recipes is a risky business, anyway, and what pleases one's own palate is not, by any means, certain to please the other fellow's. And, besides, I am not writing a cookbook.

But, nevertheless, I am going to take the risk. Here is the recipe for a chowder which has pleased many. I do not guarantee satisfaction — but I expect it.

Take a quart of clams — Cape Cod clams, of course. Then —

But, no — wait a minute. I won't take the risk, after all. I might forget something, or omit something, or make a mistake somewhere, and then think of the letters I should get. Instead I shall follow my usual custom and shift responsibility.

If you happen to own a copy of the *Boston Cooking School Cook Book*, you will find in it a recipe for clam chowder which, if followed, makes as "genuine" a Cape Cod chowder, of the best kind, as any I know — and I have known many. Stick to that formula and use Cape clams and you ought to be happy.

You will notice that the recipe calls for eight common crackers. If you live in New England, you know what a "common cracker" is. About as big as the case of an old-fashioned silver watch — a man's watch — and about as thick. If you live, not in New England but near it, you may call it a "Boston" cracker. If you live too far away, you may not be able to find it in the stores. Then you may use the ordinary pilot cracker, but, in that case, you will not need as many — say, three.

Everyone, of course, puts crackers of some sort into a chowder, but they are so often put in by the — by the what do I want to say? Why, yes, by the consumer. The consumer breaks his crackers into the chowder after it is served. It is considered bad form, we have always been told, to break crackers into one's soup, but the rule does not hold with a chowder. The proper chowder must have crackers in it, sooner or later — or both.

Down on the Cape they are put in — some of them before the chowder is brought to the table. The common crackers are split in half, the halves are soaked in enough cold milk to moisten and, when the steaming plateful is set before you, there they are, floating on top. If they are missing — well, the chowder isn't orthodox, that's all . . .

Beside clams and quahaugs, there are other varieties of shellfish in the waters bordering the Cape. Cape Cod oysters are famous and Cape Cod scallops, although not perhaps as widely advertised, are the most delicious we know. To get the full flavor of a Cape scallop, it should be cooked and eaten just after it has been cut from the shell. If kept on ice for any appreciable length of time, or "swollen" by the addition of fresh water, it is not half as good. If you are down our way early in October, when the law is "off" on scallops, ask your hostess to give you scallops brochette or fried scallops or a scallop stew. Never ate a scallop stew? Then you should. You may take my word that the finest oyster stew ever made is tasteless compared with it . . .

— *from* CAPE COD YESTERDAYS

Quahaug Chowder

CUMMAQUID, CAPE COD, MASSACHUSETTS

Okay, so I still can't bring myself to call this a *clam* chowder. Though this is not the same recipe that Joe Lincoln refers to in his essay, it remains the genuine article.

INGREDIENTS:

24 hardshell clams, shucked & chopped (liquor reserved)

4 oz. salt pork, cubed
1 onion, chopped
2 cups stock
4 potatoes, peeled & diced
2 cups evaporated milk
8 crackers
2 cups cream
Salt & pepper, to taste
2 T. butter, for garnish

IN YOUR KETTLE, render the salt pork until crisp and brown, then remove and reserve the pieces.

Discard all but 2 T. of the drippings, then sauté the onion for 3 minutes.

Stir in the stock and bring to the simmer.

Add the potatoes and cook until they are fork tender.

Meanwhile, in a small bowl soak the crackers in the evaporated milk until they are soft, then stir in the cream, browned salt pork, chopped clams, and their juices.

When the potatoes have become fork tender, add the mixture from the bowl to the kettle.

Stir, taste, and adjust the seasonings with salt & pepper.

Add the butter and simmer until it has completely melted.

Ladle into individual heated bowls.

Clam Chowder

NEW BEDFORD, MASSACHUSETTS

Whether you taste this kettle of fish along the waterfront of this historic whaling port, just west of Cape Cod, or come upon it in any one of a handful of cozy eateries around the fishing town of Provincetown at the very tip of this peninsula, you'll savor this recipe from the Portuguese fishermen who have longed called both ports their home.

INGREDIENTS:

36 hardshell clams, scrubbed & in-shells

4 oz. linguica or chourice, diced
3 onions, sliced
3 garlic cloves, minced
6 cups stock
2 potatoes, diced
4 tomatoes, peeled, seeded & diced
1 T. parsley, chopped
1 T. red pepper flakes, crushed

IN YOUR KETTLE, render the sausage until crisp and brown, then remove and reserve the pieces.

Discard all but 2 T. of the drippings, then sauté the onion and garlic for 3 minutes.

Stir in the stock and bring to the simmer.

Add the potatoes and cook until they are fork tender.

Stir in the tomatoes, parsley, red pepper flakes, and clams, then cover and cook until all the clams have opened.

Remove and discard the shells with a pair tongs. In most cases, the meat of each clam will shake loose into the broth; however, you should remove the meats of a half dozen or so clams, chop them coarsely, and return them to the kettle.

Coax any clams that have not opened with a gentle pry from the point of a knife, then remove and discard any clams do not.

Stir, taste, and adjust the seasonings with crushed red pepper.

Add the butter and simmer until it has completely melted.

Ladle into individual heated bowls.

Caribbean Clam Soup
BRIDGETON, JAMAICA

Don't be frightened-off by the thought of something as sweet as coconut in this soup. The other ingredients go a long way in balancing the taste and degree of heat. In addition, don't confuse coconut milk with either the coconut water that comes directly from the shell, or the canned cream of coconut used in many popular tropical drinks, such as a piña colada. Thicker than the water, but much thinner than the cream, the canned coconut milk for this recipe can be found in ethnic markets that specialize in Latin American or Indian foods. Now and then you can find it at your supermarket, but be certain you are buying coconut milk.

IN YOUR KETTLE, heat the oil and sauté the shallots for 3 minutes.

Add the fresh ginger, turmeric, and cumin, then gently stir another minute or so.

Add the stock, the tomatoes and their juices, the jalapeño, and the lime zest, then allow to come to the boil.

Add the clams, cover, and cook until all the clams have opened.

Remove and discard the shells with a pair tongs. In most cases, the meat of each clam will shake loose into the broth; however, you should remove the meats of a half dozen or so clams, chop them coarsely, and return them to the kettle.

Coax any clams that have not opened with a gentle pry from the point of a knife, then remove and discard any clams do not.

Stir in the lime juice and simmer another 10 minutes.

Stir, taste, and adjust the seasonings with salt & pepper.

Ladle into individual heated bowls.

Garnish with green onions.

INGREDIENTS:

36 hardshell clams, scrubbed & in shells

1 T. vegetable oil
5 shallots, chopped
1 T. ginger, peeled & chopped
1 t. ground turmeric
1/4 t. cumin seeds
2 cups stock
1 cup canned, unsweetened coconut milk
1 cup canned tomatoes, diced w/juices
1 jalapeño chili, seeded & chopped
1 t. lime zest
3 T. fresh lime juice
2 green onions, sliced

Neapolitan Clam Soup

ÍSCHIA, ITALY

Zuppe di pesce is popular throughout this Mediterranean peninsula, but on this island at the edge of the Gulf of Naples they have this distinctive recipe of their very own.

INGREDIENTS:
48 clams, scrubbed & in-shells

1/2 cup olive oil
1 ½ T. garlic, minced
2 dried red peppers, seeded
1/2 cup dry white wine
3 cups canned tomatoes
1 T. tomato paste
salt and pepper
1 T. oregano
1/4 cup parsley, chopped for garnish

IN YOUR KETTLE, heat the oil, then sauté the garlic and red pepper for 1 minute.

Add the wine and simmer until this is reduced by half.

Stir in the tomatoes, tomato paste, oregano, and chopped parsley, then cover and bring to the boil. Reduce the heat and simmer for 15 minutes.

Add the clams, cover, and cook until all the clams have opened.

Remove and discard the shells with a pair tongs. In most cases, the meat of each clam will shake loose into the broth; however, you should remove the meats of a half dozen or so clams, chop them coarsely, and return them to the kettle.

Coax any clams that have not opened with a gentle pry from the point of a knife, then remove and discard any clams do not.

Stir, taste, and adjust the seasonings with with salt & pepper.

Ladle into individual heated bowls.

Chowder Dijon

CHINCOTEAGUE, DELAWARE

Dijon mustard in seafood recipes is most often associated with mussels, but in this kettle of fish the savory flavor brings a zesty flavor to the sweet meat of the clams.

IN YOUR KETTLE, heat the oil, then sauté the leeks, onion, and celery for 5 minutes.

Stir in the garlic and sauté 1 more minute.

Add the clam liquor, stock, Dijon mustard, Worcestershire sauce, pepper, thyme, bay leaves, and parsley, then bring to the boil.

Add the potato, reduce the heat, and simmer until potato is fork tender.

Stir in the clams and simmer for 3 minutes more.

Remove and discard the bay leaves, then stir in the hot milk and cream. Simmer another 3 minutes.

Ladle into individual heated bowls. Garnish with parsley.

INGREDIENTS:

12 hardshell clams, shucked, drained & chopped coarse (liquor reserved)

1 t. olive oil
1 ½ cups leeks (white & pale green parts), sliced
1 onion, diced
1 celery rib, diced
1 garlic clove, minced
1 cup clam liquor
2 cups stock
1 t. Dijon mustard
2 t. Worcestershire sauce
1/4 t. white pepper
1 t. dried thyme
2 bay leaves
1 T. parsley, minced
1 potato, peeled & diced
2 cups hot milk
1 cup cream
2 T. parsley, chopped for garnish

Dry Clam Chowder

LUBEC, MAINE

Europeans are noted for their so-called *dry* soups, to which loaves of crusty bread broken into pieces are added as a thickener. Though some might think this is odd, it really not much different from early American recipes that include crackers, or even the table custom that many have of crumbling handfuls of crackers into their bowls.

INGREDIENTS:

48 hardshells clams, shucked & chopped coarse in their liquor

8 T. butter
8 oz. pilot crackers, crumbled
Fresh ground black pepper, to taste
4 T. fresh parsley, chopped
2 cups milk

IN YOUR KETTLE, melt 3 T. of the butter.

Remove the kettle from the heat and sprinkle a layer of crackers upon the bottom.

Cover the layer of crackers with a double layer of chopped clams and their liquor, then sprinkle with black pepper, to taste. Dot the layer with pieces of butter, and sprinkle with parslet, then repeat the process.

Make the top layer of crumbs, then add the milk.

Bring to the simmer and cook for 45 minutes.

If necessary, add milk in 1/4 cup increments to moisten to your liking.

Ladle into individual heated bowls.

Clam Chowder

MYSTIC, CONNECTICUT

As the debate continues to rage throughout New England as to which is the best of these fine kettles of fish, this recipe from the southern shorelines of the region retains the technique and ingredients of the earliest recipes; most notably, no dairy producty.

IN YOUR KETTLE, render the salt pork until crisp and brown.

Remove and reserve the browned pieces.

Add the onions and sauté 10 minutes.

Add the stock to the kettle, stir, and bring to the boil.

Stir in the reserved pieces of browned salt pork and potatoes, then simmer until the potatoes are fork tender.

Add the chopped clams and 2 cups of their steaming broth to the kettle.

Stir, taste, and adjust the seasonings with salt & pepper.

Simmer for 5 more minutes.

Remove the kettle from the heat and let the chowder stand at least one hour. The longer the chowder rests, the greater the mingling of the flavors; the longer the chowder cooks, the thicker it becomes.

Bring the kettle to the simmer.

Ladle into individual heated bowls.

INGREDIENTS:

12 hardshell clams, scrubbed, steamed & chopped coarse (broth reserved)

4 oz. salt pork, cubed
2 onions, chopped
6 cups stock
4 potatoes, peeled & cubed 1/4-inch
Salt & pepper, to taste

Manhattan Clam Chowder

NEW YORK CITY, NEW YORK

This is the recipe that revealed the elegance of this extremely fine kettle of fish. Though there are those in Manhattan who lay claim to its origin, there are others to the east at Gardners Bay on Long Island, as well as to the south in Philadelphia who share the very same tastes. And very good taste it is!

INGREDIENTS:

24 hardshell clams, steamed & chopped coarse (broth reserved)

4 oz. salt pork, cubed
I onion, chopped
I carrot, peeled & chopped
I celery rib, chopped
I green pepper, chopped
2 T. parsley, chopped
3 tomatoes, peeled, seeded & diced (w/juices)
6 cups stock
4 peppercorns
I bay leaf
1/4 t. thyme
2 potatoes, peeled & diced
1/4 t. caraway seeds (optional)
Tabasco (optional), to taste

IN YOUR KETTLE, render the salt pork until crisp and brown. Remove and reserve the browned pieces.

Add the onion and sauté 5 minutes.

Cover and bring to the simmer 3 hours.

Stir in the milk and continue to simmer, partially covered, for 2 more hours.

Remove the kettle from the heat and cool. Refrigerate chowder overnight.

To serve, stir in the cream and remaining clams, then simmer until heated throughout.

Ladle into individual heated bowls.

Garnish with paprika.

Clam Bisque

OCEAN CITY, MARYLAND

Most bisques are made with crustaceans because the shells of crabs, shrimps, lobsters, and crayfish are far more delicate and flavorful than the lime-based shells of most mollusks. Still, this kettle of fish made with clams and thickened with rice provides a surprisingly tasteful twist to the notion.

IN YOUR KETTLE, add the shucked clams and their liquor, then simmer for 5 minutes.

Remove and reserve the the cooked clams to a clean plate. Chop the clams roughly, but be careful to save all their juices. Return clams and juices to the cooked liquor.

Add the stock, rice, celery, and parsley.

Bring to the boil, reduce the heat, and simmer until the rice is tender.

Pour the bisque through a sieve into a heatproof bowl and force through the solids as much as possible.

Strain a second time from the bowl back into the kettle and discard any solids that remain in the sieve.

Simmer for 5 minutes.

Add the cream.

Stir, taste, and adjust the seasonings with salt & pepper.

Blend together with an egg beater.

Ladle into individual heated bowls.

INGREDIENTS:

24 hardshell clams, scrubbed & shucked (liquor reserved)

4 cups stock
1/2 cup rice, uncooked
1 celery rib, chopped
1 parsley sprig
1 cup cream
Salt & pepper, to taste

Clam & Spinach Soup
POVERTY BAY, NEW ZEALAND

If this recipe were made with the area's toheroa clams, then it would be the antecedent to the recipe for Bongo Bong Soup made with oysters later in this chapter.

Regardless of that, the fact that no city or town on either of New Zealand's two islands is any further than a half-day's travel from the surrounding ocean waters makes fish an integral part of the nation's diet.

INGREDIENTS:
24 hardshell clams, steamed & chopped (broth reserved)
4 anchovy fillets, chopped

4 oz. salt pork, in 1/2-inch cubes
1/2 onion, chopped fine
1 garlic clove, minced
6 T. butter
2 T. flour
4 cups stock
1 cup cream
6 oz. spinach, washed & chopped
Salt & pepper, to taste

IN YOUR KETTLE, render the salt pork until crisp and brown.

Remove and discard the brown pieces, as well as all but 1 T. of the drippings.

Add the onion and garlic, then sauté for 5 minutes.

Stir in the chopped anchovy fillets and sauté for 1 more minute. Add the butter to the kettle and allow to melt.

Sprinkle in the flour and stir with a fork to blend. Cook for 2 minutes, then slowly begin to stir in the stock.

Add the clams, spinach, and cream.

Stir, taste, and adjust the seasonings with salt & pepper.

Simmer for 5 minutes.

Ladle into individual heated bowls.

Clam Soup
MENTON, MONACO

No doubt, your first thoughts of this tiny coastal kingdom tucked between France and Italy are not of food, but more likely of the celebrated members of its royal family or the gambling tables of Monte Carlo. This recipe, though, should add a new dimension to your understanding of Mediterranean geography.

IN YOUR KETTLE, melt the butter, then sauté the onion, shallots, and garlic for 3 minutes.

Stir in the thyme, tarragon.

Sprinkle in the flour and stir to incorporate with the butter.

Slowly stir in the wine and stock, then simmer for 5 minutes.

Add the clams, cover, and cook until all the clams have opened.

Remove and discard the shells with a pair tongs. In most cases, the meat of each clam will shake loose into the broth.

Coax any clams that have not opened with a gentle pry from the point of a knife, then remove and discard any clams do not.

Stir in 1/2 cup of the cream.

In a small bowl, beat the egg yolks gently and add the other 1/2 cup of cream. Mix together, then stir into the kettle.

Cover and simmer for 5 minutes, being careful not to allow the soup to come to the boil.

Stir, taste, and adjust the seasonings with salt & pepper.

Ladle into individual heated bowls.

Garnish with a dash of Tabasco.

INGREDIENTS:

36 hardshell clams, scrubbed

2 T. butter
1 onion, minced
2 shallots, minced
1 garlic clove, minced
1/2 t. thyme, minced
1 t. tarragon, minced
1 T. flour
2 cups dry white wine
1 cup stock
1 cup heavy cream
2 egg yolks
Salt & pepper, to taste
Dash Tabasco, to taste, for garnish

Clam Soup

DUBLIN, IRELAND

"Cockles and mussels, alive, alive-o!" was the refrain sung out by Molly Malone, and those shellfish might well be the only that many think are in the diet of this island's people. After tasting this recipe, however, you might soon belive that the pot of gold at the end of the rainbow might well be this fine kettle of fish.

INGREDIENTS:

24 hardshell clams, scrubbed, steamed & chopped (broth reserved)

2 T. butter
2 T. flour
2 cups milk
2 cups reserved broth
1/2 cup whipping cream
1 egg yolk
Dash Nutmeg
Salt & pepper, to taste
2 T. parsley, chopped for garnish

IN YOUR KETTLE, melt the butter. Sprinkle in the flour and stir until thickened.

Slowly stir in the milk and cook until this thickens, too.

Add the reserved broth and bring to the simmer.

Meanwhile, in a small bowl beat together the cream and egg yolk.

Add 2 T. of the heated stock to the mixture in the bowl in order to temper the egg yolk.

Stir well, then add to the kettle and continue to stir for 3 minutes.

Taste and adjust the seasonings with nutmeg, salt & pepper.

Stir in the chopped clams, then simmer for 3 more minutes.

Ladle into individual heated bowls.

Garnish with parsley.

Clam & Mushroom Chowder

MANCHESTER-BY-THE-SEA, MASSACHUSETTS

Not too many years back, the citizens of this community just north of Boston voted to change the name of their town in order to emphasize their maritime heritage and location. After all, since 1645 the town of Manchester had been an industrious little port along the southern edge of Cape Ann long before it developed a reputation as an elegant summer resort. This rich kettle of fish further enhances their reputation.

IN YOUR KETTLE, heat the oil, then sauté the mushrooms, celery, and scallions for 3 minutes.

Meanwhile, in a small bowl mix together the cornstarch and water. Stir the mixture into the kettle and bring to the simmer until thickened.

Add the evaporated milk and reserved broth, then simmer for 5 minutes.

Stir in the clams and simmer 3 minutes more.

Stir, taste, and adjust the seasonings with cayenne, salt & pepper.

Ladle into individual heated bowls.

INGREDIENTS:

24 hardshell clams, scrubbed, steamed & chopped (broth reserved)

1 t. vegetable oil
1 cup mushrooms, washed & chopped
1 celery rib, chopped
2 scallions (white & pale green) chopped
2 T. cornstarch
2 T. water
3 cups evaporated milk
1 cup reserved broth
Cayenne pepper, to taste
Salt & pepper, to taste

Clam Soup

KUNSAN, KOREA

Aside from the use of salt pork, bacon, or even sausage, there are only a handful of recipes in this book that actually combine fish with meat or poultry. Most of those use chicken, and a couple use pork. Other than those, this is the only one that begins with the red meat of beef, which is browned to enrichen the stock.

INGREDIENTS:

24 hardshell clams, scrubbed

8 oz. beef, sliced thin
3 t. sesame oil
3 t. sesame seeds, ground
1 garlic clove, minced
2 T. soy sauce
3½ cups stock
1/4 t. dried chili pepper, ground

IN YOUR KETTLE, heat the sesame oil and brown the beef.

Stir in the sesame seeds and garlic, then sauté for 3 minutes.

Add to the kettle the soy sauce, stock, and chili pepper, then bring to the boil.

Reduce the heat, cover, and simmer for 30 minutes.

Add the clams, cover, and cook until all the clams have opened.

Remove and discard the shells with a pair tongs. In most cases, the meat of each clam will shake loose into the broth.

Coax any clams that have not opened with a gentle pry from the point of a knife, then remove and discard any clams do not.

Ladle into individual heated bowls.

Outer Banks Chowder

WANCHESE, NORTH CAROLINA

This is a chowder as pure and simple as any to be made. But though its simple list of ingredients foresakes any dairy ingredients or tomatoes, this kettle of fish requires careful attention so that it does not begin to ferment.

INGREDIENTS:

24 hardshell clams, scrubbed & shucked (liquor reserved)

4 cups stock
1 onion, chopped
1 celery rib, chopped
1 carrot, peeled & chopped
1 parsley sprig
2 potatoes, peeled & diced
Salt & pepper, to taste

IN YOUR KETTLE, add the shucked clams and their liquor, then bring to the simmer for 5 minutes.

Remove and reserve the the cooked clams to a clean plate. Chop the clams roughly, but be careful to save all their juices. Return clams and juices to the cooked liquor.

Add the stock, onion, celery, carrot, parsley, and potatoes.

Bring to the boil, then reduce the heat and simmer until the potatoes become fork tender.

Stir, taste, and adjust the seasonings with salt & pepper.

Ladle into individual heated bowls.

Rhode Island Clam Chowder

BRISTOL, RHODE ISLAND

Yachting and fishing will always remain synonymous with this colorful community, but at least half of the total fish catch for the Ocean State includes shellfish. That catch includes the quahaug, the essential ingredient in this hallmark of regional cuisine.

INGREDIENTS:

36 hardshell clams, shucked with liquor reserved

4 oz. salt pork, cubed
1 onion, sliced
1/2 cup water
4 potatoes, in 3/4-inch cubes
2 cups water
1 cup stewed tomatoes, strained
1/4 t. soda
1 cup scalded milk
1 cup scalded cream
2 T. butter
Salt & pepper, to taste
4 pilot crackers

IN YOUR KETTLE, combine the salt pork and onion with 1/2 cup of the water, then bring to the simmer for 15 minutes.

Remove the kettle from the heat, then strain the broth into a heatproof bowl and discard the solids.

Wipe clean the kettle and add the potatoes to the remaining 2 cups of water, then bring to the simmer until the potatoes are fork tender.

Meanwhile, chop fine the hard part of the clams; leave the soft parts whole.

Add the chopped clams to the kettle, along with the reserved broth.

Meanwhile, in a small saucepan scald the milk and the cream.

When the potatoes have become fork tender, stir in the soft part of the clams, along with the tomatoes, soda, milk, cream, and butter.

Stir, taste, and adjust the seasonings with salt & pepper.

Bring the kettle to the simmer for 10 minutes.

Split the crackers and place in the bottom of each bowl.

Ladle into individual heated bowls.

Mussels

On the one hand, mussels are somewhat like oysters in that they can be found in shallow coastal waters throughout the temperate zones. There are some freshwater species of mussels, but only the saltwater varieties are edible.

On the other hand, mussels are most often cooked right in their shells, and that makes things a *bit* easier for using them in a kettle of fish. Still, there are two caveats. First, you must be certain to scrub and debeard the mussels. Second, you also want to be certain not to overcook the mussels, otherwise the meats will shrink and take on a rubbery quality.

How to Scrub & Debeard a Mussel

Because these shellfish anchor themselves to rocks and wharves and seawalls and gravel, they also become an anchoring point themselves for barnacles and other mussels. To ensure that any of these other things do not become part of your kettle ingredients, you simply need to scrub the shells under running water.

1. The scrubbing itself is not at all difficult. All that is needed is a stiff-bristled brush and some running water. Most of the barnacles and sediment will wash away readily.

That done, you must remove the thread-like *beard* that each mussel uses to anchor itself to that other object.

2. To debeard a mussel, you need no other tool than your fingers. The little trick, though, is too loosely cradle the mussel in the fingers of one hand, while you grasp and pull the beard in the other. Just be certain that you do not pull so hard that you actually yank the mussel meat out of the shell.

Mussel Soup

Alexandre Dumas

Best known to most folks as the 19th-century author of such classics as *The Three Musketeers* and *The Count of Monte Cristo*, Dumas also was a noted gourmand. Though he wrote the wonderful volume entitled *Le Grand Dictionnaire de Cuisine* (*The Dictionary of Cuisine*), it was not published until 1873, some 3 years after his death. This entry comes from that work.

"When tomato time comes around, I recommend this soup, which I myself invented and perfected.

"At eleven o'clock in the morning, start a *pot-au-feu*, but in a small proportion since, as you will see, the bouillon is only a third of the preparation for this soup.

"At four in the afternoon, put 12 tomatoes and 12 white onions to boil for 1 hour in the bouillon you have made. Then put the whole through a sieve fine enough so the tomato seeds won't pass through. Put this purée on a slow fire, adding salt, pepper, and 3 or 4 ounces of meat glaze, and let it reduce.

"Put your mussels into a pot on the fire without water.

"After 15 minutes, your mussels will be cooked.

"Put their juice or sauce into your tomatoes. Bring to a boil. Remove from the fire immediately.

"Put a crushed 1/2 clove of garlic into a pot with a little oil and brown lightly. Pour the liquid into this, stirring constantly, and cook 15 minutes to homogenize. Add the mussels.

"Pardon my prolixity, I am saying all this less for the benefit of cooks among readers than for that of those who have no notion at all of cooking and must have everything explained carefully."

— *from* Le Grand Dictionnaire de Cuisine

Billi Bi

THISTLE ISLAND, SOUTH AUSTRALIA

For years, I thought this kettle of fish was an integral part of Australia's country's national song, *Waltzing Matilda;* however, neither I, nor the Australian National Dictionary Centre is certain.

If you are not fully familiar with the words to this popular tune, let me briefly explain the opening verse:

> *Once a jolly swagman camped by a Billabong*
> *Under the shade of a coolabah tree,*
> *And he sang as he watched and waited 'til his billy boiled,*
> *"Who'll come a-waltzing Matilda with me?"*

For starters, a *swagman* is a hobo, who takes his title from his backpack (*swag*). Because the slang for *swag* among swagmen is *Matilda,* the phrase *to waltz Matilda* means to take to the road! So, the swagman is singing, "Who wants to come along?"

I had thought there was some relationship between *Billabong* and this *Billi Bi,* but billabong is an aboriginal word for a section of still water adjacent to a river, cut off by a change in the water's course. In the American west, this was called an *oxbow.*

And I had also thought there was a relationship between *billy boiled* and this kettle of fish, but a billy is a tin can with a wire handle in which a swagman boiled his water. In the past, say the folks at the Australian National University, some have claimed that billy was a corruption of *bouillabaisse.* But none can prove it.

So, there you have it. We're all a little more intelligent now, but we still don't have all the answers. So, let's eat!

IN YOUR KETTLE, melt the butter, then sauté the shallots for 3 minutes.

Add the wine and bring to the simmer.

Stir in the saffron and remove the kettle from the heat.

Meanwhile, in a clean bowl make a liaison of the eggs yolks and cream, then carefully whisk into the kettle.

Return the kettle to the heat and bring to the simmer, being careful not to boil.

Add the mussels.

Stir, taste, and adjust the seasonings with salt & pepper.

Simmer until the stock has thickened.

Ladle into individual heated bowls.

INGREDIENTS:
36 mussels, scrubbed & debearded

2 T. butter
2 shallots, chopped fine
2 cups dry white wine
3 cups stock
1/2 t. saffron threads, crushed
2 egg yolks
1/2 cup cream
Salt & pepper, to taste
2 T. parsley, chopped for garnish

Mussel Soup

COFFS HARBOUR, NEW SOUTH WALES

Now that we've established that Billi Bi is probably a kettle of fish just a bit too rich for a swagman's budget, let's get right at this variation without any further explanations.

INGREDIENTS:

36 mussels, scrubbed & debearded

2 T. butter
3 small leeks (white & pale green parts), sliced thin
2 cup dry white wine
8 parsley sprigs
1 cup cream
10 saffron threads, crushed
3 cups stock
2 T. parsley, minced

IN YOUR KETTLE, bring the wine to the boil.

Add the mussels and parsley sprigs, then reduce the heat, cover, and simmer until all the mussels have opened.

Remove the kettle from the heat. Coax open any mussels with a tap of your fingers. Remove and discard all shells, as well as any mussels that do not open.

Strain the liquid into a heatproof bowl and reserve the meats of the mussels.

Wipe clean the kettle, then melt the butter and sauté the leeks for 5 minutes.

Add the reserved liquid to the kettle, along with the cream and saffron. Bring to the boil for 3 minutes, then add the stock.

Stir, taste, and adjust the seasonings with salt & pepper.

Add the reserved mussels meats and simmer for 10 minutes.

Ladle into individual heated bowls.

Garnish with fresh parsley.

Mussel Soup
ORLEANS, CAPE COD, MASSACHUSETTS

At the crook of the elbow of our peninsula is the bustling town of Orleans, which touches Cape Cod Bay (inside the arm) and the Atlantic (outside). In fact, during Colonial times a high tide enabled them to ride the waters of Jeremiah's Gutter from the bay to the ocean. On both shores of town, they have dabbled in recent years with the farming of mussels to supplement the crop seeded by nature. This recipe makes good use of the harvest.

IN YOUR KETTLE, combine the onion, parsley, and cider, then bring to the boil.

Add the mussels, then reduce the heat, cover, and simmer until all the mussels have opened.

Remove the kettle from the heat. Coax open any mussels with a tap of your fingers. Remove and discard all shells, as well as any mussels that do not open.

Strain the liquid into a heatproof bowl and reserve the meats of the mussels.

Wipe clean the kettle, then melt the butter and sauté the leeks and celery for 5 minutes.

Add the stock and milk, then simmer for 20 minutes.

Stir in the reserved mussel broth and mussel meats.

Meanwhile, in a small bowl make a liaison of the egg yolks and cream.

Stir this mixture into the kettle. Being careful not the let the soup curdle, simmer until the soup thickens.

Stir, taste, and adjust the seasonings with nutmeg, salt & pepper.

Ladle into individual heated bowls.

Garnish each with parsley.

INGREDIENTS:
36 mussels, scrubbed & debearded

1 onion, chopped
1 sprig parsley
1 cup cider
2 T. butter
2 leeks (white & pale green parts), sliced
1 celery rib, diced
2 cups stock
2 cups evaporated milk
Salt, pepper & nutmeg, to taste
2 egg yolks
1/2 cup double cream
4 T. parsley, for garnish

123

Mussel Soup
DINGLE, IRELAND

Like the recipe on the previous page, this kettle of fish brings together many of the same ingredients, including the smooth flavors of cider, leeks, nutmeg, and cream. The main difference, though, is that this soup is thickened with flour and does not have the same richness as the other thickened with eggs and cream.

INGREDIENTS:
36 mussels, scrubbed & debearded

1 onion, diced
1 parsley sprig, chopped
1/2 cup cider
3 cups milk
3 T. butter
2 leeks (white parts), sliced thin
1 celery rib, chopped
3 T. flour
Grated nutmeg, to taste
Salt & pepper, to taste
2 T. cream

IN YOUR KETTLE, combine the onion, parsley, and cider, then bring to the boil.

Add the mussels, then reduce the heat, cover, and simmer until all the mussels have opened.

Remove the kettle from the heat. Coax open any mussels with a tap of your fingers. Remove and discard all shells, as well as any mussels that do not open.

Strain the liquid through a sieve into a heatproof bowl and reserve the meats of the mussels. Use a pestle to purée the vegetables through the sieve.

Meanwhile, in a small saucepan begin to scald the milk.

Wipe clean the kettle, then melt the butter and sauté the leeks and celery for 3 minutes.

Sprinkle the flour into the kettle, then stir to incorporate with the butter and the vegetables.

Add the scalded milk slowly to the kettle.

Stir, taste, and adjust the seasonings with nutmeg, salt & pepper. Simmer for 20 minutes.

Stir in the cream, reserved mussel broth, and mussel meats. Simmer for 5 minutes.

Ladle into individual heated bowls.

Mussel Stew
GALILEE, RHODE ISLAND

Now and then, you'll come across a kettle of fish whose name defies somewhat the traditional definition. So it is with this stew, and the oyster stew, as well. Rather than have a greater proportion of solids to liquids that is supposed to be in a stew, this has a greater amount of stock.

IN YOUR KETTLE, stir together the milk and cream and bring to the simmer.

Stir in the onion, celery, mace, and bay leaf, then cover and simmer for another 30 minutes.

Strain the stock into a heatproof bowl and discard the solids.

Wash and wipe clean the kettle, then add the water and bring to the boil.

Add the mussels, then reduce the heat, cover, and simmer until all the mussels have opened.

Remove the kettle from the heat. Coax open any mussels with a tap of your fingers. Remove and discard all shells, as well as any mussels that do not open.

Strain the broth into a heatproof bowl and reserve the meats of the mussels.

Wash and wipe clean the kettle. Add the stock, butter, and 1/2 cup of the reserved broth, then bring to the simmer.

Stir the mussel meats into the kettle, then simmer for 5 minutes.

Stir, taste, and adjust the seasonings with salt & peppers.

Ladle into individual heated bowls.

Garnish with butter and paprika.

INGREDIENTS:
36 mussels, scrubbed & debearded

3 cups milk
3 cups cream
1 onion, chopped
1 celery rib, chopped
1/2 blade mace
Bay leaf
2 cups water
4 T. butter
Salt & white pepper, to taste
Red pepper flakes (crushed), to taste
Butter, for garnish
Paprika, for garnish

Mussel Stew

PORTO RECANATI, ITALY

Halfway down the back calf of this peninsular country sits this community on the Adriatic Sea. The kettle of fish which it offers up has not only the familiar tastes which we associate with Italy, but also the proportion of ingredients which we more readily proclaim to be a stew.

INGREDIENTS:

24 mussels, scrubbed & debearded

2 T. olive oil
1 onion, sliced thin
1 T. celery, diced
3 garlic cloves, minced
2 T. basil, chopped
2 t. red pepper flakes, crushed
8 plum tomatoes, peeled, seeded & diced
1/2 cup dry white wine
1 cup stock
Lemon zest, garnish
Parsley, chopped for garnish

IN YOUR KETTLE, heat the oil, then sauté the onion over medium heat for 5 minutes.

Add the celery, garlic, basil, and red pepper flakes, then stir and bring to the simmer for 3 minutes.

Stir in the tomatoes and simmer another 5 minutes.

Stir in the wine, cover, and simmer for 30 minutes.

Add stock and simmer 20 minutes more.

Remove the kettle from the heat. Coax open any mussels with a tap of your fingers. Remove and discard all shells, as well as any mussels that do not open. Return the meats of the mussels to the kettle.

Simmer for 5 minutes.

Ladle into individual heated bowls.

Garnish each with lemon zest and parsley.

Mussel Soup
CONCARNEAU, FRANCE

The closest body of water to Dijon, France is the Côte d'Or; the largest, Lac Léman in Switzerland. While neither of those can be noted for mussels, the landlocked Dijon brings to this recipe that fabled blend of herbs, wine, and dried mustard which bears its name. In fact, many people readily associate mussels and Dijon. They will not be disappointed with this kettle of fish, and neither will you.

INGREDIENTS:
36 mussels, scrubbed & debearded

1 onion, diced
1 parsley sprig, chopped
1/2 dry white wine
3 cups milk
3 T. butter
2 leeks (white parts), sliced thin
1 celery rib, chopped
3 T. flour
2 T. Dijon mustard
Salt & pepper, to taste
2 T. cream

IN YOUR KETTLE, combine the onion, parsley, and wine, then bring to the boil.

Add the mussels, then reduce the heat, cover, and simmer until all the mussels have opened.

Remove the kettle from the heat. Coax open any mussels with a tap of your fingers. Remove and discard all shells, as well as any mussels that do not open.

Strain the liquid through a sieve into a heatproof bowl and use a pestle to force the vegetables through the sieve. Reserve the meats of the mussels.

Meanwhile, in a small saucepan, begin to scald the milk.

Wipe clean the kettle, then melt the butter and sauté the leeks and celery for 3 minutes.

Sprinkle the flour into the kettle, then stir to incorporate with the butter and the vegetables.

Add the scalded milk slowly to the kettle.

Add the Dijon mustard to the kettle.

Stir, taste, and adjust the seasonings with salt & pepper.

Simmer for 20 minutes.

Stir in the cream, reserved mussel broth, and mussel meats.

Simmer for 5 minutes.

Ladle into individual heated bowls.

Oysters

Because the oyster can thrive in a wide range of temperatures from 90°F down to those below freezing, this little treasure can be found in bays and estuaries throughout many parts of the world. From Sweden to Spain, from New England to Texas, from Charlotte Sound to San Diego Harbor, and from Asia to Australia, the delectable oyster boasts of a culinary history that is both long and far-reaching. And because of the varying mineral content in these wordly waters, gourmands claim to be able distinguish its origin simply by taste.

Despite such worldwide appeal, however, the oyster has two apparent shortcomings. One seems to be the relative difficulty one experiences in opening an oyster's rustic shell; the other, the limited role an oyster plays when cooked in a kettle of fish.

How to Shuck an Oyster

First, note that there is a flat shell on the top of the oyster, as well as a deeper, bowl-shaped bottom shell. This bottom shell will retain much of the prized liquor. Second, note that the best tool for opening these shells is the "church key" can/bottle opener that has the pointed end to puncture the top of a beverage can.

Keeping in mind that you don't want to startle the oyster into closing its shell any tighter, take the oyster in your gloved hand and look closely for the "rear" end of the oyster, where the shells are joined together by its hinge muscle.

Insert the point of the "church key" between the top and bottom shells at the hinge, then pry this rear end open. Then, insert the point of your knife and sever the hinge.

Once the knife is inside, run the blade deeper around the perimeter to cut the muscles that hold the 2 shells together.

Lift off the top shell and remove the oyster meat with the point of the knife or a fork.

The tradition method of using an oyster knife is done this way.

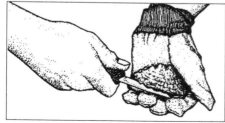

1. Take the oyster in your gloved hand and force your oyster knife between the oyster shells. Because this lip is not as smooth and easy to penetrate as is the lip of a hardshell clam, you must take *extra* care and caution when inserting the sharp knife. A poor placement can cause the oyster knife to slip and cut a hand.

2. Insert the point of your knife and sever the hinge, then run the blade deeper around the perimeter to cut the muscles that hold the 2 shells together.

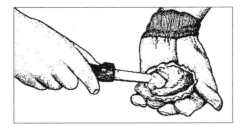

Lift the shell and remove the oyster with the point of the knife or fork.

Cooking Oysters

In my opinion, an oyster has a more distinctive and appealing taste when eaten raw on the halfshell than when cooked. Heat seems to bring out the fish taste in an oyster, and most recipes indicate that the oysters should only be cooked to a point where their edges just begin to curl. In fact, the recipes for oyster stew do not appear to have changed very much at all throughout the ages.

When you consider that the *art* of cooking is probably not much more than 300 years old and that cookbooks are relatively recent additions to that art, there is not much versatility when it comes to preparing oysters.

In the 1700s, Custis' *Booke of Cookery* provided this instruction for making an oyster stew:

"Take your oysters open & pick them very clean & save the liquor that comes out of them. When you open them set on a scyllet of water, & make it boyle hot not to fast, then put in your oysters & make them boyle up, then take them up & put them in a cullender, & poure cold water on them this is to plump & keepe them from shrinking then set them a stewing in theyr owne liquor & as much water as will cover them, or put to the liquor white wine in the roome of water, put in a whole ounion some whole pepper, & whole mace, when you sevre them up, put in butter & garnish your dish with beaten & sifted ginger."

If you carefully read that recipe, you'll see that boiling the oysters was the fashionable way to prepare them; however, a generation or so later the recipe in Raffald's *English House-keeper*, appears to turn down the heat just a bit:

"When you have opened your oysters, put their liquor into a tossing pan with a little beaten mace, thicken it with flour and butter, boil it three or four minutes, toast a slice of white bread, and cut it into three-cornered pieces, lay them round your dish, put in your oysters and shake them round in your pan, you must not let them boil, for if they do it will make them hard and look small, serve them up in a little soup dish or plate."

Since then, the ingredients and instructions do not seem to have changed that much at all.

129

The Wellfleet Oysterman

HENRY DAVID THOREAU

Having walked about eight miles since we struck the beach and passed the boundary between Wellfleet and Truro (a stone post in the sand), we turned inland over barren hills and valleys — where the sea for some reason did not follow us — and discovered two or three sober-looking houses within a half mile, uncommonly near the coast. Their garrets were apparently so full of chambers that their roofs could hardly lie down straight, and we did not doubt that there was room for us there.

Houses near the sea are generally low and broad. These were a story and a half high, but if you merely counted the windows in their gable-ends you would think that there were many stories more, or that the half-story was the only one thought of being illustrated. The great number of windows in the ends of the houses and their irregularity in size and position — here and elsewhere on the Cape — struck us agreeably, as if each of the various occupants who had their *cunabula* behind had punched a hole where his necessities required it and without regard to outside effect. There were windows for the grown folks and windows for the children. A certain man had a large hole cut in his barn-door for the cat and smaller one for the kitten. Sometimes they were so low under the eaves that I thought they must have perforated the plate beam for another apartment, and I noticed some which were triangular to fit that part exactly. The ends of the houses had thus as many muzzles as a revolver, and if the inhabitants have the same habit of staring out the windows that some of our neighbors have, a traveller must stand a small chance with them.

Generally, the old-fashioned and unpainted houses on the Cape look more comfortable, as well as picturesque, than the modern and more pretending ones, which were less in harmony with the scenery and less firmly planted . . .

We knocked at the door at the door of the first house, but its inhabitants were all gone away. In the meanwhile, we saw the occupants of the next one looking out the window at us, and before we reached it an old woman came out and fastened the door of her bulkhead and went in again. Nevertheless, we did not hesitate to knock at her door, when a grizzly-looking man appeared, whom we took to be 60 or 70 years old. He asked us, at first, suspiciously, where we were from and what our business was; to which we returned plain answers.

"How far is Concord from Boston?" he inquired.

"Twenty miles by railroad."

"Twenty miles by railroad," he repeated.

"Didn't you ever hear of Concord of Revolutionary fame?"

"Didn't I ever hear of Concord? Why I heard the guns fire at the battle of Bunker Hill. [They heard the sound of heavy cannon across the Bay.] I am almost 90; I am 88 year old. I was 14 year old at the time of the Concord Fight — and where were you then?"

We were obliged to confess that we were not in the fight.

"Well, walk in, we'll leave it to the women," said he.

So we walked in, surprised, and sat down, an old woman taking our hats and bundles, and the old man continued, drawing up to the large, old-fashioned fireplace.

"I am a poor good-for-nothing crittur, as Isaiah says; I am all broken down this year. I am under petticoat government here."

The family consisted of the old man, his wife, and his daughter, who appeared nearly as old as her mother, a fool, her son (a brutish-looking, middle-aged man with a prominent lower face who was standing by the hearth when we entered, but immediately went out), and a little boy of ten.

While my companion talked with the women, I talked with the old man. They said that he was old and foolish, but he was evidently too knowing for them.

"These women," said he to me, "are both of them poor good-for-nothing critturs. This one is my wife. I married her 64 years ago. She is 84 year old and as deaf as an adder, and the other is not much better."

He thought well of the Bible, or at least he *spoke* well and did not *think* ill of it, for that would not have been prudent for a man of his age. He said that he had read it attentively for many years, and he had much of it at his tongue's end. He seemed deeply impressed with a sense of his own nothingness and would repeatedly exclaim:

"I am a nothing. What I gather from my Bible is just this: that man is a poor good-for-nothing crittur, and everything is just as God sees fit and disposes."

"May I ask your name?" I said.

"Yes," he answered, "I am not ashamed to tell my name. My name is — . My great-grandfather came over from England and settled here."

He was an old Wellfleet oysterman, who had acquired a competency in that business, and had sons still engaged in it.

Nearly all the oyster shops and stands in Massachusetts, I am told, are supplied and kept by natives of Wellfleet, and a part of this town is still called Billingsgate from the oysters having been formerly planted there, but the native oysters are said to have died in 1770. Various causes are assigned to this, such as a ground frost, the carcasses of blackfish kept to rot in the harbor, and the like, but the most common account of the matter is — and I find that a similar superstition with regard to the disappearance of fishes exists almost everywhere — that when Wellfleet began to quarrel with the neighboring towns about the right to gather them, yellow specks appeared in them, and Providence caused them to disappear.

A few years ago sixty thousand bushels were annually brought from the South and planted in the harbor of Wellfleet till they attained "the proper relish of Billingsgate," but now they are imported commonly full-grown and laid down near their markets at Boston and elsewhere, where the water, being a mixture of salt and fresh, suits them better. The business was said to be still good and improving.

The old man said that the oysters were liable to freeze in the winter, if planted too high, but if it were not "so cold as to strain their eyes" they were not injured. The inhabitants of New Brunswick have noticed that "ice will not form over an oyster-bed, unless the cold is very intense indeed, and when the bays are frozen over the oyster-beds are easily discovered by the water above them remaining unfrozen, or as the French residents say, *degèle*." Our host said that they kept them in cellars all winter.

"Without anything to eat or drink?" I asked.

"Without anything to eat or drink," he answered.

"Can the oysters move?"

"Just as much as my shoe."

But when I caught him saying that they "bedded themselves down in the sand, flat side up, round side down," I told him that my shoe could not do that without the aid of my foot in it; at which, he said that they merely settled down as they grew. If put down in a square, they would be found so, but the clam could move quite fast. I have since been told by oystermen of Long Island, where the oyster is still indigenous and abundant, that they are found in large masses attached to the parent in their midst and are so taken up with their tongs; in which case, they say, the age of the young proves that there could have been no motion for five or six years at least.

And Buckland in his *Curiosities of Natural History* (page 50) says: "An oyster who has once taken up his position and fixed himself when quite young can never make a change. Oysters,

132

nevertheless, that have not fixed themselves, but remain loose at the bottom of the sea, have the power of locomotion They open their shells to their fullest extent, and then suddenly contracting them, the expulsion of the water forwards gives a motion backwards. A fisherman at Guernsey told me that he had frequently seen oysters moving in this way."

Some still entertain the question "whether the oyster was indigenous in Massachusetts Bay" and whether Wellfleet harbor was a "natural habitat" of this fish. But to say nothing of the testimony of old oysterman — which, I think, is quite conclusive (though the native oyster may now be extinct there) — I saw that their shells opened by the Indians were strewn all over the Cape. Indeed, the Cape was at first thickly settled by Indians on account of the abundance of these and other fish. We saw many traces of their occupancy after this, in Truro, near Great Hollow, and at High-Head, near East Harbor River — oysters, clams, cockles, and other shells, mingled with ashes and the bones of deer and other quadrupeds. I picked up half a dozen arrow-heads and in an hour or two could have filled my pockets with them. The Indians lived about the edges of the swamps, then probably in some instances ponds, for shelter and water.

Moreover, Champlain, in the edition of his *Voyages* printed in 1613, says that in the year 1606 he and Poitrincourt explored a harbor (Barnstable Harbor?) in the southerly part of what is now called Massachusetts Bay — in latitude 42°, about five leagues south, one point west of *Cap Blanc* (Cape Cod) — and there they found many good oysters, and they named it *"le Port aux Huistres"* (Oyster Harbor). In one edition of his map (1632), the *"R. aux Escailles"* is drawn emptying into the same part of the bay, and on the map *"Novi Belgii,"* in Ogilby's *America* (1670), the words *"Port aux Huistres"* are placed against the same place. Also William Wood, who left New England in 1633, speaks, in his *New England's Prospect* (published in 1634) of "a great oyster-bank" in Charles River, and of another in the Mistick, each of which obstructed the navigation of its river. "The oysters," says he, "be great ones in form of a shoehorn; some be a foot long; these breed on certain banks that are bare ever spring tide. This fish without the shell is so big, that it must admit of a division before you can well get it into your mouth." Oysters are still found there. (Also, see Thomas Morton's *New English Canaan*, page 90.)

Our host told us that the sea-clam, or hen, was not easily obtained. It was raked up, but never on the Atlantic side, only cast ashore there in small quantities in storms. The fisherman sometimes wades in water several feet deep and thrusts a pointed stick into the sand before him. When this enters between the valves of a clam, they close upon it and the clam is drawn out. It has been known to catch and hold coot and teal which were preying on it. I chanced to be on the bank of the Acushnet at New Bedford one day since this, watching some ducks, when a man informed me that, having let out his young ducks to seek their food amid the samphire (*Salicornia*) and other weeds along the riverside at low tide that morning, at length he noticed that one remained stationary amid the weeds, something preventing it from following the others. Going to it, he found its foot tightly shut in a quahog's shell. He took up both together, carried them to his home, and his wife opening the shell with a knife released the duck and cooked the quahog.

The old man said that the great clams were good to eat, but that they always took out a certain part which was poisonous before they cooked them. "People said it would kill a cat." I did not tell him that I had eaten a large one entire that afternoon, but began to think that I was tougher than a cat.

He stated that peddlars came round there and sometimes tried to sell the women folks a skimmer, but he told them that their women had got a better skimmer than they could make in the shell of their clams. It was shaped just right for this purpose. They call them "skim-alls" in some places. He also said that the sun-squall was poisonous to handle. When the sailors came across it, they did not meddle with it, but heaved it out of their way. I told him that I had handled it earlier that afternoon and that I had felt no ill effects as yet. But he said it made the hands itch, especially if they had previously been scratched, or if I put it into my bosom I should find out what it was . . .

— *from* CAPE COD

Oyster Stew

WELLFLEET, MASSACHUSETTS

Here on the Cape, there has long been a good-natured rivalry between the bayside oystermen of Wellfleet and those of Cotuit on Nantucket Sound. In both places they farm this shellfish these days. When it comes to taste, though, there are no losers. And the same can be said of *all* the oysters in the world, many of which find their way into this traditional kettle of fish.

IN YOUR KETTLE, heat the reserved liquor and bring to the simmer.

Add the oysters and cook just until the edges begin to curl.

Remove and reserve the oysters on a warm plate.

Add to the kettle the butter and milk, then bring to the simmer for 5 minutes.

Stir, taste, and adjust the seasonings with salt & pepper.

Return the oysters to the kettle and simmer for 3 more minutes.

Ladle into individual heated bowls.

INGREDIENTS:

12 oysters, shucked & drained (liquor reserved)

2 T. butter
6 cups milk
Salt & pepper, to taste

Oyster Soup
GOWER, WALES

The Welsh recipe for this kettle of fish is among the handful that normally calls for mutton stock as its cooking liquid. More often than not, though, you won't have that rare ingredient on hand, so you might subsitute any brown meat stock of your choice, or simply rely upon your fish stock.

INGREDIENTS:

16 oysters, shucked & drained (liquor reserved)

2 T. butter
2 T. flour
8 cups stock
1/2 onion, grated
1/2 t. mace
1/2 t. black pepper

IN YOUR KETTLE, first make a light brown roux by melting the butter over medium heat, then sprinkling in the flour. Continue to stir the mixture so that it does not burn; however, cook until the roux has the color of a peanut butter.

Gradually add the stock to the kettle and continue to stir so that the roux mixes with the liquid.

Bring the stock to the boil, then reduce the heat.

Stir in the the onion, mace, and pepper, then simmer for 15 minutes.

Meanwhile, divide the oysters and their liquor among the individual bowls.

Strain the broth through a sieve into a heatproof bowl.

Ladle over the oysters into the individual heated bowls.

Christmas Oyster Stew

SEPT-ÎLES, QUEBEC, CANADA

This traditional *Soupe aux Huitres de Noel* is generally made with the fresh oysters of winter; however, there is nothing preventing you from enjoying this recipe at any other time throughout the year. In some recipes, the recipe has included the kernels of 2 fresh ears of corn, so I suspect that it has also been prepared when that crop is in season.

IN YOUR KETTLE, melt the butter, then sauté the carrots and celery for 3 minutes.

Add to the kettle the milk and cream, then cover and bring to the simmer for 15 minutes.

Add the oysters and their liquor, then simmer just until the edges of the oysters begin to curl.

Taste and adjust the seasonings with salt & pepper.

INGREDIENTS:

24 oysters, shucked & drained (liquor reserved)

4 T. butter
2 carrots, peeled & grated
2 celery ribs, diced fine
2 cups milk
2 cups cream
Salt & pepper, to taste

137

Bongo Bong Soup
CHICAGO, ILLINOIS

Legend has it that this kettle of fish was originally the New Zealand recipe made with toheroa clams and first tasted by a gentleman named Vic Bergeron during World War II. Later, he became known as Trader Vic and created this recipe with oysters for his chain of so-called "tiki" restaurants worldwide.

Whether or not that's true, this recipe was passed along by a friend, and you'll notice that the ingredients are also quite similar to the Rockefeller Oyster Soup.

INGREDIENTS:

24 oysters, shucked & liquor reserved

5 cups half-and-half
1/2 cup spinach, washed, stemmed & puréed
4 T. butter
2 t. A-1 sauce
Garlic salt, to taste
Cayenne pepper, to taste
Salt & pepper, to taste
4 t. cornstarch
4 T. water
Whipped cream

IN YOUR KETTLE, add the half-and-half and bring to the simmer.

Add the spinach and oysters to poach together just until the edges of the oysters begin to curl.

Remove the kettle from the heat. In a blender, purée the half-and-half, spinach, and oysters, then add the butter and A-1 sauce.

Return to the kettle heat and bring to the simmer.

Stir, taste and adjust the seasonings with garlic salt, cayenne, and salt & pepper.

Simmer for 5 minutes.

Meanwhile, in a small bowl dissolve the cornstarch in the water, then stir into the kettle and simmer until thickened.

Meanwhile, heat the broiling element of your stove.

Ladle into individual heated bowls.

Top with whipped cream, then place under the broiler until cream has slightly browned.

Chesapeake Oyster Soup

NEWPORT NEWS, VIRGINIA

The Old Dominion has long been noted for its sumptuous foods, not the least of which are its hams and peanuts. From the mouth of the bountiful Chesapeake comes this recipe for a kettle of fish which is second to none, and part of its flavor does come from a ham.

IN YOUR KETTLE, bring the water to the boil, then add the onions pierced with cloves, along with ham.

Reduce the heat, then simmer until the liquid reduces by half.

Remove and discard the onion and cloves.

Meanwhile, in a small bowl whisk the flour into the cream, then add the egg yolks and beat well.

Stir this mixture into the kettle and simmer until the soup thickens.

Being careful not the let the soup curdle, add the oysters and simmer until the edges just curl.

Stir, taste, and adjust the seasonings with salt & pepper.

Ladle into individual heat bowls.

INGREDIENTS:

24 oysters, shucked & drained (reserve liquor for other use)

6 cups water
2 onions
8 whole cloves, stuck into the onion
1 lean ham slice, chopped
1 T. flour
4 oz. cream
3 egg yolks, beaten well
Salt & pepper to taste

Oyster & Artichoke Bisque

DUXBURY, MASSACHUSETTS

Though you can make this kettle of fish with fresh artichokes, I have found that it works just as well with frozen artichoke hearts. Most important, however, is that you do not use any sort of marinated artichoke hearts which will bring to the kettle their own seasoned taste.

INGREDIENTS:

24 oysters, shucked, drained & chopped (liquor reserved)

4 T. butter
1 onion, chopped
1 celery rib, chopped
1/2 green bell pepper, seeded & chopped
8 bacon slices
4 artichoke hearts, cooked & chopped
1 cups oyster liquor
1 cup stock
2 t. basil, chopped
2 cups cream
Cayenne pepper, to taste
Salt & pepper, to taste
2 T. parsley, chopped for garnish

IN YOUR KETTLE, melt the butter, then sauté the onion, celery, and bell pepper for 5 minutes.

Add to the kettle the bacon slices and chopped oysters, then bring to the simmer for 5 minutes.

Stir in the chopped artichoke hearts, then bring to the boil for 5 minutes. Continue to stir to prevent any scorching and sticking.

Reduce the heat, then stir in the basil and simmer for 5 minutes.

Add the cream to the kettle, then bring the kettle just to the boil.

Stir, taste, and adjust the seasonings with cayenne, salt & pepper.

Remove the kettle from the heat and allow to stand for 10 minutes.

Ladle into individual heated bowls.
Garnish with parsley.

Oyster Jalapeño Chowder
PADRE ISLAND, TEXAS

I continue to be amazed at the number of people — myself included — who forget the fact that the Lone Star State indeed has a coastline. It's not that we never knew, but more a result of the fact that so much of the lore is based upon the western aspects of the state's culture. Still, this kettle of fish is a pleasant reminder that there is a Texas shoreline along the bountiful Gulf of Mexico.

INGREDIENTS:

24 oysters, shucked & drained (liquor reserved)

3 cups stock

3 red-skinned potatoes, diced

1 onion, chopped

1 bay leaf

6 jalapeño peppers, seeded & diced

1 cup kernel corn

1 roasted red bell pepper, seeded & chopped

2 cups cream

Salt, to taste

1 T. butter

1 t. marjoram, chopped for garnish

IN YOUR KETTLE, bring 2 cups of the stock to the boil, then add the potatoes.

Reduce the heat and simmer the potatoes until fork tender.

Remove and reserve the potatoes in a clean bowl.

Add the remaining stock to the kettle, along with the chopped onion and bay leaf, then simmer for 15 minutes.

Remove and discard the bay leaf.

Stir in the jalapeño peppers and corn, then simmer for 5 minutes.

Add the cream and reserved liquor, then bring to the simmer for 5 minutes.

Stir, taste, and adjust the seasonings with salt.

Add the butter and oysters, then simmer until the butter has melted and the edges of the oysters just begin to curl.

Ladle into individual heated bowls.

Garnish each with marjoram.

Chinese Oyster Stew

ZHANJIANG, CHINA

For more than 2,000 years the Chinese have been cultivating fish and shellfish alike, especially carp and oysters. This recipe brings together many of the nation's traditional flavors in a rather light kettle of fish.

INGREDIENTS:
24 oysters, shucked & in their liquor

4 cups stock
2 T. soy sauce
1/4 t. ginger root, grated
2 cups Chinese cabbage, chopped
8 oz. mushrooms, sliced
1/2 cup bean sprouts
4 scallions (entire), in 1-inch pieces

IN YOUR KETTLE, combine the stock, soy sauce, and ginger, then bring to the boil.

Add to the kettle the cabbage, mushrooms, bean sprouts, and oysters, then cover and simmer for 5 minutes.

Ladle into individual heated bowls.

Garnish each with chopped scallion.

Yucatan Oyster Stew

MÉRIDA, MEXICO

In the shallow, tropical waters surrounding this Mexican peninsula plump oysters still abound. They are not particularly large, but they impart a rich flavor to this kettle of fish.

IN YOUR KETTLE, melt the butter, then sauté the onion, green pepper, and garlic for 5 minutes.

Add the tomatoes and bring to the simmer for 3 minutes.

Stir in the stock and bring to the boil.

Add the potatoes, then reduce the heat and simmer until they are fork tender.

Stir in the green olives, capers, salt, marjoram, cayenne pepper, and vinger, then simmer for 3 minutes more.

Add the oysters and simmer until their edges just begin to curl.

Ladle into individual heated bowls.

INGREDIENTS:

12 oysters, shucked & drained (liquor reserved)

2 T. butter
1 onion, chopped
1 green bell pepper, seeded & chopped
2 garlic cloves
3 tomatoes, peeled, seeded & diced
4 cups stock
2 potatoes, peeled & diced
1/2 cup stuffed green olives, sliced
2 T. capers
1 t. salt
1/4 t. marjoram, crushed
1/4 t. Cayenne pepper
2 t. vinegar

Hazelnut Oyster Stew

COOS BAY, OREGON

Time and time again in the history of America's settlement we are reminded of the contributions which the Native Americans have made to our culture. More often than not, these have come in the form of teaching the peoples of the Old World how to adapt to the climate and soil of the New. Seldom, though, are we provided with a legitimate recipe which has been adapted to modern day cooking. I think it's dafe to say that this kettle of fish belongs in that category.

In other places in this book you will find grain-based thickeners that have become rather traditional, such as flour, hominy, or rice. At one time, however, nuts served the same purpose, especially when food was gathered, rather than grown.

To replace the greens that would have been gathered for this dish, broccoli leaves should be used. While you could use the stems or the flowerets, they do not provide the same texture.

INGREDIENTS:

16 oysters, shucked & drained (reserve liquor)

8 cups stock
1/2 cup hazelnuts, chopped
1 onion, chopped
1 cup broccoli leaves, chopped
Salt & pepper, to taste

IN YOUR KETTLE, bring the stock to the boil, then add the hazelnuts and onion.

Reduce the heat, cover, and simmer for 30 minutes.

Stir in the broccoli. If necessary, add enough water to make 8 cups, then simmer another 20 minutes.

Add the oysters and simmer just until the edges of the oysters begin to curl.

Stir, taste, and adjust the seasonings with salt & pepper.

Ladle into individual heated bowls.

Cream of Oyster Soup

RIVERHEAD, LONG ISLAND, NEW YORK

Some might think that there is only a slight distinction to be made between a traditional Oyster Stew and this kettle of fish. And they would be right. This recipe not only produces a thicker stock, but also requires that the oysters be cut into pieces and cooked a bit longer. You should be able to taste the difference, and you should be pleased, as well.

IN YOUR KETTLE, first make a light roux by melting the butter over medium heat, then sprinkling in the flour. Continue to stir the mixture so that it blends smoothly, but does not turn color.

Gradually stir in the milk and cream. Allow to simmer and thicken.

Stir, taste and adjust seasonings with celery salt, as well as salt & pepper.

Remove the kettle from the heat.

Use scissors to cut the shucked oysters into small pieces directly into the kettle, then add the reserved oyster liquor.

Return the kettle to the heat and simmer for 10 minutes.

Ladle into individual heated bowls.

Garnish each with a pat of butter.

INGREDIENTS:

12 oysters, shucked & drained (liquor reserved)

2 T. butter
1 T. flour
3 cups milk
1 cup cream
Dash celery salt
Salt & pepper, to taste
4 t. butter, garnish

145

Oyster & Brie Soup

WESTPORT, MASSACHUSETTS

Often overlooked by a great many people who travel the main roads further inland, this quaint seacoast community is blessed to be a bit off the beaten path; however, it does not lack for summer visitors, who tend to arrive by sea as much as by land.

INGREDIENTS:

24 oysters, shucked & liquor reserved

2 cups water
4 T. butter
1 onion, chopped coarse
1 celery rib, chopped coarse
1/4 cup flour
8 oz. brie, cubed
2 cups heavy cream
1/4 cup champagne
4 scallions (entire), chopped
Salt, to taste
White pepper, to taste
Red pepper flakes, crushed, to taste
4 slices crisp bacon, crumbled for
 garnish

Before preparing this recipe, combine the oysters, reserved liquor, and water in a small bowl and refrigerate for 1 hour.

IN YOUR KETTLE, melt the butter, then sauté the onion and celery for 3 minutes.

Sprinkle the flour into the kettle, then stir to incorporate thoroughly with the butter and vegetables.

Meanwhile, strain the reserved liquor and water through a sieve into a clean bowl, then reserve the oysters.

Gradually, stir the liquor and water into the kettle, then bring to the simmer.

Add the cubed brie and stir until the cheese has melted.

Remove the kettle from the heat, then strain the stock through a sieve into a heatproof bowl. Discard the solids.

Return the strained stock to the kettle and bring to the simmer.

Stir in the cream and simmer for 3 minutes.

Add the champagne and scallions, then simmer another 2 minutes.

Stir, taste, and adjust the seasonings with salt & peppers.

Add the oysters to the kettle and simmer until their edges just begin to curl.

Ladle into individual heated bowls.

Garnish each with chopped bacon.

Rockefeller Oyster Soup

NEW ORLEANS, LOUISIANA

Contrary to popular opinion, the original recipe for "Oysters à la Rockefeller" — created a century ago by Jules Alaciatore for a restaurant called Antoine's in New Orleans — never included spinach among its ingredients. At that time, snails from Europe were becoming more difficult to import, and the chef hoped to create a dish from the local abundance of oysters. To make his oysters different from all the others being served, he created a secret sauce from scallions, celery, chervil, tarragon leaves, bread crumbs, Tabasco, and butter. The flavor of his well-guarded recipe proved to be so rich that he named his dish after the man he believed to be the richest in the world. In the years since, however, the recipe has changed somewhat to include both spinach and bacon, neither of which was part of his secret.

In addition, Alaciatore became an oyster pioneer of yet another sort. With the exception of oyster stew, this shellfish generally had been served uncooked.

INGREDIENTS:

1/2 pint oysters, liquor reserved

2 slices bacon
1 scallion (white part), chopped
1 potato, peeled & diced
2 cups stock
1 t. lemon juice
1/2 t. tarragon
1 cup evaporated milk
1 cup water
5 spinach leaves, washed & stemmed
Salt & pepper, to taste
Dash of Pernod

IN YOUR KETTLE, render the bacon until crisp and brown.

Remove and reserve bacon on a paper towel to drain. Remove and discard all but 1 T. of the drippings.

Add scallion and sauté 3 minutes.

Stir in the stock and bring to the boil.

Add the diced potato, reduce the heat, and simmer until the potato is fork tender.

Stir in the lemon juice, tarragon, and evaporated milk, then continue to simmer.

Meanwhile, in a small saucepan bring the water to the boil and blanch the spinach for 3 minutes.

Drain the spinach, chop, then add to the kettle.

Wipe clean the saucepan and bring the reserved liquor to the simmer. Add the oysters and simmer just until the edges begin to curl.

Add the oysters and liquor to the kettle.

Stir, taste, and adjust the seasonings with salt & pepper.

Simmer for 3 more minutes.

Ladle into individual heated bowls.

Garnish each with chopped bacon.

Oyster Soup

GAY HEAD, MARTHA'S VINEYARD, MASSACHUSETTS

The tribal seat of the Wampanoag Nation is in this up-island town set upon the majestic, colorful cliffs that face the setting sun and the Vineyard Sound. Though this kettle of fish might not be a pure Native American dish, its use of ground grain as a thickener is much like that of the hazelnuts used by the Native Americans of the Pacific Northwest.

INGREDIENTS:

24 oysters, shucked & drained (liquor reserved)

2 T. butter

2 cups milk

1/4 cup cornmeal

Salt & pepper, to taste

IN YOUR KETTLE, melt the butter, then add the reserved liquor and bring to the simmer.

Meanwhile, in a small bowl first mix together 1/4 cup of the milk with the cornmeal, then stir in the remainder of the milk.

Add the cornmeal and milk mixture to the kettle, then bring to the simmer.

Stir, taste, and adjust the seasonings with salt & pepper.

Add the oysters to the kettle and simmer for 20 minutes.

Ladle into individual heated bowls.

Oyster Stew

CAPE FEAR, NORTH CAROLINA

This recipe takes the one from the previous page just one step
further by incorporating the corn meal into dumplings. This is not
an usual item in many regions along the eastern U.S. shoreline.

IN YOUR KETTLE, render the salt pork until crisp and brown.

Add the water and oyster liquor.

Stir, taste, and adjust the seasonings with salt & pepper.

Bring to the boil.

Meanwhile, in a bowl mix the dumplings by beating eggs together with the milk and melted butter.

Reduce the heat to the simmer, then stir in the oysters.

Spoon the dumplings on top of the stew, cover, and steam until the dumplings are cooked.

Ladle into individual bowls.

INGREDIENTS:

The Kettle of Fish:
24 oysters, shucked with their liquor

4 oz. salt pork, 1/2-inch cubes
1 cup water
Salt & black pepper, to taste

The Dumplings:
4 eggs
1 ½ cups milk
6 T. butter, melted
1 ½ cups corn meal

Scallops

To begin with, let's understand how to pronounce this word. *Scallop* rhymes with *call up,* as in: "I'm going to *call up* everyone in New England and tell each one that you're just learning how to say this word!" If you insist upon saying *scallop* any other way, then we're *never* going to be able to see eye-to-eye.

But now that we understand each other, let's make certain that we know a little about this tasty little morsels from the sea.

In brief biological terms, scallops are more closely related to oysters than to any other sort of shellfish; however, the muscle which holds to two shells together is much larger. And this is the prized meat.

Unlike oysters, though, scallops cannot survive for long outside of the water, and so they are seldom sold in their shells. That means that your fishmonger sells them already shucked.

The other key facts you should know about scallops concern their size. The *bay scallops* that live within the familiar grooved shells provide a muscle meat that ranges from 1/2-inch to 1-inch in diameter, while the larger *sea scallops* with the smoother shells can be as large as 3 inches across. As their names suggest, the bays live in shallower waters (predominantly from Cape Cod to Cape Hatteras), and the sea scallops are in deeper waters offshore from the St. Lawrence River to the eastern coast of Florida.

Because a scallop season might not always yield a bumper crop, now and then some rather unscrupulous folks will try to make-up for the scarcity of scallops by trying to dupe consumers. For example, if scallops are soaked in water for a certain length of time, they not only lose some of their flavor, but also absorb a great deal of the liquid. As a result, the weight of a pound of scallops might be more water than meat. In addition, some people try to sell codfish cheeks as the genuine article, or else punch cyclindrical pieces of flesh from a skate or a shark. While it's worthwhile to know such things, it's more important to realize that most fishmongers take pride in the quality of their product and would never deal in such deception.

Nantucket Scallop Chowder
NANTUCKET ISLAND, MASSACHUSETTS

Though this island is so compact that it is a town, a county, and an island all in one, Nantucket is the largest scallop fishery along the entire eastern seaboard of the United States, and the shellfish itself is nothing less than gold in this economy. As for this kettle of fish, it remains the island's treasure. As you work your way through its 3 distinct and deliberate stages, take your time and do not allow anything to boil except for the potatoes.

INGREDIENTS:

16 oz. bay scallops

6 T. butter
1 onion, sliced thin
2 cups milk
2 cups cream
1 cup water
1 T. salt
1 potato, peeled & in 1/2-inch cubes
Salt & pepper, to taste
4 T. butter, for garnish
Paprika, for garnish

IN YOUR KETTLE, melt 4 T. of the butter, then sauté the onion for 10 minutes.

Stir in the milk and the cream, then partially cover and bring to the simmer for 15 minutes.

Remove the kettle from the heat.

Strain the stock through a fine sieve into a heatproof bowl. Discard the solids.

Meanwhile, in a saucepan bring the water to the boil. Add the salt and potatoes, then cook until potatoes are fork tender.

Drain the water from the potatoes and reserve them on a plate.

Wipe clean the kettle, then melt the remaining 2 T. of butter and sauté the scallops on each side until they are opaque.

Add the potato and the stock to the kettle, then bring to the simmer.

Stir, taste, and adjust the seasonings with salt & pepper.

Simmer for 5 minutes.

Ladle into individual heated bowls.

Garnish each with a pat of butter and a sprinkle of paprika.

Scallop Chowder
NEW BEDFORD, MASSACHUSETTS

The historic rivalry between New Bedford and Nantucket as to which was the greater whaling port has its counterpart in the debate over which is the capital of the scallop industry along the eastern seaboard. Perhaps we could give one trophy to the New Bedford draggers for their harvest of sea scallops and award another to the island for its bay scallops; however, don't say that it was my idea.

Meanwhile, the ingredients in this kettle of fish are very similar to the Nantucket chowder, but the process is less ritualistic.

INGREDIENTS:

24 oz. sea scallops, cut into 1/2-inch pieces

2 T. butter
1 onion, chopped
3 cups milk
3 cups cream
6 red-skinned potatoes, cubed
Salt & pepper, to taste
Paprika, for garnish

IN YOUR KETTLE, heat the butter, then brown the pieces of scallops.

Meanwhile, in a separate saucepan begin to cook the potatoes until they are fork tender.

When the scallops have begun to caramelize and brown, add the onions and sauté for 3 minutes.

Stir in the milk and bring it to the simmer, but not the boil.

Add the cooked potatoes to the kettle.
Stir, taste, and adjust the seasonings with salt & pepper.
Add the cream and simmer until heated throughout.
Ladle into individual heated bowls.
Garnish with paprika.

Scallop Soup
KURE, JAPAN

This particular kettle of fish uses *dashi* as its cooking liquid, but you could also make this with a fish consommé.

IN YOUR KETTLE, bring the *dashi* to the simmer.

Add the leek and carrot, then simmer for 5 minutes.

Add the scallops and poach for 3 minutes, but do not be concerned if the stock should become a bit cloudy.

Taste and adjust the seasonings with salt.

Remove and distibute the scallops in equal servings.

Ladle the *dashi* and vegetables into individual heated bowls.

INGREDIENTS:

16 oz. scallops

8 cups *dashi*
1 leek (white & pale green), washed & julienned
1 carrot, peeled & julienned
Salt, to taste

Scallop Stew

ST. CATHERINES ISLAND, GEORGIA

Though the original recipe for this kettle of fish utilizes the small, calico scallop from warmer waters, you'll find that this also works well with lobster meat, crab meat, or even shrimp.

INGREDIENTS:

12 oz. calico scallops

1 T. olive oil
1/2 onion, diced
1 leek (white & pale green parts), sliced
1 celery rib, sliced thin
1/2 green pepper, diced
1 medium tomato, seeded & diced
1 garlic clove, minced
3 cups stock
1 t. black pepper
1/2 t. dried thyme
1 t. Dijon mustard
1 t. Worcestershire
1 T. parsley, minced
2 bay leaves
1 cup milk

IN YOUR KETTLE, heat the oil, then sauté the onion, leek, celery and pepper about 3 minutes.

Stir in the tomato and garlic, then sauté for 1 minute.

Add the stock, thyme, pepper, mustard, Worcesteshire, parsley and bay leaves. Bring to the simmer for 15 minutes.

Remove the kettle from the heat and add the scallops. Stir and allow this to stand for 5 minutes.

Meanwhile, warm the milk in a separate saucepan.

Remove and discard the bay leaf.

Stir in the heated milk.

Ladle into individual heated bowls.

Cold Scallop Soup

SCITUATE, MASSACHUSETTS

When cooked properly, even these large sea scallops remain sweet and succulent; if overcooked, however, they can become just another something in the stock. I've found that this particular kettle of fish is almost foolproof, because you can watch the poaching of the scallops carefully, then never worry about their cooking any more beyond that.

INGREDIENTS:

8 sea scallops, in 1/2-inch pieces

1 T. butter
1 onion, sliced
2/3 cup milk
2 bay leaves
3 cups stock
2 bunches of watercress, washed and picked over
1 potato, diced
Salt & pepper
3 T. sherry
2 t. cornstarch
4 T. heavy cream
Watercress, for garnish

IN YOUR KETTLE, melt the butter, then sauté the onion for 5 minutes.

Meanwhile, in a separate saucepan bring the milk and bay leaves to the simmer, then add the scallops and poach for 5 minutes.

Remove and reserve the scallops on a clean plate.

Add the poaching liquid to the kettle, along with the stock, watercress, and potato.

Stir, taste, and adjust the seasonings with salt & pepper.

Bring the kettle to the boil, then reduce the heat and allow to simmer until the potatoes are fork tender.

Stir in the sherry.

Process the soup in batches in a blender until smooth, then return to the kettle.

Meanwhile, in a small bowl combine 1/2 cup of the soup with the the cornstarch, then mix into the kettle.

Bring the kettle to the boil, reduce the heat, and simmer 5 minutes.

Remove the kettle from the heat and cool, then refrigerate for at least 2 hours.

Chop the reserved scallops, then add to the kettle, along with the cream. Stir thoroughly.

Ladle into individual chilled bowls.

Garnish with watercress.

Cream of Scallop Soup
LITTLEHAMPTON, ENGLAND

Some might view this kettle of fish as an Anglicized version of Coquille St. Jacques, and they would not be that far astray, for there are countless recipes that bear that name. In France, however, *Coquille St. Jacques* is the name for the scallop, not a recipe.

One of the fisherman apostles of early Christianity, James was beheaded by King Herod and later canonized as patron saint of shellfish and the gatherers of shellfish alike. Those who later made pilgrimages to his shrine each wore a scallop shell — a *coquille* — as a badge. Over the years, this symbolic shell of St. James — *coquille St. Jacques* — became the idiom for the scallop itself. And so, many confuse this one ingredient with any number of recipes which include it within the name, such as *Coquille St. Jacques au gratin* or *Créme de Coquille St. Jacques.*

INGREDIENTS:

12 sea scallops, chopped coarse

4 cups stock
Salt & pepper, to taste
1 bay leaf
1 clove
1 T. onion, chopped
1 T. butter
1 T. flour
1 cup heavy cream
1 yolk
Parsley, garnish

IN YOUR KETTLE, combine the stock, salt & pepper, bay leaf, clove, and onion, then simmer gently for 20 minutes.

Remove the kettle from the heat, then strain the stock through a sieve into a heatproof bowl. Discard the solids.

Wipe clean the kettle, then make a white roux from the flour and butter. Melt the butter, then sprinkle in the flour and stir until thickened.

Gradually stir the stock back into the kettle until all has been added, then cover and bring to the simmer for 20 minutes.

Meanwhile, in a small bowl make a liaison with the egg yolk and cream. Carefully, blend this into the soup.

Stir in the scallop meats and simmer for 5 minutes.

Stir, taste, and adjust the seasonings with salt & pepper.

Ladle into individual heated bowls.

Garnish with chopped parsley.

Scallop Chowder

BLOCK ISLAND, RHODE ISLAND

This recipe brings together many of the ingredients one would find in Créme de Coquille St. Jacques; namely, the wine and cheese. In this case, the sharp cheddar is punctuated by zesty Dijon, then enhanced with the sweetness of onions.

IN YOUR KETTLE, melt the butter, then sauté the onions for 5 minutes.

Stir in the chopped scallops and sauté until they just become opaque.

Add the milk, cover, and bring to the simmer for 20 minutes.

Stir in the shredded cheddar until completely melted.

Add the mustard, wine, and chervil.

Stir, taste, and adjust the seasonings with salt & pepper.

Ladle into individual heated bowls.

Top each with a toasted crouton.

INGREDIENTS:

24 oz. sea scallops, chopped coarse

6 T. butter
4 large onions, sliced
5 cups milk
1 cup cheddar cheese, shredded
1/2 t. Dijon mustard
2 T. dry white wine
1 t. chervil, chopped
Salt & pepper, to taste
Croutons, for garnish

Scallop Soup
CANET-PLAGE, FRANCE

This is yet another variation of the cream soup made with scallops. Though they are most definitely similar in their ingredients, their proportions lend a distinct nuance to each kettle of fish.

INGREDIENTS:

16 oz. sea scallops, in 1/2-inch pieces

3 T. butter
3 shallots, chopped
1/2 cup mushrooms, chopped
4 parsley sprigs
1/4 t. cayenne pepper
2 cups dry white wine
Salt & pepper, to taste
3 egg yolks
1 cup cream

IN YOUR KETTLE, melt the butter, then sauté the shallots and mushrooms for 5 minutes.

Add the cayenne pepper and wine, then bring to the boil.

Add the scallops, reduce the heat, and simmer for 5 minutes.

Stir, taste and adjust the seasonings with salt & pepper.

Remove the kettle from the heat, then strain the stock through a sieve into a heatproof bowl. Remove and reserve the scallops on a clean plate, then discard the solids.

Return the stock to the kettle and bring to the simmer.

Meanwhile, in a small bowl beat the egg yolks slightly, then mix in the cream. Spoon some of the simmering stock into the bowl to temper the eggs and cream, then stir this into the kettle of stock.

Cook slowly until the stock has thickened.

Meanwhile, chop the scallops roughly.

Add the scallops to the kettle and stir.

Simmer for 3 minutes.

Ladle into individual heated bowls.

Cold Scallop Soup

LA TESTE, FRANCE

About this point, you must be asking: "How many variations can there be of this kettle of fish?" Jillions! This, however, is the last — until we leave France. Indeed, the serving temperature for this recipe is different, but the subtle flavors also make this one worthy of your consideration.

IN YOUR KETTLE, melt the butter, then sauté the onion and celery for 3 minutes.

Add the peppercorns, salt, thyme, and wine, then bring to the boil.

Add the scallops, reduce the heat, and simmer for 5 minutes.

Remove the kettle from the heat, then strain the stock through a sieve into a heatproof bowl. Remove and reserve the scallops on a clean plate, then discard the solids.

Wipe clean the kettle and heat the olive oil. Add the flour and make a white roux, being careful not to brown the flour.

Slowly stir the stock into roux, then bring to the boil. Reduce the heat and simmer until the stock has thickened.

Add the scallops to the kettle and stir.

Remove the kettle from the heat and allow to cool. Place in the refrigerator to chill at least 2 hours.

Stir the cream into the soup.

Ladle into individual chilled bowls.

Garnish with parsley.

INGREDIENTS:

16 oz. scallops

1 T. butter
2 cups Chablis
1 onion, chopped
2 celery ribs, chopped
16 whole black peppercorns
1/4 t. salt
1/4 t. thyme, crushed
2 T. olive oil
2 T. flour
2 cups cream
2 T. parsley, chopped

Cockle Soup

YOUGHAL, IRELAND

The twist to the preparation of this particular kettle of fish is that it treats the cockle much as we have treated a hardshell clam or a mussel; namely, it is steamed in its shell and helps to create its own broth. Whenever the occasion arises, I prefer this method, because that broth includes the taste of juices that might otherwise have been lost in the shucking.

INGREDIENTS:

16 cockles, scrubbed

6 T. butter
2 onions, diced
3 celery ribs, chopped
2 cups water
4 cups milk
4 T. cornstarch
Salt & pepper, to taste
4 t. butter, for garnish
Parsley, chopped for garnish

IN YOUR KETTLE, melt the butter, then sauté the onion and celery for 5 minutes.

Add the cockles and water, then cover and bring to the boil until all the cockles have opened.

Coax any cockles that have not opened with a gentle pry from the point of a knife, then remove and discard any cockles do not.

Remove and reserve the cockle meats to a dish and keep warm. Discard the shells.

Remove the kettle from the heat, then strain the stock through a colander into a heatproof bowl and discard the solids.

Return the stock to the kettle, bring to the boil, and allow it to reduce to 2 cups.

Stir in the milk, reduce the heat, and allow the kettle to simmer.

Meanwhile, in a small bowl mix the cornstarch with an equal amount of milk, then stir this paste into the soup.

Simmer until thickened.

Stir, taste and adjust the seasonings with salt & pepper.

Return the cockles to the kettle and simmer for 3 more minutes.

Ladle into individual heated bowls.

Garnish each with a pat of butter and a sprinkle of parsley.

Abalone

Unlike the other shellfish mentioned prior to now in this book, the abalone — like the conch — is a cephalopod which lives within a single shell, and this particular shell is a beauty. In fact, its iridescent qualities long made the abalone more profitable in the jewelry industry than in the food trade. Nonetheless, it has enjoyed a following on both sides of the Pacific, as well as in Europe and the Mediterranean.

More closely related to the snail than the clam, this mild-flavored, but rather rubbery shellfish must be tenderized or cooked before it can even be chopped. And while canned abalone is readily available in a great many supermarkets (you just need to look for it!), the fresh meat is not particularly difficult to prepare. Be certain to scrape off the black film of the meat and rinse well, then use the fine blade on a food chopper to process the meat and save the juices.

Abalone Chowder

MONTEREY, CALIFORNIA

The most commercially popular species of this particular shellfish in the United States is the red abalone, which is harvested off the Monterey peninsula. The ingredients in this kettle of fish look as familiar as those in a New England chowder.

IN YOUR KETTLE, render the salt pork until crisp and brown.

Discard all but 2 T. of the drippings, then sauté the onions and abalone for 10 minutes.

Add the water to the kettle and bring to the boil.

Add the potatoes and bay leaf. Reduce the heat, cover, and simmer until the potatoes are fork tender.

Meanwhile, in a small saucepan heat the milk and butter. When the butter has melted completely, add this to the kettle.

Stir, taste, and adjust the seasonings with salt & pepper.

Add the parsley and simmer for 3 minutes.

Ladle into individual heated bowls.

Garnish with chives.

INGREDIENTS:

16 oz. abalone meat, tenderized & in 1/4-inch pieces

4 oz. salt pork, diced
1 onion, chopped
2 cups boiling water
2 potatoes, peeled & diced
1 bay leaf
2 cups evaporated milk
1 T. butter
Salt & pepper, to taste
3 T. parsley, chopped
4 T. fresh chives, chopped for garnish

Abalone Cream Soup

POINT ARGUELLO, CALIFORNIA

Given the close relationship of sorts between the abalone and the conch, it remained a surprise to me that I could not find any recipe for conch which also made use of cream in its stock. Not having found any law against that either, I also tried this recipe with conch and found it to be just as good. Surprised? I think not.

INGREDIENTS:

16 oz. abalone, tenderized & in
  1/4-inch pieces

1 T. butter
1 T. green pepper, chopped
3 scallions (white part), chopped
2 celery ribs, diced
3 cups stock
1/4 t. thyme
1 tomato, peeled, seeded & chopped
Juice of 1/2 lemon
1/2 cup heavy cream
1/4 t. salt
2 egg yolks, beaten slightly

IN YOUR KETTLE, melt the butter, then sauté the green pepper, scallions, and celery for 5 minutes.

Stir in the stock, thyme, and tomato, then cover and bring to the simmer for 10 minutes.

Remove the kettle from the heat, then purée the soup in small batches with a blender.

Return the soup to the kettle.

Stir in the abalone meat and juices, then cover and bring to the simmer for 15 minutes.

Remove the kettle from the heat and strain the soup through a sieve into a heatproof bowl. Discard all the solids and return the strained soup to the kettle.

Bring the kettle to the simmer, then stir in the lemon juice, cream, and salt.

Meanwhile, in a small bowl beat the egg yolks slightly, then add a small amount of the heated soup. Blend them together, then stir into the kettle and simmer another 2 minutes.

Ladle into individual heated bowls.

Conch

As with scallops, you must be certain to pronounce this shellfish properly: it's *konK* (as in *bonk!*), not *konCH.* Okay? Now let's get on with it.

If you were not surprised to learn that how to say the name of this shellfish, you still might be caught off-guard to discover that it's in the same biological family as the squid. But more on that in a couple of pages.

As kids, we used to bring live conchs home from the beach and boil them to clean out their shells. None of us kids thought much of eating one, because they truly had a fishy smell; however, that comes from boiling them in the shell.

In Key West, where the native islanders are called *Conchs* and the fishery has now been severely restricted, they have an easier — but more tedious — method of getting the meat from its shell. They simply hook a piece of the protruding meat, then hang it up somewhere. The pull of gravity will eventually tire the conch and force it to give up (drop!) the shell.

Still another method is to pour some salt into the shell. This will cause the conch to crawl out.

As with the abalone, the conch really ought to be tenderized; however, all this can be avoided if you simply ask your fishmonger to order you some. Shell and cleaned, the conch meat comes in a 5-pound box, generally from Jamaica. Use what you need, then freeze the rest.

Unlike the abalone, though, the conch does have a relatively strong flavor, and a little can go a long way. You'll find that most of the recipes have a heavy dose of pepper or other spice to help offset that taste.

Keys Conch Chowder

KEY WEST, FLORIDA

As with every other recipe included in this book, any attempt to present this as the *definitive* one would only invite a blizzard of correspondence on the subject. Please, then, accept these next 3 only as variations upon a theme.

That said, I do want to point out that the best place to enjoy conch chowder in Key West is a little spot called B.O.'s Fish Wagon, which is located — as of this writing — at the corner of Caroline & William, not far from where the shrimpboats tie up to the pilings. This is not B.O.'s recipe, but I can't eat any sort of conch without thinking of his place.

INGREDIENTS:
16 oz. conch steak, chopped

6 cups water
1/4 cup Key Lime juice
1 T. salt
1/3 cup olive oil
1 green pepper, diced
1 onion diced
3 celery ribs, diced
2 garlic cloves, chopped
1/2 t. red pepper flakes, crushed
1/4 t. thyme
1 cup parsley, chopped
1/2 cup rice, uncooked

Prepare the conch steak by placing it upon a plate, rubbing it with the salt, and allowing it to stand for 15 minutes.

Rinse the conch steak well. Using a coarse blade, chop the conch in a food processor.

IN YOUR KETTLE, combine the conch meat, water, lime juice, and salt, then bring to the boil.

Cover, reduce the heat, and simmer for 30 minutes.

Meanwhile, in a small skillet heat the oil, then sauté the pepper, onion, celery, garlic, thyme, and 1/2 cup of parsley for 5 minutes.

Stir the sautéed vegetables into the kettle, then simmer 1 hour.

Add the rice, stir, and simmer another 30 minutes.

Stir in the remaining parsley.

Ladle into individual heated bowls.

Keys Conch Soup

BIG PINE KEY, FLORIDA

Barley is one of those ingredients we often associate with other kinds of soups, but seldom with a kettle of fish. Unlike corn, which — we are reminded time and time again — was a new concept to settlers when they arrived upon these shores, barley was something they brought *to* this continent from the Old World. Given the taste and texture of conch, barley does make a fine complementary ingredient to this thicker kettle of fish.

Prepare the conch steak by placing it upon a plate, rubbing it with the salt, and allowing it to stand for 15 minutes.

Rinse the conch steak well. Using a coarse blade, chop the conch in a food processor.

INGREDIENTS:

16 oz. conch steak, chopped

1 cup barley, uncooked
2 T. salt
4 oz. salt pork, diced
2 onions, chopped
1 sweet red pepper, chopped

IN YOUR KETTLE, cook the barley according to directions on the package.

Remove the kettle from the heat, then pour the cooked barley and its water into a heatproof bowl.

Wipe clean the kettle, then render the salt pork until crisp and brown.

Discard all but 2 T. of the drippings, then sauté the onions and pepper for 5 minutes.

Add the conch to the kettle, along with the barley and its liquid.

Stir well, then cover and bring to the simmer until the conch meat is cooked.

Ladle into individual heated bowls.

Conch Soup

HOPE TOWN, GREAT ABACO ISLAND, THE BAHAMAS

Generally, you will come upon two basic variations of a kettle of fish made with conch. One is white; the other, red. Sound familiar? If so, then you already know the essential difference among the ingredients.

INGREDIENTS:

16 oz. conch steak, chopped

4 oz. salt pork, diced
1 onion, diced
1 sweet red pepper, diced
1 t. flour
2 tomatoes, peeled, seeded & chopped
6 cups water
2 potatoes, peeled & diced
4 T. butter, garnish

Prepare the conch steak by placing it upon a plate, rubbing it with the salt, and allowing it to stand for 15 minutes.

Rinse the conch steak well. Using a coarse blade, chop the conch in a food processor.

IN YOUR KETTLE, render the salt pork until crisp and brown.

Discard all but 2 T. of the drippings, then sauté the onion and pepper for 5 minutes.

Sprinkle the flour into the kettle and stir to incorporate with the drippings and vegetables.

Stir in the tomatoes and water, then bring to the simmer for 5 minutes.

Add the conch and potatoes to the kettle and bring to the boil.

Reduce the heat and simmer for 1 hour.

Ladle into individual heated bowls.

Garnish each with a pat of butter.

Squid

When spring comes to Nantucket Sound and the shallow waters begin to warm, the annual migration of fish begins to arrive from the south. Before the striped bass come the blue fish. And before the blues come the squid. Just offshore the fishermen have strung their nets and await their catch of something more than baitfish.

For centuries, however, the peoples of Asia and the Mediterranean have long savored this simple and abundant catch. Though it does have fins, the squid's 10 tentacles — or feet — place it in the same category of cephalopods as the conch and the snail.

The cigar-shaped body is relatively hollow, except for a clear piece of cartilage and its legendary sac of ink. Its large head has two eyes and a beak, which are surrounded by the tentacles. And overall, a mantle of thin skin covers the body. Generally speaking, this is probably the easiest to clean of all the fish in this book.

The only cautionary note about squid is that you should either cook it very quickly, or else simmer it for 2 hours or more.

How to Clean a Squid

1. Grab the tentacles in one hand and the fins in another, then gently pull the head away from the body.

2. Being certain to cut a piece which holds the tentacles together as one, slice through just below the eyes. Discard the head and gizzards.

Fold back the tentacles and feel for the beak at their center. This can be simply removed by squeezing it between your 2 thumbnails. Discard the beak and rinse the tentacles.

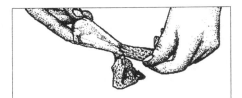

3. Peel and discard the membrane which covers the mantle, then feel inside to find the thin, clear cartilage that looks like a piece of plastic. Remove and discard the cartilage.

Rinse the mantle to wash out any ink from the sac within.

Red Squid Stew

NEW BEDFORD, MASSACHUSETTS

Most recipes will call for the mantle to be sliced across into rings, but a few will suggest you keep it whole. Nearly all of them indicate that the tentacles should remain as a single piece, otherwise they will float throughout your kettle of fish.

Though the dollop of *aïoli* might provide a finishing touch of elegance to some, I always think of this recipe as a hearty kettle of fish, rich with tomatoes and red wine. Just thinking of it makes my mouth water!

INGREDIENTS:

8 squid, cleaned & cut into 1/2-inch rings

4 T. olive oil
16 garlic cloves, peeled
5 T. flour
Bouquet garni
4 cups full-bodied red wine
4 tomatoes, peeled, seeded & chopped
16 mushrooms, quartered
2 T. parsley, chopped
Salt & pepper, to taste
4 T. *aïoli*, for garnish

IN YOUR KETTLE, heat the olive oil, then sauté the garlic for 3 minutes.

Dredge the squid in flour, then add to the kettle and brown.

Stir in the wine, tomatoes, and *bouquet garni*, then cover and bring to the simmer for 30 minutes.

Remove and discard the *bouquet garni*.

Use a slotted spoon, to remove and divide the garlic and squid among the four heated bowls.

Add the mushrooms and parsley to the soup, then simmer for 3 minutes.

Stir, taste and adjust the seasonings with salt & pepper.
Ladle the soup in the individual heated bowls.
Garnish with *aïoli*.

Portuguese Squid
FALL RIVER, MASSACHUSETTS

This kettle of fish is especially good when prepared with squid, but it is even better than that if you are able to sneak in a handful of hardshell clams, oysters, or shrimp.

IN YOUR KETTLE, heat the oil, then sauté the onions, pepper, and olives for 3 minutes.

Add the potatoes, black pepper, fish stock, lemon juice, and orange juice, then cover and bring to the simmer for 15 minutes.

Stir in the parsley and squid, then simmer another minute.

Ladle into individual heated bowls.

Garnish with hard-boiled egg.

INGREDIENTS:

24 oz. whole squid, cleaned & cut into rings

1 T. olive oil
1/2 red onion, sliced
1 large red bell pepper, sliced
4 black olives, sliced
1 lb red-skinned potatoes, diced in 1/2-inch cube
1/4 t. black pepper
2 cups stock
1 T. lemon juice
2 T. orange juice
2 T. parsley, minced
1 hard-boiled egg, chopped for garnish

Squid Stew

WOODS HOLE, CAPE COD, MASSACHUSETTS

As simple as this recipe is, the key to this kettle of fish is in cooking the squid just enough. This will be done if you do remove the kettle from the heat and allow the squid to cook in that short time. Have faith and don't think you'll accomplish anything by allowing the squid to boil; it will just become rubbery.

INGREDIENTS:

4 whole squid, cleaned & cut into 1-inch rings

1 T. butter
1 onion, chopped
1/4 t. allspice
1/2 cup tomato paste
6 cups stock
Dash of Worcestershire
1/4 t. saffron threads
1/2 cup sherry
Salt & black pepper, to taste
1 cup quick rice

IN YOUR KETTLE, melt the butter, then sauté the onions until thoroughly browned.

Add to the kettle the tomato paste and stock along with the saffron and allspice, then bring to the simmer for 30 minutes.

Stir in the Worcestershire and sherry, then taste and adjust the seasonings with salt & pepper.

Bring the kettle to the boil.

Add the squid, cover, and remove the kettle from the heat.

Meanwhile, ladle 1 cup of the stock into a small saucepan and cook the rice according to directions.

When the rice is cooked, divide it among the individual heated bowls and ladle the stew on top.

Squid Stew

MADEIRA, PORTUGAL

Here is a recipe that requires that you actually stew the squid for some 2 hours or so, which is the only other way to assure that it comes out tender. Meanwhile, the other elements that distinguish this particular kettle of fish from others of the region is the inclusion not only of curry powder, but also ginger.

IN YOUR KETTLE, heat the olive oil, then sauté the onion, garlic, and pepper for 5 minutes.

Stir in the curry and ginger, then sauté 2 more minutes.

Stir in the bay leaf, tomatoes, and stock, then cover and bring to the simmer for 25 minutes.

Add the squid and wine, then cover and simmer gently for 2 hours.

Add the potatoes, then cover until they are fork tender.

Stir, taste, and adjust seasonings with salt.

Ladle into individual heated bowls.

INGREDIENTS:

4 squid, cleaned & sliced in 1/4-inch rings; tentacles, 1-inch lengths

2 T. olive oil
1 onion, peeled & chopped
2 garlic cloves, peeled & minced
1 green bell pepper, cored, seeded & cut into strips
1/2 t. curry powder
1/4 t. ginger, ground
1 bay leaf
2 tomatoes, peeled, seeded & chopped
4 cups stock
1/2 cup dry white wine
1 large potato, peeled & cut in 1-inch cubes
Salt, to taste

Lobster

No matter where you travel, it seems that the one word that *must* precede lobster is *Maine*. And with due reason. At last count, there were nearly 6,000 lobstermen licensed in the state of Maine, whose rocky seacoast (including all the bays, inlets, and islands) measures about 3,500 miles long. Still, the American lobster — the two-clawed beauty we expect to be served in a restaurant — swims in the cold waters from The Maritime Provinces down as far as the Outer Banks of North Carolina. There is a similar species in Norwegian waters and another off the European coast.

The *spiny lobster* lives in the Gulf of Mexico, the Caribbean, and Atlantic waters from the Carolinas to Brazil; its *rock lobster* relation roams the Pacific shores of South Africa and Australia.

For those who do not understand the difference between the American lobster and the spiny lobster, the former has two large, meat-filled claws: a *crusher* and the *quick*. In fact, the anatomy is very much like the much smaller *crawfish*. The spiny lobster lacks the large claws and has two long antennae. In this respect, it is more like a *shrimp* or *prawn*. Otherwise, their bodies are rather similar with the bulk of the meat being in the tail. There is, however, meat to be found in the 4 pairs of walking legs and the body cavity. Beyond that, there are gourmands who prize the green tomalley (the liver), as well as the coral roe of the females.

Finally, there is a smaller form of this crustacean called the *lobsterette*, which is found on both sides of the Atlantic and sometimes called the *Danish lobster*.

How to Cook a Lobster

Keep in mind that most lobsters are a brownish green, and only turn red upon cooking. A rare find, though, is a lobster with a blue shell, which tastes no different than the others.

As with the cooking of live crabs, cooking live lobsters presents a moral question for those who despise the thought of plunging a living being into boiling water. In each instance, however, there is a quick and relatively painless way to dispatch the animal beforehand. Using a small, sharp knife, plunge the point of the blade into the space between the eyes of the lobster. If this does not appeal to you, there is the alternative of placing the lobsters into a kettle of cold water, then bringing that to the boil; however, that process seems to be more of an moral illusion that anything else.

A lobster should be cooked for no longer than 12 minutes per pound, then plunged into cold water to retard any further cooking.

How to Clean a Lobster

1. Begin by removing the tail from the body, which is done simply by bending the top of the tail backward from the bottom of the body.

2. The meat of the tail can be removed in 2 ways. One is to cut through the bottom of the tail with a pair of ktichen shears, then remove the meat. The other is to break off the tail fan, then force a fork or your finger into the tail and push the meat out the other end.

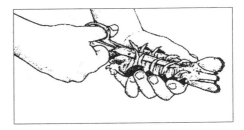

3. Remove the claws by twisting their *knuckles* (or arms) free from the body. The meat from the claws and knuckles can best be reached by using a lobster cracker, then removed with a pick.

4. Only the most patient folks will then work their way through the body itself to the precious, tiny pieces of meat, as well as the tomalley and roe. The best way to benefit from the 8 legs is simply to break each at their joints and suck out the meat.

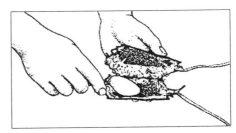

Lobster Stew

CHATHAM, CAPE COD, MASSACHUSETTS

"If you like the taste of a lobster stew, served by a window with an ocean view," crooned Patti Page, "you're sure to fall in love with old Cape Cod." Oddly enough, though, there are two ironies of sorts to her words. The first is that the writer of those lyrics had never been to the Cape before he had penned them. The second is that there are only two restaurants (of the *hundreds* on the peninsula!) from which you can see the Atlantic Ocean. Any others are on a harbor, a bay, or a sound. So much for semantics.

Meanwhile, any true lobster lover knows that there is a great deal of flavor to be derived from the fat that lines the inside of a lobster shell, as well as a distinctive color that comes from the roe. This recipe makes full use of those elements of the lobster that are often neglected by novices, or else put into a stock by chefs.

INGREDIENTS:
2 (1¼-lb.) lobsters, cooked & picked
Lobster coral & fat

4 T. butter
3 cups milk
1 cups heavy cream
Dash ground mace
Salt & white pepper, to taste
Butter, for garnish
Paprika, for garnish

IN YOUR KETTLE, melt the butter, then sauté for 2 minutes any coral and fat from the lobsters.

Add into the kettle the lobster meat and sauté for 5 minutes.

Meanwhile, in a small saucepan combine the milk and cream over low heat.

When the milk and cream begin to bubble around the edge, pour into the kettle.

Stir, taste, and adjust the seasonings with mace, salt & white pepper.

Though this stew will be ready to serve when heated through, it is best cooled, refrigerated overnight, and reheated the next day.

Ladle into individual heated bowls.

Garnish each with butter and paprika.

Lobster Stew

MAHONE BAY, NOVA SCOTIA

If there is a coastline any more rugged than that of downeast Maine, then it can only belong to Nova Scotia. Fortunately, though, its coastline outside the Gulf of Maine is on the western edge of the warmer Gulf Stream, so its weather is it more moderate. Still, this maritime province produces an important catch of cod, haddock, and the lobster we love.

IN YOUR KETTLE, melt the butter, then sauté the onion for 3 minutes.

Add the water and potatoes, then bring to the boil.

Reduce the heat, cover, and simmer until the potatoes are fork tender.

Add to the kettle the milk and lobster, then simmer for 5 minutes.

Stir, taste, and adjust the seasonings with salt & pepper.

Ladle into individual heated bowls.

INGREDIENTS:

2 (1¼-lb.) lobsters, cooked & picked

4 T. butter
1 onion, chopped fine
2 cups water
2 potatoes, peeled & chopped
2 cups milk
Salt & pepper, to taste

Lobster Chowder

EASTPORT, MAINE

As with many chowders made with the succulent meat of a Maine lobster, this one can also be made with — or by substituting — some other crustaceans, such as shrimp or crab, or even the simple scallop.

INGREDIENTS:

16 oz. lobster meat, in 1-inch pieces

2 T. butter
1 leek (white & pale green), washed & sliced
1 celery rib, sliced thin
Dash of nutmeg
1 potato, peeled & diced
3 cups stock
2 cups hot milk
1 cup warm cream
Paprika, for garnish

IN YOUR KETTLE, melt the butter, then sauté the leeks and celery for 3 minutes.

Stir in the potato, pepper, nutmeg, stock, and juice, then bring to the boil.

Reduce the heat, cover, and simmer for 20 minutes.

Meanwhile, in a small saucepan heat the milk.

Stir into the kettle the hot milk and lobster meat, then remove the kettle from the heat and let stand for 5 minutes.

Wipe clean the saucepan, then heat the cream.

Stir into the kettle the warm cream.

Ladle into individual heated bowls.

Garnish with paprika.

176

Lobster Bisque

MATTAPOISETT, MASSACHUSETTS

While much attention is often paid to nearby New Bedford as an historical port, other havens — such as Fairhaven, Marion, and Mattapoisett — along the western shoreline of Buzzards Bay were home to the builders and captains of vessels that plied the waters of the world.

INGREDIENTS:

2 (1½-lb.) cooked lobsters, cleaned & in 1-inch pieces
Reserved shells chopped

4 cups cream
2 cups milk
2 onions, peeled & sliced thin
1 garlic clove, crushed
2 parsley sprigs
1 bay leaf
2 cloves
4 whole black peppercorns
2 T. butter, softened
2 T. cracker crumbs
2 egg yolks, beaten
2 T. dry sherry
Salt & pepper, to taste
Parsley, for garnish

IN YOUR KETTLE, mix together the cream and milk, as well as the onion, garlic, parsley sprigs, bay leaf, cloves and peppercorns, then bring to the simmer.

Stir the chopped shells into the kettle, then partially cover and bring to the simmer for 45 minutes. Watch carefully and stir occasionally.

Remove the kettle from the heat. Strain the stock through a sieve into a heatproof bowl, then use a pestle to force the solids. Discard any solids that remain in the sieve, then return the stock to the kettle and bring to the simmer.

Meanwhile, in a small bowl make a paste of the butter and cracker crumbs, then blend in 1/2 cup of the strained stock.

Sir the paste into the kettle, along with the lobster meat.

Meanwhile, in a small bowl whisk together the yolks and sherry. Temper the egg with 1/2 cup of the heated stock, then stir into the kettle.

Simmer for 5 minutes.

Stir, taste, and adjust the seasonings with salt & pepper.

Ladle into individual heated bowls.

Garnish with parsley.

Lobster Bisque

SMØLA, NORWAY

Known as a *hummer* in Norway, a single 1½-pound lobster can provide enough meat for a hearty mid-day meal from this kettle of fish. Unlike most recipes for a bisque, however, this one does not create a new stock from the lobster's shell or body pieces.

INGREDIENTS:

16 oz. lobster meat, cooked & in 1/2-inch pieces

2 T. olive oil
2 celery ribs, chopped
1 carrot, peeled & diced
1 onion, diced
2 T. parsley, chopped
4 cups stock
1 bay leaf
6 whole black peppercorns
4 T. butter
4 T. flour
3 cups milk
1 cup cream, hot
Cayenne pepper, to taste
Salt, to taste
4 T. dry sherry, for garnish

IN YOUR KETTLE, heat the olive oil, then sauté the celery, carrot, onion, and parsley for 5 minutes.

Add the stock, bay leaf, and black peppercorns, then cover and bring to the simmer for 30 minutes.

Meanwhile, in a saucepan prepare a roux by melting the butter, then incorporating the flour. Cook only until the flour turns a light brown, then slowly add the milk. Bring to the simmer and stir until thickened.

Stir in the cayenne pepper, then remove the saucepan from the heat.

Remove the kettle from the heat, then strain the stock through a sieve into a heatproof bowl. Remove and discard the bay leaf and peppercorns, then force the vegetables through the sieve with a pestle. Discard any solids that remain.

Return the stock and vegetables to the kettle, then stir in the thickened milk mixture and bring to the simmer.

Meanwhile, in a small saucepan bring the cream to the simmer.

Stir the kettle, taste, and adjust the seasonings with salt & pepper.

Add the lobster meat, then simmer another 5 minutes.

Ladle into individual heated bowls.

Garnish each with 1 T. of sherry.

Lobster Soup

EDGARTOWN, MARTHA'S VINEYARD, MASSACHUSETTS

While the science of mariculture has enabled the profitable farming of all sorts of finfish and shellfish alike, lobsters have proven to be the somewhat of an exception. Being cannibalistic, lobsters do not particularly enjoy the cramped quarters and waters of a breeding tank. Still, the first and only lobster hatchery in the world was built back in the 1940s on the island of Martha's Vineyard, where it still remains in operation as a research facility.

IN YOUR KETTLE, melt the butter, then sauté the celery, onion, and carrot for 5 minutes.

Stir in the lobster shells and body, along with the white wine, then simmer for 10 minutes.

Meanwhile, in a small bowl combine the flour and water to make a thin paste, then stir into the kettle and gradually add the stock.

Stir in the sprigs of thyme and parsley, then simmer for 30 minutes.

Remove the kettle from the heat, then strain the stock through a colander into a heatproof bowl.

Add to the kettle the milk and lobster meat, then bring to the simmer.

Return the strained stock to the kettle and simmer for 5 minutes.

Meanwhile, in a small bowl make a liaison with the egg yolk and cream, then blend this into the kettle. Do not allow this to come to the boil.

Stir, taste and adjust the seasoning.

(If you wish, anchovy paste may be added, to taste, just before serving.)

Ladle into individual heated bowls.

Garnish each with chopped cucumber.

INGREDIENTS:

1 (1½-lb.) cooked lobster, cleaned & in 1-inch pieces
Reserve shells, pounded
Reserve body

2 T. butter
2 celery ribs, diced
1 onion, chopped
1 carrot, diced
1/2 cup dry white wine
2 T. flour
2 T. water
4 cups stock
1 cup milk
2 thyme sprigs
2 parsley sprigs
2 egg yolks
3/4 cup cream
Anchovy paste (optional)
1 cucumber, peeled & diced fine

Lobster Soup

SASEBO, JAPAN

As with the Lobster Consommé on the opposite page, this recipe is about as light and delicate a kettle of fish as you might make and still have it display some substance. That said, neither is something that I would take the time to prepare and present properly unless I was certain that it would be appreciated by the other diners. Nonetheless, I include it here to help keep your collection complete.

INGREDIENTS:

6 oz. uncooked lobster meat, diced

2 cups water
1/2 t. salt
8 dried mushrooms
4 cups *dashi*
1 t. soy sauce
1-inch piece of cucumber, peeled & sliced thin
2 t. lemon zest

IN YOUR KETTLE, bring the water to the boil.

Meanwhile, in a small bowl soak the mushrooms in warm water to soften.

Combine the lobster meat with the salt, then shape into 8 oval patties. Place a wire cake rack over the top of the boiling kettle, then arrange the lobster patties on the rack to be cooked by the steam.

Remove the kettle from the heat and the wire rack from the kettle, then discard the water. Reserve the patties on a clean plate.

Wipe clean the kettle, then add 1 cup of *dashi* to the kettle, along with the soy sauce, and bring to the boil.

Reduce the heat, then add to the kettle the softened mushrooms and simmer for 2 minutes.

Stir in the remaining *dashi*, then simmer for another minute.

With a slotted spoon, remove the mushrooms and divide among 4 individual heated bowls.

Divide the lobster patties and the cucumber slices among the bowls as well.

Ladle the *dashi* into the individual heated bowls.

Garnish each with lemon zest.

Lobster Consommé
ROCKPORT, MASSACHUSETTS

The key to making a rich lobster consommé from a lobster stock is to include in this recipe the roe found in the female lobsters. The frugal way to do this is to ask your fishmonger for a female cull, which is a lobster that has lost one or both of her claws. The lobster tail will have enough meat for this recipe, and you'll still have the riches to be found in the body.

INGREDIENTS:

2 (1¼-lb.) female lobsters, cleaned & tail meat in 1-inch pieces
Reserve roe

5 cups crustacean stock
2 egg whites
1 onion, chopped
1 celery rib, chopped
2 T. parsley, chopped
1 tarragon sprig, chopped
Salt, to taste
Blanched tarragon, for garnish

IN YOUR KETTLE, bring the stock to the simmer.

Meanwhile, in a large bowl combine the egg whites, onion, celery, parsley, tarragon, reserved roe. Use your hands to knead the ingredients together and make certain that the egg whites cover the vegetables, herbs, and roe as much as possible.

Stir the mixture into the warm stock.

Bring the kettle to the simmer, then carefully move it to one side of the burner so that the heat is not directly beneath the center of the kettle. Stir and allow to cook for 45 minutes.

Every 10 minutes or so, adjust the kettle around the burner so that the heat does not cook in the same place.

After this time, a thick froth will have risen to the top of the stock. Create an opening in the froth so that the stock can continue to simmer to the surface, then simmer another 10 minutes or so until only a few particles of vegetables, herbs, roe, and egg can be seen in the clear broth.

Place a fine sieve over a heatproof bowl. Being careful not to disturb the thickened layer of froth, ladle the consommé into the sieve.

Wipe clean your kettle, then add the consommé and bring to the simmer.

Taste and adjust the seasoning with salt.

Divide the tail meat among the individual heated bowls.

Ladle the consommé into each.

Garnish with a tarragon leaf.

Crawfish

For the longest time I thought that there was some distinct difference between *crawfish* and *crayfish;* perhaps one was from saltwater and the other from freshwater. But I was wrong about that. A crawfish is a crayfish, and a crayfish is a crawfish. And I was wrong in thinking that these things that look like tiny lobsters were esteemed only by the folks of Louisiana when, in fact, these freshwater crustaceans are found on every continent of the world, except Africa. Though it is true that Louisiana farms them, as well as fishes them, the state of Oregon is not that far behind.

Because some species do have claws and others do not, most recipes call for the tail meat, which is most easily removed from the small body. In some respects the texture is like that of lobster, but there is also a similarity to that of shrimp.

Crawfish Stew

GRAND ISLE, LOUISIANA

The hallmark of Louisiana cooking is not necessarily that of the red pepper sauce that might first spring into your mind, but more likely the region's distinguishing use of roux. Everything — from etoufée to jambalaya — seems to begin with this quintessential blend of oil and flour that came from the cooks of France. And though *roux* is the word for "red" in the mother tongue, the full range of Louisiana roux extends from white to dark brown. That color is not simply a matter of aesthetics, but also an indication of taste.

IN YOUR KETTLE, make a dark brown roux by heating the oil over medium-high, then gradually whisking in the flour. Continue to stir and cook until the roux is nut brown, but not chocolate brown.

Stir in the onions, celery, bell pepper, and garlic, then sauté for 3 minutes.

Stir in the crawfish meat and cook until it just turns pink.

Add the tomato sauce, then begin to gradually stir in all of the stock and bring to the boil.

Reduce the heat and simmer for 30 minutes.

Add the scallions and parsley.

Stir, taste, and adjust the seasonings with salt, cayenne pepper, and Tabasco.

Cook the rice according to the directions on the package.

Ladle stew over rice into individual heated bowls.

INGREDIENTS:

24 oz. crawfish tails, uncooked & cleaned

2/3 cup vegetable oil
2/3 cup flour
2 onions, chopped
2 celery ribs, chopped
1 green bell pepper, chopped
4 garlic cloves, minced
1/4 cup tomato sauce
12 cups stock
2 scallions (entire), chopped
2/3 cup parsley, chopped
Salt, to taste
Cayenne pepper, to taste
Tabasco, to taste
1½ cups rice, cooked

Crawfish Soup

GDANSK, POLAND

If you have always thought of central Europe as a region that existson a diet of industrial strength, then you will certainly change your thinking after trying this kettle of fish. The soup itself is more a bisque, and the garnish of stuffed shells adds a delightful taste.

INGREDIENTS:

The Kettle of Fish:
12 crawfish, uncooked

1/2 cup dill, chopped
1 T. salt
2 cups water
2 T. butter
3 cups stock
1/4 cup sour cream
3 t. flour
3 t. dill, chopped for garnish

The Stuffing:
3 t. butter
1 egg yolk, hard-cooked
3 t. breadcrumbs
1/2 t. dill, minced
Salt & pepper, to taste

IN YOUR KETTLE, combine the water, dill, and salt, then bring to the boil.

Add the crawfish and cook for 5 minutes.

Remove the kettle from the heat. Strain the broth through a colander into a heatproof bowl and reserve.

Clean the crawfish and reserve the meat on a clean dish. Also reserve 4 of the shells. Rinse them under running water and set aside.

Using a mortar and pestle, pound the remaining shells, claws, and body fats.

Wipe clean the kettle, then melt the butter and sauté the pounded shells for 30 minutes.

Stir the reserved broth into the kettle, then simmer until reduced to about 1 cup. Skim the surface regularly and reserve the melted butter in a small bowl.

Strain the reduced broth through a sieve into a heatproof bowl, then return it to the kettle, along with the stock and simmer for 5 minutes.

Meanwhile, in a small bowl combine the sour cream and flour, then stir into the simmering kettle.

Add to the kettle the reserved crawfish meat, the dill, and the butter skimmed from the kettle, then simmer another 10 minutes.

Meanwhile, in a small bowl cream the butter. Blend in the hard-cooked egg yolks. Add the breadcrumbs and dill. Mix well, taste and adjust the seasonings with salt & pepper.

Spoon equal amounts of the stuffing into each shell.

Add the stuffed shells to the kettle, then allow them to simmer in the soup for 3 minutes.

Ladle into individual heated bowls.

Garnish each with a floating, stuffed shell. Sprinkle with chopped dill.

Crawfish Bisque

FRANÇOIS, MARTINIQUE, THE LESSER ANTILLES

Words cannot describe how the flavors blend together in this kettle of fish from the Windward Islands. Though you might have to shop around some to locate the fish and the coconut milk, I do believe that you'll discover this *bisque de cribiches* is worth all the effort.

INGREDIENTS:

24 oz. crawfish meat

3 T. butter
1 onion, chopped
2 garlic cloves
1 fennel sprig
2 T. red pepper flakes, crushed
4 cups stock
1 cup coconut milk
2 egg yolks
Salt & pepper, to taste

IN YOUR KETTLE, melt the butter, then sauté the onion and garlic for 5 minutes.

Add to the kettle the fennel sprig, red pepper flakes, and stock, then bring to the simmer for 30 minutes.

Remove the kettle from the heat, then strain the stock through a sieve into a heatproof bowl. Discard the solids and return the stock the the kettle.

In a blender, purée the crawfish meat with 1 cup of the stock, then add to the kettle.

Stir in the coconut milk and bring to the simmer.

Meanwhile, in a small bowl beat the egg yolks with a little of the stock to temper the eggs.

Stir the egg mixture into the kettle and simmer until thickened.

Stir, taste, and adjust the seasonings with salt & pepper.

Ladle into individual heated bowls.

Shrimp

Though most of the recipes in this book advise you to cook the shrimp until they "just become pink," you ought to keep in mind that some species of shrimp are pink to begin with. These are the tasty delights found around the Tortugas and in Florida waters; however, there are shrimp from Maine which also have a natural color that is dark pink. Among the 6 species of shrimp, the colors range from white to brown to pink, depending upon the mineral content of the water, as well as the diet of the shrimp itself. The so-called *tiger* shrimp seen in most supermarket fish departments are those bred on farms in southeast Asia.

And as I've noted before, there often is a distinction so fine among shrimp, crawfish, and spiny lobsters, that it's not uncommon for one to be called by the name of the other.

How to Peel & Devein a Shrimp

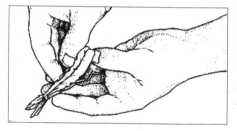

1. More often than not, you'll be buying shrimp which have already had their heads removed. Though you might find the whole shrimp available to you, the head sections (with their 5 pairs of walking legs) are more useful to the shrimp than the cook. They have no real food value except for making stocks. If you're given the option, then, purchase them without their heads.

2. Remove the legs simply by grabbing them between your fingers and giving a gentle tug. The shell itself is just as easily removed by peeling it back from the leg section with your thumbs. For most of these recipes, you'll also want to tug off the tail.

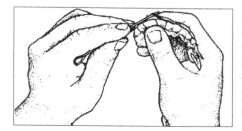

3. The black line along the length of the shrimp is the vein, easily removed with the point of a paring knife or toothpick. In small shrimp, this might not even be visible or worth the effort of removing. In fact, removing the vein is often more a matter of aesthetics than taste.

4. If a recipe indicates that you *butterfly* the shrimp, simply slice through the back of the shrimp without cutting it into halves.

Shrimpball Soup

ZHANJIANG, CHINA

This recipe does take a little bit of time to prepare, mainly because you must cool the prepared stock in order to skim it sufficiently. If you do have the time to do this ahead of time, then bringing everything together is relatively, and you'll present a kettle of fish that's both interesting and enjoyable .

INGREDIENTS:

Uncooked shells from 3 lbs. shrimp
8 oz. uncooked shrimp, peeled,
  deveined & chopped fine

1/4 cup peanut oil
1/2 onion, chopped
1 garlic clove
1 T. gingerroot, grated
2 T. soy sauce
1/4 cup sherry
4 cups stock
2 T. water chestnuts, chopped
2 scallions (white parts), chopped
4 t. cornstarch
1 egg
4 lemon slices, for garnish

IN YOUR KETTLE, heat the peanut oil, then sauté the shells until they turn pink. sauté another minute

Add the onion, garlic, and ginger, then sauté 2 minutes more.

Stir in the soy sauce, sherry, and sauce, then bring to the simmer for 30 minutes.

Remove the kettle from the heat, then strain the stock through a sieve into a heatproof bowl and allow to cool.

Meanwhile, in another bowl mix together the shrimp, water chestnuts, scallions, cornstarch, and egg, then form them into balls about the size of a walnut.

Skim the cooled stock, then return it to the kettle and bring to the simmer.

Add the shrimp balls to the kettle and poach for 10 minutes.

Ladle the soup into individual heated bowls and divide the shrimp balls equally among them.

Garnish each with a lemon slice.

Calico Stew

ANCHOR BAY, CALIFORNIA

The ingredients in this kettle of fish remind me very much of a Portuguese recipe that relies upon pork, rather than chicken for the added richness. You might try it with "the other white meat," as well as with scallops, crab meat, or lobster.

IN YOUR KETTLE, heat the oil, then brown the pieces of chicken.

Add the scallion, carrot, and garlic, then sauté for 3 minutes.

Stir in the corn, tomato, snow peas, parsley, thyme, and stock, then bring to the simmer for 10 minutes.

Add the milk and shrimp, then simmer until the shrimp just become pink.

Ladle into individual heated bowls.

INGREDIENTS:

12 extra large uncooked shrimp, peeled & deveined
8 oz. chicken breast, boned & in 1-inch pieces

1 t. olive oil
1/4 cup scallion, chopped
1 carrot, sliced
1 garlic clove, minced
1 ear corn kernels
1 tomato, seeded & diced
4 oz. snow peas
1 T. parsley
1/4 t. dried thyme
1 cup stock
1/2 cup milk

Shrimp Soup
CHIBA, JAPAN

Essentially, this *Ebi no Suimono* is a heated broth within which you poach the shrimp. This does require some prep time, not only to poach and chill the shrimp, but also to configure them into their little pinwheels.

INGREDIENTS:
8 large shrimp, shelled & deveined (tail on)

2 T. cornstarch
1 oz. canned bamboo shoot (soft part)
4 cups stock
8 toothpicks
Lemon zest

IN YOUR KETTLE, bring the stock to the boil.

Arrange the shrimp in pinwheel pairs (positioning the heads within the opposing tails), then fasten each pair with 2 toothpicks. Dredge in cornstarch, then cook in stock for 4 minutes.

With a slotted spoon, remove the shrimp to a piece of paper towel to drain. Place on a plate and chill for 2 hours in the refrigerator. Do not discard the stock.

To serve, bring the stock again to the boil.

About 1½ inches from its point, cut a piece of bamboo shoot then julienne this into pieces about 1/10-inch thick.

Carefully remove the toothpicks from the shrimp, then arrange each pair with the bamboo shoot in separate bowls.

Ladle the stock over the shrimp and bamboo.

Garnish with lemon zest.

Shrimp Pozole

YÁVAROS, MEXICO

Hominy is misunderstood by most well-meaning folks around New England, but they'd probably be amazed to discover that it was introduced to the settlers from Europe in the 1620s by the Native Americans who called their parched corn *rockahominie* and their hulled corn *tackhummin*. Hominy, after all, is nothing other than dried, hulled kernels of white corn.

As popular as the dish has been in the history of the American South, so it is with the peoples of Mexico who can lay claims just as strong to this form of grain. By including hominy in this kettle of fish, the stew becomes known as a *pozole*, which can be made with either other forms of fish, or even meat or poultry.

IN YOUR KETTLE, heat the olive oil, then sauté the onion for 5 minutes.

Add to the kettle the hominy, tomatoes, ancho chili peppers, cumin, and stock, then cover and bring to the simmer for 5 minutes.

Stir in the fish and simmer until the fish begins to flake.

Stir, taste, and adjust the seasonings with Tabasco.

Ladle into individual heated bowls.

Garnish each with the juice of 1/4 lime.

INGREDIENTS:

16 oz. uncooked shrimp, peeled & deveined

2 T. olive oil

1 onion, peeled & sliced

1 cup canned hominy, rinsed & drained

2 tomatoes, peeled, seeded & diced

4 ancho chili peppers, stemmed, seeded & chopped

1 t. cumin, ground

3 cups stock

Tabasco, to taste

1 lime, quartered

Cream of Shrimp Soup
DAUPHIN ISLAND, ALABAMA

From the barrier islands in the gulf just off the coastline of Alabama and Mississippi comes a kettle of fish so rich and tasty that you'll find yourself thinking about it for days after you've finished the last spoonful. Before long, you'll be making up occasions and reasons to prepare this recipe once again.

INGREDIENTS:
8 oz. uncooked shrimp, peeled & deveined

1 T. butter
1 T. flour
3 cups stock
1 egg yolk
1 T. cream
Salt & pepper, to taste
4 T. sour cream, for garnish
Parsley, for garnish

IN YOUR KETTLE, melt the butter over medium heat. Add the flour and stir in thoroughly to make a roux.

Slowly stir in the stock, then bring to the simmer for 5 minutes.

Remove the kettle from the heat and allow to cool for 5 minutes.

Meanwhile, in a small bowl combine the egg yolk and cream.

When the thickened stock has cooled, stir in the egg and cream mixture thoroughly.

Return the kettle to the heat and bring to the simmer.

Stir, taste, and adjust the seasonings with salt & pepper.

Stir in the shrimp and simmer until the shrimp just turn pink.

Ladle into individual bowls.

Garnish each with a dollop sour cream and a sprinkle of parsley.

Creamed Shrimp Soup
SAGRES, PORTUGAL

Though the shrimp off the cosat of Portugal are a bit different from those we are used to, there is nothing lost in this kettle of fish. As you will see, though, the presentation of this recipe calls for you to butterfly the shrimp before adding them to the kettle. This causes them to appear larger than they truly are, and it's a style you can add to any other shrimp recipe in this book.

IN YOUR KETTLE, heat the butter and olive oil, then sauté the onion and garlic 3 minutes.

Stir in the tomato paste and sauté for 3 minutes more.

Add to the kettle the tomatoes, wine, and fish stock, then bring to the boil.

Stir in the red pepper flakes, then reduce the heat, cover, and simmer for 30 minutes.

Stir, taste, and adjust the seasonings with salt & pepper.

Remove the kettle from the heat and allow to cool.

Strain the soup through a sieve into a bowl, then use a pestle to force the vegetables through the sieve.

Return the strain soup to the kettle and bring to the simmer.

Add the shrimp to the kettle and cook until they just turn pink.

Ladle into individual heated bowls.

Garnish each by floating 1 T. of heavy cream atop the soup.

INGREDIENTS:

8 uncooked shrimp, peeled, deveined & butterflied

2 T. butter
2 T. olive oil
1 onion, sliced thin
2 garlic cloves, mashed
4 T. tomato paste
4 tomatoes, peeled, seeded & chopped
1 cup dry white wine
5 cups stock
1/2 t. red pepper flakes, crushed
Salt & pepper, to taste
4 T. heavy cream, for garnish

Shrimp Stew

MEMPHIS, TENNESSEE

Forget the simple fact that the only shoreline along this state comes from the flow of the "mighty Mississip," not exactly a natural habitat for shrimp. Still, this city is just across the line from the state of Mississippi itself, and it wouldn't take long today to bring up fresh crustaceans from the Gulf.

That said, this kettle of fish is but another variation of a basic recipe found in several other pages of this book.

INGREDIENTS:

16 oz. cooked shrimp, peeled & deveined

4 oz. salt pork, 1/4-inch cubes
1 cup onion, chopped
1/2 green bell pepper, chopped
2 cups water
2 potatoes, peeled & cubed
1½ cups canned tomatoes, chopped & with juices
1 bay leaf
Tabasco, to taste
Salt & pepper, to taste
2 T. parsley, chopped

IN YOUR KETTLE, render the salt pork until crisp and brown, then sauté the onion and green pepper for 10 minutes.

Add the water to the kettle and bring to the boil.

Add the potatoes, tomatoes with juices, and bay leaf.

Stir, taste, and adjust the seasonings with Tabasco, salt & pepper.

Simmer until potatoes are fork tender.

Remove and discard bay leaf.

Stir in the shrimp and parsley, then simmer another 3 minutes.

Ladle into individual heated bowls.

Shrimp & Corn Chowder

CAPE MAY, NEW JERSEY

From the shoreline of the Garden State, this especially fine kettle of fish combines the best of the area's two resources: the fertile farmland and the sea. Though you might expect that this is simply a corn chowder with shrimp added, the taste is not that simple.

IN YOUR KETTLE, combine the corn and onion with 1 cup of the scalded milk, then simmer for 20 minutes.

Meanwhile, in a small saucepan melt the butter, then sprinkle in the flour and stir to make a roux. Cook over low heat about 2 minutes.

Slowly add the remaining 1½ cups scalded milk to make a white sauce, whisking each time to keep the mixture smooth.

When all the milk has been added, taste and adjust the seasonings with salt & pepper.

Simmer another 5 minutes to ensure that the flour has cooked.

Remove the white sauce from the heat and keep warm.

Remove the kettle from the heat, then strain the stock through a sieve into a heatproof bowl. Use a pestle to force the onion and corn through the sieve into the bowl.

Return the stock to the kettle, then stir in the warm white sauce and bring to the simmer.

Meanwhile, in a small bowl combine the egg yolk and cream, then stir into the chowder.

Add the chopped shrimp and simmer until the shrimp meat just turns pink.

Stir, taste, and adjust the seasonings with salt & pepper.

Ladle into individual heated bowls.

Garnish with grated nutmeg.

INGREDIENTS:

8 oz. uncooked shrimp, peeled, deveined & chopped

1 cup kernel corn
2 onion slices
2½ cups milk, scalded
1 T. butter
1 T. flour
Salt & white pepper, to taste
1 egg yolk
1/2 cup cream
Salt & white pepper, to taste
Grated nutmeg, for garnish

Shrimp Soup
GUINCHO, PORTUGAL

As basic as this recipe remains, it also serves as a reminder that a great many kettles of fish can — and *will* — create their own rich stocks as they evolve.

INGREDIENTS:

16 oz. uncooked shrimp, shell-on

4 cups water
2 T. olive oil
2 onions, peeled & chopped
2 garlic cloves, peeled & minced
2 tomatoes, peeled, seeded & chopped
1 T. parsley, minced
1 bay leaf
2 T. tomato paste
Cayenne pepper, to taste
Salt & pepper, to taste
1/2 cup dry white wine
2 T. coriander, chopped for garnish

IN YOUR KETTLE, combine the water and shrimp, then bring to the simmer until they just turn pink.

Remove the kettle from the heat, then strain the broth through a colander into a bowl. Drain the shrimp and set aside to cool.

Wipe clean the kettle, then heat the olive oil and sauté the onions and garlic for 5 minutes.

Stir in the tomatoes, parsley, bay leaf, and tomato paste, then cover and bring to the simmer for 20 minutes.

Stir in the reserved broth and the wine, then simmer uncovered for 1 hour.

Meanwhile, shell and devein the shrimp.

Stir, taste, and adjust the seasonings with cayenne, salt & pepper.

Add the shrimp to the kettle, then simmer another 5 minutes.

Ladle into individual heated bowls.

Garnish with coriander.

Shrimp Chowder

MARION, MASSACHUSETTS

The recipes in this book do not get much simpler than this one; however, that should remain a secret from your family and friends. The subtle, zesty flavors will not only keep them guessing, but also convince them that you have worked *especially* hard to create for them this taste.

IN YOUR KETTLE, melt the butter, then sauté the onion for 5 minutes.

Sprinkle in the flour and stir to incorporate with the butter and onion.

Add the dry mustard, paprika, and sugar.

Gradually stir in the milk and cream, then bring to the simmer. Continue to stir until thickened.

Stir, taste, and adjust the seasonings with salt & pepper.

Add the shrimp and cook until heated throughout.

Ladle into individual heated bowls.

INGREDIENTS:

16 oz. cooked shrimp, peeled, deveined & chopped

1 onion, chopped
4 T. butter
4 T. flour
1/4 t. dry mustard
1/4 t. paprika
1/2 t. sugar
3 cups milk
1 cup cream
Salt & pepper, to taste

Hot & Sour Shrimp Soup

SHAOXING, CHINA

The Shanghai region along the East China Sea is more noted for its seafood, while the Szechuan province nearly a thousand miles inland is more reknowned for its hot and sour recipes.

Set in a basin that is ringed with mountains and connected to the east by gorges created from the Yangtze River, Szechuan is blessed with both fertile soil and a warm, humid climate that enable crops — especially its famous spices — to grow throughout most of the year. This same climate, though, has always made it difficult to keep food fresh, and so the province is also know for its food preservation techniques of salting, drying, smoking, and pickling. And from these factors we discover the essence of this characteristic known as *hot & sour*. While such ingredients as chilis and peppercorns (along with pungent garlic and spring onions) provided the hot, the residual pickling vinegar of preserved ingredients lent a recipe the sour. Combine that with a fresh catch of shrimp from the coast and you will have a fine kettle of fish.

INGREDIENTS:

8 oz. shrimp, peeled, deveined & split
  lengthwise

4 cups stock
1 T. soy sauce
1 T. cornstarch
1/2 t. salt
2 eggs, beaten
1½ T. vinegar
Black pepper, to taste
Watercress sprigs, garnish

IN YOUR KETTLE, bring the stock to the boil.

Meanwhile, in a small bowl combine the soy sauce, cornstarch, and salt into a paste.

Add 4 T. of the stock to thin the mixture in the bowl.

When the stock has come to the boil, stir in the cornstarch/soy paste, then reduce the heat and simmer for 5 minutes.

Meanwhile, in a small bowl beat the eggs with a fork.

Stir the stock and slowly add the beaten eggs while stirring.

Add the vinegar to the kettle.

Stir, taste, and adjust the seasonings with pepper.

Add the shrimp and simmer until they just become pink.

Ladle into individual heated bowls.

Garnish with watercress.

Shrimp Soup

GEORGETOWN, GUYANA

This South American nation just south and east of Venezuela has a rich mixture of cultures, as well as a major crop of rice, but you'd have a difficult time discovering that from the ingredients in this kettle of fish. In fact, fishing is not even considered a major industry in this country. Still, you'll enjoy this kettle of fish.

IN YOUR KETTLE, bring the stock to a boil.

Add the spinach, onion, and ham, then reduce the heat and simmer for 15 minutes.

Stir in the okra and simmer another 5 minutes.

Add the shrimp and shallots, then simmer for 15 minutes.

Stir, taste, and adjust the seasonings with thyme & pepper.

Ladle into individual heated bowls.

INGREDIENTS:

8 large shrimp, peeled & deveined

6 cups stock
16 oz. spinach, washed and stemmed
1 onion, chopped
8 oz. smoked ham, chopped
8 pieces of okra, stemmed
8 shallots, chopped
Thyme, to taste
Pepper, to taste

Shrimp Soup
PISCO, PERU

The Humboldt — or Peru — Current flows north from the regions of the South Pole along the western coast of South America, where it not only keeps this otherwise tropical region just a bit cooler than others, but also brings rich foods to feed the tuna, swordfish, and shrimp. In the 1960s, Peru exported fish meal and fish oil for poultry and pig food, but by the early 1970s they had nearly depleted their fish stocks. Faced with that situation, they fished only to feed people, at home and abroad.

INGREDIENTS:
18 shrimp, peeled & deveined

4 t. olive oil
1 onion, chopped
2 garlic cloves, chopped
2 T. tomato sauce
4 cups stock
1/3 cup green peas
1/3 cup kernel corn
4 potatoes, peeled & diced
1 t. salt
1/4 t. chili powder
1/4 t. marjoram, ground
4 oz. cream cheese, softened
2 T. milk
3 eggs

IN YOUR KETTLE, heat the olive oil, then sauté the onion and garlic for 5 minutes.

Add the tomato sauce and stock, then bring to the boil.

Stir in the peas, corn, potatoes, salt, chili powder, and marjoram, then allow the stock to return to the boil.

Reduce the heat and simmer for 15 minutes.

Meanwhile, in a small bowl combine the cream cheese and milk into a smooth paste, then add to the kettle.

Add the shrimp and simmer until they just become pink.

Meanwhile, in a small bowl beat the eggs. While stirring, slowly add 1 cup of the soup to the bowl to temper the eggs.

Stir the kettle of soup and slowly add the tempered eggs to the rest of the ingredients.

Simmer for 3 more minutes.

Ladle into individual heated bowls.

200

Shrimp Soup

CASCAI, PORTUGAL

The shrimp of the eastern Atlantic are somewhat different from those we know on this side of the ocean, but either species does well in this kettle of fish. Basically a puréed soup, the recipe is best prepared with the traditional kitchen tools.

INGREDIENTS:

16 oz. uncooked shrimp, shells on

2 T. olive oil
1 onion, chopped
1 carrot, chopped
2 tomatoes, peeled, seeded & chopped
1/4 cup white wine
1 T. port wine
4 cups stock
1/2 cup rice, uncooked
Salt & pepper, to taste
4 t. butter, for garnish

IN YOUR KETTLE, add the olive oil, then sauté the onion, carrot, and tomatoes for 10 minutes.

Add the wines, stir, and bring to the simmer for 3 minutes.

Add the shrimp and cook until they just become pink.

Remove and reserve the shrimp to a clean plate.

Stir in the stock, then bring to the boil.

Add the rice.

Stir, taste, and adjust the seasonings with salt & pepper.

Meanwhile, remove the shells from the shrimp. Reserve 4 whole shrimp, then roughly chop the rest. Using a mortar and pestle, pound the chopped shrimp, then add to the kettle.

Simmer until the rice is tender.

Remove the kettle from the heat, then strain the soup through a sieve into a heatproof bowl. Use a pestle to forth the solids through the sieve.

Return the puréed soup to the kettle, then bring to the simmer for 3 minutes.

Ladle into individual heated bowls.

Garnish each with a pat of butter and a whole shrimp.

Shrimp & Tomato Soup

ALEXANDRE DUMAS

From Dumas' *Le Grand Dictionnaire de Cuisine* comes this fine kettle of fish, exactly as he prescribed. All I have done is list the ingredients separately.

INGREDIENTS:

16 oz. uncooked shrimp, cleaned & deveined

2 cups water
2 lemon slices
Bouquet garni
4 tomatoes, peeled, seeded & diced
4 onions, sliced
1 T. butter
1 garlic clove
Pepper, to taste
1 cup bouillon

"Bring salted water to a boil with 2 slices of lemon and a mixed bouquet. Put your shrimp into the boiling water.

"Into another pot put the tomatoes from which you have squeezed the water, 4 big white onions (sliced), a piece of butter, 1 clove of garlic, and a mixed bouquet.

"Your tomatoes and onions cooked, put them though a fine sieve, add a piece of meat glaze and a pinch of pepper, return to the fire and let all this thicken to a purée. Then add an equal portion of bouillon and 1/2 glass of the water in which the shrimps were cooked. Stir to a boil. Add your shrimps, and your soup is done."

Shrimp & Corn Soup

ZAMBOANGA, MINDANAO ISLAND, THE PHILLIPINES

Of the 7,000 islands that make up the Pacific archipelago named The Phillipines by Magellan, Mindanao is the second largest. Zamboanga City, one of its busiest ports, sits at the tip of the Zamboanga Peninsula.

IN YOUR KETTLE, heat the oil, then sauté the onion and garlic for 5 minutes.

Add the shrimp to the kettle and sauté until they just become pink.

Stir in the stock, broth, pepper, and corn, then bring to the boil.

Reduce the heat, cover, and simmer for 10 minutes.

Stir in the spinach, cover, and simmer for 3 more minutes.

Ladle into individual heated bowls.

INGREDIENTS:

8 oz. uncooked shrimp, peeled, deveined & chopped

2 T. oil
1/2 onion, sliced
2 garlic cloves, chopped
2 cups stock
2 cups clam juice
1/2 t. black pepper, ground coarse
1 cup kernel corn
1/2 cup spinach, washed and stemmed

203

Shrimp Chowder

CEDAR KEY, FLORIDA

It's a long way around from Bahia Mar Marina in Fort Lauderdale to this spot off the upper, west coast of Florida, but for some reason I always think of Travis McGee whenever I think of Cedar Key. Though Bahia Mar is the homeport where John D. MacDonald had his detective keep his boat, the *Busted Flush*, I'm not entirely certain that there is a smooth transition now into the recipe for this especially fine kettle of fish. But here it is.

INGREDIENTS:

16 oz. uncooked shrimp, peeled & deveined

4 cups stock
2 T. butter
2 celery ribss, chopped
1 onion, chopped
1 carrot, peeled & chopped
1/2 t. curry powder
1 t. chili powder
1/4 t. thyme
2 garlic cloves, chopped
1/4 cup flour
1 tomato, peeled, seeded & chopped
1 green bell pepper, seeded & chopped
2 T. parsley, chopped for garnish
1 potato, peeled & diced
Salt & pepper, to taste

IN YOUR KETTLE, melt the butter, then sauté the celery, onion, and carrot 5 minutes.

Stir in the curry, chili powder, thyme, and garlic, then sauté another 2 minutes.

Sprinkle in the flour and stir well to incorporate with the butter and vegetables.

Slowly stir in the stock and bring to the simmer for 15 minutes.

Add to the kettle the tomato, green pepper, and potato, then continue to simmer until the potatoes are fork tender.

Stir, taste, and adjust the seasonings with salt & pepper.

Add the shrimp and simmer until they just turn pink.

Ladle into individual heated bowls.

Garnish each with parsley.

Shrimp Stew

ST. HELENA ISLAND, SOUTH CAROLINA

The barrier islands south of Charlston remain rich in the heritage of the West Africans who had been brought to this low-country as slaves to the rice farmers. Though these wonderful people came from their own societies with their own languages, they learned to communicate with one another in a new tongue that their masters could not comprehend. This was called *gullah*, a melodic, sing-song language that combined an English vocabulary with words and speech patterns from their African homeland. Over the years, this transplanted society translated itself into a whole culture and cuisine throughout the low-country of South Carolina and Georgia, much of which remains today. "Ef oona ent kno weh onna da gwine," say many of the Gullah-speaking descendants, "oona should kno weh oona come from."*

This kettle of fish is just the sort of thing to savor while you ponder your own direction.

IN YOUR KETTLE, add the water and liquid shrimp & crab boil, then bring to the boil.

Add to the kettle the onions and potatoes, then reduce the heat and simmer for 10 minutes.

Stir in the sausage and corn, then cover and simmer another 10 minutes.

Add the lemon slices and shrimp, then cover until the shrimp just turn pink.

Ladle into individual heated bowls.

INGREDIENTS:

24 oz. uncooked shrimp, shells-on

6 cups water
Liquid shrimp & crab boil, to taste
2 onions, quartered
4 potatoes, quartered
16 oz. smoked sausage, in 1-inch pieces
4 ears of corn, shucked & broken in half
1 lemon, sliced

* If you don't know where you are going, you should know where you are coming from.

205

Crab

Related more closely to the lobster than to the shrimp, these crustaceans are characterized by their rather broad bodies and jointed legs. Though some live on land or burrow between rocks, others summer in the tidal waters of estuaries, then winter in the depths of the ocean.

Florida is most known for the claws of its stone crab; Alaska, for the long spiny legs of its king crab; and the Pacific Northwest, for the succulent meat of its Dungeness crab. More ubiquitous, though, is the blue crab, which dwells in the Atlantic waters from the Chesapeake down around to the Gulf of Mexico, Blue crabs are the most commercial crustaceans behind the shrimp and the lobster. They have been found as far south as Uruguay, as far north as Nova Scotia, and as far east as Denmark. And throughout these Atlantic shores they are sought out little boys with dipnets to deep-sea trawlers with seines.

The Delicate Meats

As with lobster, the meat of the crab can be found throughout various parts of its body, not all of which are accessible to the impatient. This is one reason why the meats of both can be on the pricey side. Still, if you have the patience and the right picking tools, there is a wealth of flavor and texture in the crab body, and the remains will help you concoct a delectable stock.

Lump meat is generally the most expensive of the lot. These are large pieces of body meat that are adjacent to the backfin.

Backfin meat consists of the lump meat, as well as the large white flakes that are in the body.

Special meat refers to the flakes of white body meat by themselves.

Claw meat is the brown, least expensive meat of the crab.

How to Dress and Clean A Crab

As with the cooking of live lobsters, cooking live crabs presents a moral question for those who despise the thought of plunging a living being into boiling water. In each instance, however, there is a quick and relatively painless way to dispatch the animal beforehand. Using a small, sharp knife, plunge the point of the blade into the space between the eyes of the crab. That done, you may cook the crab in better conscience.

To dress the crab without cooking:
1. Place the crab on its back and use a sharp knife cut (front to rear) between its legs. Some recipes will call for the crab to be halved, such as this.

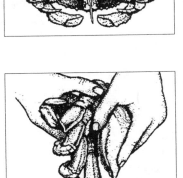

2. Remove the split back shell.

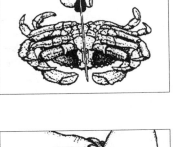

3. Remove the spongy viscera and feathery gills.

To clean the crab after cooking:
1. Follow the steps above, then remove the thin shell of the body where the legs are attached and pick out the meat.
    2. Use a mallet or cracker to break the leg shells and pick clean the meat.

Crab Soup

OSSABAW ISLAND, GEORGIA

The recipe for this fine kettle of fish is best, I think, when made with large pieces of white backfin meat; however, it can also be adapted to be prepared with shrimp, scallops, or even some combination of any and all.

INGREDIENTS:

8 oz. crab meat, picked & cleaned

1 T. safflower oil
1 celery rib, chopped
4 oz. snow peas, slivered
1/4 scallion, sliced
1 garlic clove, minced
2 cups stock
1 T. Dijon mustard
Dash of white pepper
3/4 cup peas
3 cups hot milk
1 hard-cooked egg, chopped coarse for garnish
1/4 t. paprika

IN YOUR KETTLE, heat the oil, then sauté the celery, snow peas and scallion for 3 minutes.

Stir in the garlic, then sauté for 1 minute.

Add the stock, parsley, Dijon mustard, and pepper, then stir and bring to the simmer for 10 minutes.

Meanwhile, in a separate saucepan heat the milk.

Remove the kettle from the heat, then stir in the peas, crab meat and hot milk. Allow this to stand for 5 minutes.

Ladle into individual heated bowls.

Garnish with chopped egg and paprika.

She-Crab Soup
CHARLESTON, SOUTH CAROLINA & SAVANNAH, GEORGIA

The taste of some kettles of fish is worth dying for, and She-Crab Soup is certainly one of them. Still, to avoid dying in the clenched hands of some cook from Charleston or from Savannah (both of which boast of this soup's creation in the early 1800s), I give thanks to the folks of good taste in both those fine cities.

As for the soup itself, there is a distinguishable tang to its flavor that sets it apart from all other crab soups, and this — as well as its orange color — comes from the roe of the female crab. In some states, though, the taking of female crabs with mature eggs is illegal, so cooks have devised a range of legal alternatives, including the use of crumbled, hard-cooked egg yolk to lend the kettle some color. The taste, however, is pale in comparison to the true ingredients.

IN YOUR KETTLE, heat the butter, then sauté the onion, mace, and celery for 3 minutes.

Stir in the crab meat and roe, then sauté another 5 minutes.

Meanwhile, in a separate saucepan heat the milk.

Add the hot milk to the kettle, then stir in the cream and Worcestershire.

In a small bowl, dissolve the flour in the water, then whisk into the kettle.

Stir in the sherry and the crumbled egg yolks, then simmer for 30 minutes.

Stir, taste, and adjust the seasonings with salt & pepper.

Ladle into individual heated bowls.

INGREDIENTS:
12 oz. crab meat
2 T. crab roe

2 T. butter
1 onion, grated
1/2 t. mace
2 celery ribs, grated
4 cups milk
1 cup cream
2 T. Worcestershire sauce
3 T. flour
3 T. water
4 T. sherry
Yolks of 3 hard-cooked eggs
Salt & pepper, to taste

She-Crab Soup

TIDEWATER, VIRGINIA

Slightly different from the traditional recipe, this version can also be made with chopped shrimp meat.

INGREDIENTS:

12 oz. white crab meat

2 T. crab roe
3 T. butter
2 cups milk
2 mace blades
1 T. lemon zest
2 cups cream
1/4 cup crackers, crumbled
Salt & pepper, to taste
2 t. sherry

IN YOUR KETTLE, melt the butter.

Stir in the milk, mace, and lemon zest, then bring to the simmer for 5 minutes.

Stir in the crab meat and cream, then simmer 10 more minutes.

Add the crumbled crackers.

Stir, taste and adjust the seasonings with salt & pepper.

Remove the kettle from the heat and allow to stand for 5 minutes.

Stir in the sherry.

Ladle into individual heated bowls.

Crab Soup

CORNWALL, ENGLAND

Though this recipe comes from the shores of England, it is identical to a recipe which I have for Scotland's Partan Bree. The title for that recipe, so I am told, comes from the Gaelic word for "crab" (*partan*) and a corruption of the Gaelic word for "broth" (*brigh*). Call it whatever you will, this is a fine kettle of fish.

IN YOUR KETTLE, melt the butter, then add the milk and rice.

Stir, taste, and adjust the seasonings with nutmeg, salt & pepper.

Bring to the boil, then reduce the heat and simmer until the rice is cooked.

Meanwhile, pick over the crab meat to remove any pieces of shell and cartilage, as well as to separate the white meat of the claws from the darker meat of the back.

When the rice is cooked, stir the dark crab meat into the kettle.

Remove the kettle from the heat, then strain the soup through a sieve into a heatproof bowl. Use a pestle to force through the solids.

Return the strained soup to the kettle, then stir in the stock and bring to the simmer.

Add the anchovy paste and the claw meat to the kettle.

Stir, taste, and again adjust the seasonings with nutmeg, salt & pepper.

Stir in the cream and simmer for 5 minutes.

Ladle into individual heated bowls.

Garnish each with nutmeg.

INGREDIENTS:

1 large crab, cooked, picked & cleaned

2 cups milk
1/2 cup long grain rice, uncooked
1 T. butter
Nutmeg, to taste
Salt & pepper, to taste
2 cups stock
1/2 t. anchovy paste
1/2 cup cream

Crab & Wild Rice Stew

FANNY BAY, VANCOUVER ISLAND, BRITISH COLUMBIA

This especially fine kettle of fish combines 2 of my very favorite foods: Dungeness crab and wild rice. While you might get away with using the flavorful white meat from some other sort of crab, there can be no substitution here of regular rice for wild rice.

In fact, the so-called wild rice is not really a rice at all, but the grain from a tall water grass that grows along the northern United States. Sometimes known as *Canadian rice* or *Indian rice* (and sometimes even *Tuscarora rice* for the Tuscarora tribe), this ingredient had also been called *water rice, water oats,* and — by the French — *crazy oats*. In the late 1770s, though, the newly-independent Americans had settled upon the name *wild rice*. These days it is cultivated mostly in paddies throughout Minnesota.

Be certain that you buy this true grain, and not some "wild rice" subsitute sold by the large, commercial rice companies which specialize in seasoned, quick-cooking products.

INGREDIENTS:

16 oz. crab meat, picked & cleaned

1/3 cup wild rice, uncooked
2 cups crab stock
3 t. butter
1 T. onion, minced
1/4 cup flour
3 cups stock
Salt & pepper, to taste
1/2 carrot, peeled & grated
2 T. slivered almonds
1½ cups half-and-half
3 t. dry sherry
2 T. chives, minced for garnish

IN YOUR KETTLE, combine the wild rice and crab stock, then bring to the boil.

Reduce the heat, cover, and simmer until the rice has split its hulls and most of the stock has been absorbed.

Remove the kettle from heat. Fluff the rice with a fork, then pour into a clean bowl and cover tightly with plastic wrap.

Wipe clean the kettle and return to the heat. Melt the butter and sauté the onion for 3 minutes.

Sprinkle the flour into the kettle, then stir to incorporate with the butter and onion.

Slowly whisk in the stock until it thickens slightly.

Return the rice to the kettle.
Stir, taste, and adjust the seasonings with salt & pepper.
Add the carrot and almonds, then simmer for 5 minutes.
Stir in the half-and-half, as well as the sherry.
Add the crab meat, then simmer for 5 minutes.
Ladle into individual heated bowls.
Garnish each with chives.

Crab Stew

NEW BERN, NORTH CAROLINA

Behind the fabled Outer Banks of North Carolina lie the protected waters of Pamlico Sound and the coastal plain, where you'll find this historic community at the confluence of the Neuse and Trent Rivers. Sometimes battered by hurricanes, but never defeated, these are the sort of people who have seen the worst of what the nearby waters can present, but who still know how to make the best of what it offers up for harvest. This kettle of fish is testimony to that.

INGREDIENTS:
- 12 crabs, dressed & washed
- 4 oz. salt pork, cubed
- 4 onions, sliced
- 6 cups water, boiling
- Salt & pepper, to taste
- 4 T. vinegar
- Catsup, to taste
- Worcestershire sauce, to taste
- Tabasco, to taste
- 1 cup corn meal

IN YOUR KETTLE, render the salt pork until crisp and brown.

Cover the bottom of the kettle with a layer of crabs, then top that with a layer of sliced onion. Continue to add alternate layers of crabs and onion.

Add enough boiling water to cover up to 1 inch above the top layer.

Stir, taste, and adjust the seasonings with salt & pepper.

Add the vinegar.

Bring the kettle to the boil, then reduce the heat and simmer for 15 minutes.

Stir, taste, and adjust the seasonings with catsup, Worcestershire, and Tabasco.

Simmer another 15 minutes.

Sprinkle in the corn meal and simmer until thickened.

Ladle into individual heated bowls.

213

Crab Chowder

BEAUFORT, SOUTH CAROLINA

If you are fortunate to visit both Beaufort, North Carolina, and Beaufort, South Carolina, you had better be certain ahead of time that you understand how to pronounce the names of these two destinations. In North Carolina, it's pronounced *BOE-fort* (with a long O), but further down in South Carolina, it's *BYOU-fort* (with a long U) or sometimes *BYOU-forD* (with the long U, as well as a D on the end).

INGREDIENTS:

24 oz. crab meat, cleaned & picked

4 T. butter
2 onions, chopped
4 T. flour
2 cups milk
2 cups cream
2 t. Worcestershire sauce
1 cup kernel corn
1 cup fresh butter beans, cooked
Salt & pepper, to taste

IN YOUR KETTLE, melt the butter, then sauté the onions for 5 minutes.

Sprinkle the flour into the kettle, then stir well to incorporate with the butter and onion.

Slowly stir in the milk and cream, then continue to stir until thick and smooth.

Stir in the Worcestershire sauce.

Add the corn, beans, and crab meat.

Stir, taste, and adjust the seasoning with salt & pepper.

Bring to the simmer for 5 minutes.

Ladle into individual heated bowls.

Crab Bisque

KITTY HAWK, NORTH CAROLINA

While we are on the topic of differences between the Carolinas, let's consider a moment here what difference there is between the Crab Chowder on the opposite page and the Crab Bisque presented here. Aside from some subtleties of spice, and a distinct absence of vegetables, this recipe is more likely to be considered something less than a bisque by those who insist that the rich creaminess of a bisque must be further enhanced by the inclusion of puréed meat or pulverized shells. Nonetheless, this *is* a fine kettle of fish.

IN YOUR KETTLE, melt the butter.

Sprinkle the flour into the kettle and stir to incorporate with the butter.

Gradually stir in the milk and bring to the simmer. Continue to stir until thickened.

Stir in the salt, red pepper flakes, mace, and nutmeg.

Add the crab meat, then gradually stir in the cream.

Simmer over low heat for 10 minutes.

Ladle into individual heated bowls.

Garnish each with 1 t. of sherry.

INGREDIENTS:

16 oz. back fin crab meat, cleaned & picked

4 T. butter
2 T. flour
2 cups milk
1 t. salt
1/4 t. red pepper flakes, crushed
1/4 t. mace
1/4 t. nutmeg
3 cups light cream
4 t. sherry, for garnish

215

Crab Chowder

SNOW HILL, DELAWARE

Much like the Shrimp Stew presented from Peru, the richness of this recipe comes in part from the addition of softened cream cheese. A bit different, though, is the inclusion of the cauliflower. Although this is the only recipe in this entire book which calls for cauliflower, the texture does mix well with that of the crabmeat.

INGREDIENTS:

8 oz. crab meat, cleaned & picked

4 T. butter
2½ cups cauliflower flowerets
4 T. flour
1/4 t. white pepper
2 cups stock
2 cups milk
3 oz. cream cheese w/chives, softened & cubed
1/4 cup dry white wine
2 T. fresh parsley, for garnish

IN YOUR KETTLE, melt the butter, then sauté the cauliflower flowerets for 5 minutes.

Sprinkle in the flour and pepper, then stir well to incorporate with the butter.

Slowly add the stock and the milk, then bring to the simmer. Continue to stir until thickened.

Meanwhile, in a small bowl gradually combine the cream cheese with 1 cup of the heated stock and milk from the kettle.

Add the cream cheese mixture to the kettle and stir until melted.

Stir in the crab meat and wine, then simmer for 5 more minutes.

Ladle into individual heated bowls.

Garnish each with parsley.

Crab Soup

OAK HARBOR, WASHINGTON

This recipe could be prepared with any crab meat other than that of a Dungeness; however, I have done that and still prefer this original version.

IN YOUR KETTLE, combine the water and crab seasoning, then bring to the boil.

Add the Dungeness crab and cook for 5 minutes.

Remove the crab from the kettle and set aside to clean.

Strain the stock into a heatproof bowl and reserve.

Wipe clean the kettle and melt the butter. Sprinkle in the flour, then stir well to make a white roux.

Slowly stir in the milk and simmer until thickened.

Add the reserved stock, along with the creamed corn and green onions. Simmer for 10 minutes.

Meanwhile, when the Dungeness crab has cooled, remove the meat from its shells.

Stir, taste, and adjust the seasonings with salt & pepper.

Stir both kinds of crab meat into the kettle, then simmer for 10 minutes.

Ladle into individual heated bowls.

INGREDIENTS:

16 oz. Dungeness crab, uncooked
8 oz. lump crab meat, cleaned & picked

2 cups water
1 T. crab boil seasoning
4 T. butter
4 T. cup flour
2 cups milk
3 cups creamed corn
4 scallions (white & green), chopped

Crab & Artichoke Bisque

PACIFIC GROVE, CALIFORNIA

Traditionally, this kettle of fish is finished with a topping of a sauce that is made simply with roasted red pepper and olive oil; however, you might simply use a *rouille* if you have made and reserved that ahead of time.

INGREDIENTS:

The Kettle of Fish:
16 oz. lump crab meat, cleaned & picked

4 T. butter
4 T. flour
16 oz. artichoke hearts, chopped
2 cups stock
1 cup heavy cream
1 cup milk
2 T. basil, chopped
Tabasco, to taste
Seasoned salt, to taste
White pepper, to taste

The Sauce:
1 roasted red bell pepper
2 T. olive oil

IN YOUR KETTLE, melt the butter.

Sprinkle in the flour and stir until thoroughly incorporated into a white roux, then cook for 3 minutes.

Slowly stir in the stock, cream, and milk, then bring to the simmer

Add the fresh basil.

Stir, taste, and adjust the seasonigns with Tabasco, salt & pepper.

Add the chopped artichoke hearts and simmer for 5 minutes.

Meanwhile, purée the roasted red pepper and olive oil.

Stir in the crab meat, then simmer another 5 minutes.

Ladle into individual heated bowls.

Garnish wish roasted pepper sauce or *rouille.*

Crab & Asparagus Soup
QUEENSLAND, AUSTRALIA

This recipe requires a little work, but it is not at all difficult. What's more, you'll discover that the taste is not only delicious, but quite unlike any other kettle of fish in this book.

IN YOUR KETTLE, melt the butter, then sauté the onion, celery, carrot, garlic, and shallot for 3 minutes.

Sprinkle in the flour, then stir to incorporate thoroughly with the butter and vegetables.

Slowly stir in the evaporated milk, then bring to the simmer. Continue to stir until thickened.

Add the sherry, Worcestershire sauce, lemon zest, and bay leaf, then simmer for 5 minutes.

Stir, taste, and adjust the seasonings with salt & pepper.

Add the blanched asparagus and crab meat, then cover and simmer for 20 minutes.

Ladle into individual heated bowls.

INGREDIENTS:

16 oz. crab meat, cleaned & picked

3 T. butter
1 onion, chopped
2 celery ribs, chopped
1/2 carrot, peeled & chopped fine
3 garlic cloves, chopped
2 shallots, chopped
3 T. flour
4 cups evaporated milk
2 T. dry sherry
1 t. Worcestershire sauce
1 t. lemon zest
1 bay leaf
Salt & white pepper, to taste
1 cup asparagus spears, blanched & sliced

Crab & Pumpkin Soup

PLYMOUTH, MASSACHUSETTS

Off the rocky shoreline of this historic town, the rock crabs have long been considered a "trash fish" of sorts, a by-catch brought up by fishermen in pursuit of more lucrative commercial fish. In truth, though, these crabs are not a whole lot different from the highly-prized stone crabs of the southern waters. Rock crab would be appropriate for this recipe, but any variety of crabmeat will do.

INGREDIENTS:

8 oz. crab meat, picked & cleaned

2 T. butter
1 onion, sliced
1 t. cumin seeds, crushed
1/4 t. nutmeg
1/4 t. paprika
1/4 t. cayenne pepper
1/2 t. dried basil
4 cups stock
16 oz. canned pumpkin
1/2 cup heavy cream
Salt & pepper, to taste

IN YOUR KETTLE, melt the butter, then sauté the onion for 5 minutes.

Stir in the cumin seeds, nutmeg, paprika, cayenne, and basil, then saute for another minute.

Add to the kettle the stock and the canned pumpkin, then mix, cover, and bring to the simmer for 20 minutes.

Remove the kettle from the heat. Purée small batches of the soup in a blender, then return to the kettle and bring to the simmer.

Add the crab meat and simmer for 3 minutes.

Add to the kettle the cream.
Stir, taste, and adjust the seasonings with salt & pepper.
Simmer for 5 minutes.
Ladle into individual heated bowls.

Cooking with a Variety of Seafoods

If this were a textbook, then it would be simple to begin this chapter by encouraging you to bring together now whatever you might have read and learned in previous chapters. But this is *not* a textbook, and there's a very strong likelihood that you might have jumped right to this chapter with an eye toward preparing a fine kettle of fish with a tasty variety of finfish and/or shellfish. In that case, it might be wise for me to point out a few things already mentioned in other places.

For starters, I assume that you are not using any sort of commercially-prepared cooking liquid, such as chicken stock or even bottled clam juice. If you haven't had the opportunity to create your own, then you might be better off using plain water. After all, most of these fish will bring their own special flavors to your kettle.

By the same token, keep in mind that other ingredients bring both flavor and texture to a recipe. While it is one thing to cook them sufficiently to bring out those flavors, it is quite another to boil the living heck out of them and create a vegetable porridge.

Finally, keep in mind that not all ingredients cook at the same rate to reach their desired state of doneness; all of which means that — unless specifically directed — not everything ought to be tossed into your kettle at the same time. This especially true of the finfish and shellfish, some of which require very little cooking. For example, mussels will become very rubbery when they are overcooked, as do squid. In the case of squid, though, it should either be cooked very quickly, or else stewed for 2 hours or so. When in doubt about an ingredient, look back at the previous pages on those subjects.

Some Final Words about Kettles of Fish

As familiar as the title of this book might first have seemed to you, I did not apply it to this work with my tongue too firmly planted in my cheek. Believe me, I hope that I don't create in your kitchen any sort of confusing muddle that some imply from the familiar old phrase, "a fine kettle of fish," or even "a pretty kettle of fish." While it's also a tidy coincidence that folks in parts of the U.S. refer to some of their seafood soups as *muddle*, the title of this book truly traces back to the sort of Old World picnic by the riverside, which the French called a *fete champêtre*. On those occasions, a salmon would be caught, boiled, then dined upon. Such an awkward party led to the coining of the phrase, "a pretty kettle of fish."

While we're at it, let's take a look at that word *chowder*, which most will tell you derives from the French word *chaudiére*, a large cauldron. There are those who maintain that sailors of Breton made a communal stew in such a kettle. During the 1600s and 1700s, they carried this custom to Newfoundland, then down through Nova Scotia, into New England. If so, then the origins of chowder predate this fabled food of New England. Back in Britanny, though, there is no longer any existence of the phrase *faire la chaudiére*.

And as to the French word for a cauldron, it is not *chaudiére*, but *chaudron*. To the north, in fact, the English-speaking folks of Devonshire and Cornwall called the fish peddlar a *jowter*, and there are those who will insist that *chowder* is a derivation of that.

As to whether or not New Englanders found their inspiration from the Bretons, the ingredients published in the *Boston Evening Post* in 1751 included thyme, sweet marjoram, and savory. There was neither milk, nor cream, but red wine, thickened with biscuit. This made not only for a hearty consistency, but also for a sensible meal aboard a ship. It did not easily slop over the sides of the bowl, and it did not require precious water.

In 1800, Amelia Simmons' *American Cookery* (recognized as the first American cookbook) notes that potatoes were to be served on the side; not until the 1840s did they become an essential ingredient. Lacking that starch, the chowders often were thickened with ketchup; not the kind we know today, but the kind described in the Finishing Touches chapter of this book. In fact, it was not until the end of the 19th century that either milk or cream became a significant ingredient in any recipes.

Well, there you have it: enough basic cookery and history to enable you to begin this cookbook with these recipes that come toward the end. As always, I do hope that you enjoy them, and I hope you'll find some time to return to the very beginning.

A *Pretty* Kettle of Fish

THE BOSTON TRANSCRIPT

Many years ago, legend says, a fishmonger returned to his Marseilles home pushing his little cart before him. "Hey, mama," he called from the street, "I didn't sell all my stock and tomorrow's a feast day!"

Mama told papa off in good fishwife terms. She didn't want fish on a feast day any more than the customers.

"Give it here!" she ordered, and in a fine frenzy threw the entire stock — fish, bivalves and crustaceans — into a pot with whatever else came to her angry hands. Covering the kettle she pushed it to the back of the stove and went on with her pre-feast visiting. When she returned in the evening she found her old man sniffing the celestial aroma that emanated from the pot.

"That's a fine kettle of fish, mama. What did you put in it?"

Mama, now calm, could not recall. All she could mutter was "bouillabaisse," a word that seems to mean different things to different Frenchmen; but in Provençal means *over a low fire*. The dish was so good that all who shared in it forgot the festival meat.

Bouillabaisse entered the United States at New Orleans or New England. The South's claim is valid and is based upon the fact that Southerners have made more of the dish. Over the years, several tidy fortunes have been made by those who excelled in its preparation. New England's pretensions, though, are not to be dismissed lightly.

When the Pilgrims were bumped on the cold and lonely shore they quickly learned they would have to eat fish or starve while they were learning to fire their blunderbusses with enough accuracy to bring down red meat. And what were they trying to make when they cooked a mess of fish and shellfish in a big pot called a *chaudière*? Were they clumsily trying to put together a bouillabaisse? Whatever they were cooking up they, or their descendants, called it a *chowder*, after the kettle in which it was cooked — a dish entirely unknown to the rest of the world. And let it be added that the best damn chowder ever made is only a pale, feeble imitation of a bouillabaisse.

The Provençal fishwife never could recall all she had put into her pot and French cooks have been guessing ever since. They call for *rascasse, chapon, fielas, cabillaud, boudreuil* and *whiting*, with *langouste* and *huitres* added. In America we have plenty of whiting, and the *cabillaud* is our old friend the cod.

Down in New Orleans they begin by tearing up the French recipes and coming forth with a very nice one of their own calling for redfish, red snapper, green trout, sheepshead and blackfish, with handfuls of crabs, crayfish and lake shrimps added. The working recipe they guard. Cape Cod cooks, with deep bows to Mme. Foyot, of Marseilles, and to Mme. Begue and MM. Antoine and Gallatoire, of New Orleans, assemble their fishes, the cod, hake and haddock, striped bass and yellow-tail flounders, omitting the oily fishes. They have also the fine North Atlantic lobsters, those grown in cold shallow waters with paper-thin shells, excellent oysters, scallops, clams, quahaugs, mussels and a few crabs. "If it's variety we have it, and if it's freshness we have that, too."

To be a veritable bouillabaisse, we believe, the pot should contain at least one fish, one bivalve and one crustacean, in addition to other indispensable ingredients. Nevertheless variety enriches the dish.

The service varies. In France it comes to the table with glassyeyed head of a fish bobbing about and many a hungry diner has decided at that point he could never care for a bouillabaisse. New World cooks are prone to leave shrimps, crabs or lobster halves, still in their original jackets, floating about presumably to please the eye. The Cape Cod bouley is edible down to the last morsel.

A resident native observing the preparation sniffed appreciatively and sighed. "You know, mister, during the war I ate so much fish my stomach still rises and falls with the tides."

Bouillabaisse Cape Cod

INGREDIENTS:
2 pounds firm fish
6 oysters and/or
  6 clams and/or
  6 mussels
1 cup crabmeat and/or
  1 cup lobster and/or
  1 cup shrimp

2 tomatoes, peeled
2 onions, sliced
1/2 cup olive oil
1 lemon, juice only
1 bay leaf
1 clove garlic, crunched
2 tblsp. parsley, minced
1/2 cup pimientos, chopped
1/2 cup white wine
Heavy pinch of saffron
Light pinch of thyme
4 slices garlic bread, toasted

Routine: Cut heads tails and fins from fish and place in one quart of water and boil until liquid is reduced to a pint, drain and save liquid. Cut fish into pieces for serving, brush with olive oil, sprinkle with salt, pepper, crumbled bay leaf and thyme, and let stand a while. Put the olive oil and fish stock into a large pot, adding onions, garlic, tomatoes, parsley and lemon juice and let the whole simmer for about an hour. Wet the saffron in a small part of the wine and add with fish and shellfish, pimientos, and continue simmering until fish is done, rolling the pot to distribute the saffron. just before removing from the fire add the balance of the wine and serve over the garlic toast.

— *From* THE BOSTON TRANSCRIPT

Kakavia

LEVKÁS, GREECE

Though *bouillabaise* comes to the minds of many folks when they consider the "quintessential" kettle of fish, we must give credit where credit is due. And to do so, we must look back before 600 B.C. and before the French villagers of Marseilles first tasted the *kakavia* created by the Greeks.

Like the *bouillabaise* that takes its name from the *bouillet* in which it is cooked, so the *kakavia* takes its name from the kettle they call the *kakavi*. More importantly, though, the two kettles of fish are alike in the fact that they make use in the full range of the bounty from the sea, as well the tastes of the simple fishing villagers from which they originate. Quintessential as they are, these fine kettles of fish are by no means elegant.

INGREDIENTS:

32 oz. of 3 or 4 kinds of fish fillets, in 1-inch pieces
1 lobster, cut up & claws cracked
8 oz. uncooked shrimp, peeled & deveined
8 oz. scallops

1/4 cup olive oil
1/2 cup scallions (white & pale green), sliced
2 tomatoes, peeled, seeded & chopped
1/2 fennel rib, chopped
2 parsley sprigs
1 bay leaf
2 thyme sprigs
1/2 cup dry white wine
4 cups stock
Salt & pepper, to taste
4 thick slices bread, toasted

IN YOUR KETTLE, heat the olive oil, then sauté the scallions for 5 minutes.

Add the tomatoes, fennel, parsley, bay leaf, thyme, wine, and stock, then bring to the boil.

Stir, taste, and adjust the seasonings with salt & pepper.

Reduce the heat, then simmer for 45 minutes.

Meanwhile, lightly salt the fish and let stand. After 10 minutes, rinse the fish with water, then reserve on a clean plate.

Remove the kettle from the heat. Strain the stock through a sieve into a heatproof bowl. Use a pestle to force through as much of the solids as possible, then discard those solids that remain.

Return the stock to the kettle and bring to the boil.

With a slotted spoon, gently add the reserved fish to the kettle, reduce the heat, and simmer for 5 minutes.

Stir in the lobster, cover, and simmer another 5 minutes.

Add the shrimp and scallops, then simmer 5 minutes more.

Stir, taste, and adjust the seasonings with salt & pepper.

Place a toasted slice of bread into the bottom of each bowl, then divide the fish among them.

Ladle the soup into the individual heated bowls.

Traditional Bouillabaisse

MARSEILLES, FRANCE

Though the *kakavia* belongs to all those ports where fishermen still fish, the true recipe for a *bouillabaisse* is made in only one place: Marseilles, France. All the others remain only derivatives of the *kakavia* and variations of this unique recipe, which uses a minimum of 5 varieties of finfish and only a sparse amount of shellfish. Moreover, the true stock for this kettle of fish is not made from the customary frames and trimmings of large fish, but of tiny Mediterranean fish.

For the record, the true French recipe would include fish from this group available in United States waters: *baudroie* (goosefish), *congre* (conger eel), *dorade* (walleye), *grondin* (flying fish), *langouste* (spiny lobster), and *merlan* (kingfish), as well as fish from this group (that would require some approximate substitutition): *felian* (small eel), *galinette* (grouper), *rascasse* (sea bass), *rougier* (eel), *sard* (haddock or cod), and *turbot* (flounder).

INGREDIENTS:

The Stock:

Frames & trimmings, rinsed & chopped in 3-inch pieces

3 T. olive oil
6 garlic cloves, chopped
I fennel bulb, chopped coarse
I onion, chopped coarse
4 thyme sprigs
I T. orange zest
6 cups water

The Kettle of Fish:
32 oz. assorted fish fillets

3 T. olive oil
3 leeks (white & pale green), washed & chopped fine
8 tomatoes, peeled, seeded & diced
1/4 cup Pernod
6 cups stock
1/2 T. saffron threads, crushed
8 1/2-inch slices of French bread
2 cups *rouille*

To make the stock:

IN YOUR KETTLE, heat the olive oil, then sauté the garlic, fennel, onion, thyme, and orange zest for 10 minutes.

Stir the fish frames and trimmings into the kettle, then sauté another 10 minutes.

Add the water and simmer for 30 more minutes.

Remove the kettle from the heat and strain the stock through a sieve into a heatproof bowl.

To make the kettle of fish:

IN YOUR KETTLE, heat the olive oil, then sauté the leeks for 10 minutes.

Stir in the tomatoes, Pernod, stock, and saffron, then simmer for 20 minutes.

Meanwhile, in a large skillet arrange the fillets in a single layer, then ladle just enough of the simmering stock to cover the fish. Bring the skillet to the simmer.

In a large bowl, place 1/2 cup of the *rouille*, then spread each slice of French bread with *rouille*. Be certain, though, to reserve some of the sauce for the garnish.

226

When the fillets just become opaque, whisk the stock from skillet into the bowl of *rouille,* then stir the mixture into the kettle.

Place 2 slices of French bread in the bottom of each bowl.

Divide the fillets among each serving.

Ladle into the individual heated bowls.

Garnish with a dollop of *rouille.*

Bouillabaisse

NICE, FRANCE

Most of the same flavors and textures are found in this fine kettle of fish; however, the requisite stock is whatever you might have prepared and and preserved.

INGREDIENTS:

32 oz. assorted fish fillets
2 crabs, cleaned & halved

2 T. olive oil
1 onion, sliced
1 leek (white & pale green), washed & chopped fine
2 garlic cloves, crushed
1 tomato, peeled, seeded & diced
6 cups stock
1/2 T. saffron threads, crushed
1/2 T. summer savory, crushed
1 T. parsley, chopped
1/8 t. fennel seed, crushed
1/8 t. dried thyme
Salt & pepper, to taste
8 1/2-inch slices of French bread
1 cup *rouille*, for garnish
2 T. parsley, chopped for garnish

IN YOUR KETTLE, heat the olive oil, then sauté the onion, leek, garlic, and tomato for 5 minutes.

Stir in the saffron, savory, parsley, fennel seed, and thyme.

Layer the firmer fillets on top of the vegetables and herbs, then top with the crabs and add the stock. Cover and bring to the boil for 5 minutes.

Add the softer fillets, then simmer for 5 minutes.

Taste and adjust the seasonings with salt & pepper.

Simmer for 5 more minutes.

Place 2 slices of French bread in the bottom of each heated bowl.

Divide the fillets and crabs among each serving.

Ladle into the individual heated bowls.

Garnish each with a dollop of *rouille* and parsley.

228

Caldeirada

GUINCHO, PORTUGAL

Caldeirada is to Portugal what *bouillabaisse* and *kakavia* are to France and Spain. Depending upon the catch of the day, this kettle of fish generally has a 50/50 mix of lean and oily finfish, as well as clams, mussels, squid and octopus.

IN YOUR KETTLE, heat the olive oil, then sauté the onions, garlic, and green pepper for 10 minutes.

Stir in the parsley, bay leaf, peppercorns, tomatoes, tomato paste, wine, and water, then bring to the simmer for 10 minutes.

Add the squid and clams, cover, simmer for 30 minutes.

Place the pieces of fish in the kettle, then add the shrimp, mussels, and black pepper.

Cover and simmer until the mussels open and the fish flakes with a fork.

Slowly stir to mix all the ingredients together.

Ladle into individual heated bowls.

Garnish with coriander.

INGREDIENTS:

8 oz. squid, cleaned & sliced 1/2-inch rings; tentacles chopped
12 hardshell clams, scrubbed
24 oz. assorted whitefish (cod, monkfish, hake, flounder, or haddock)
24 oz. assorted oily fish (mackerel, swordfish, or tuna)
8 oz. uncooked shrimp, shell-on
12 mussels, scrubbed & debearded

3 T. olive oil
3 onions, peeled & chopped
4 garlic cloves, peeled & minced
1 sweet green pepper, cored, seeded & chopped
3 parsley sprigs
1 bay leaf
6 whole black peppercorns
3 tomatoes, peeled, seeded & chopped
3 T. tomato paste
1½ cups dry white wine
2 cups stock
1/4 t. black pepper
1/4 cup coriander, chopped for garnish

Seafood Stew

FLORES ISLAND, THE AZORES

Unless you look at the globe, you might be unaware that this group of islands in the North Atlantic is just about midway between North America and Europe. In fact, this westernmost island is only 1200 miles from Newfoundland, which is only two-thirds the distance from Cape Cod to Key West; the easternmost islands are only 800 miles or so from Portugal.

As for this *Sopa de Peixe*, the recipe calls for an equal amount of lean and oily finfish. Though some might be tempted to add shellfish, including squid and octopus, those ingredients truly belong in the *caldeirada*.

INGREDIENTS:

4 oz. haddock fillets, in 1½-inch pieces
4 oz. pogy fillets, in 1½-inch pieces
4 oz. grouper fillets, in 1½-inch pieces
4 oz. mackerel fillets, in 1½-inch pieces
4 oz. shark or swordfish fillets, in 1½-inch pieces
4 oz. eel, skinned & in 1-inch chunks

2 T. olive oil
2 yellow onions, chopped
3 garlic cloves, minced
1 bay leaf
3 plum tomatoes, peeled, seeded & chopped
2 T. parsley, minced
Cayenne pepper, to taste
1/3 cup dry white wine
2 cups stock
2 potatoes, peeled & sliced
1 T. cider vinegar
Salt & pepper, to taste

IN YOUR KETTLE, heat the butter and olive oil, then sauté the onions and garlic for 15 minutes.

Stir in the bay leaf, tomatoes, parsley, cayenne, wine, and stock, then bring to the simmer for 30 minutes.

Add the fish, potatoes, and vinegar. Bring to the simmer and cook until potatoes are fork tender and the fillets flake at the touch of a fork.

Remove and discard the bay leaf.

Stir, taste, and adjust the seasonings with salt & pepper.

Ladle into invidual heated bowls.

Tuna Soup

FORT-DE-FRANCE, MARTINIQUE

Though French is the official language of this island, there remains a strong element of Creole about the population. That element of the culture is apparent in some of the flavors found in this kettle of fish.

IN YOUR KETTLE, melt the butter, then sauté the the onion, green pepper, celery, and garlic for 3 minutes.

Sprinkle the flour into the kettle and stir well to incorporate it with the butter and vegetables.

Gradually stir in the stock, then bring to the simmer.

Add the fish, thyme, and cayenne pepper.

Stir, taste, and adjust the seasonings with salt & pepper.

Add the capers, stir again, and bring to the simmer for 10 minutes.

Ladle into individual heated bowls.

INGREDIENTS:

8 oz. fish, in 1/2-inch pieces
4 oz. tuna steak, in 1/2-inch cubes

2 T. butter
1 onion, minced
1/2 green pepper, minced
1/2 cup celery, minced
2 garlic cloves, minced
2 T. flour
4 cups stock
1/4 t. cayenne pepper
1/4 t. thyme
Salt & pepper, to taste
1/4 cup capers, drained

Romesco
CATALONIA, SPAIN

This Mediterranean region of the country sits just south of coastal France and just across the water from Italy. As a result, it shares some of the same language, tastes, and fish from the sea. What sets this kettle of fish apart from the others, though, is *picada*, a sauce that might be considered Spain's equivalent to *rouille* or *aïoli*. (*See* Finishing Touches.)

INGREDIENTS:
32 oz. assorted fish fillets

1 T. olive oil
1 cup *picada*
6 cups stock
Salt & pepper, to taste

IN YOUR KETTLE, heat the oil almost to the smoking point.

Keeping in mind that you are about to mix a cooler liquid into the hot oil, carefully stir in the *picada* and cook for 2 minutes.

Stir in 2 cups of the stock and bring to the simmer.

Add the fish and poach for 10 minutes.
Remove and distribute the fish among individual heated bowls.
Add the remaining stock to the kettle and bring to the simmer.
Stir, taste, and adjust the seasonings with salt & pepper.
Ladle soup over the fish in the individual heated bowls.

Seafood Soup

CHICAGO, ILLINOIS

This soup brings together a blend of fish textures that are not limited to the 3 kinds of fish specifically named in this recipe. In addition, it derives a Mediterranean flavor from the distinctive taste of both fennel and fennel seed, not to mention the other ingredients often found in the same combination.

IN YOUR KETTLE, heat the olive oil, then sauté the mushrooms until they are golden.

Remove and reserve the mushrooms on a clean plate.

Add the bacon and render until it is crisp and brown.

Stir in the onion, fennel, bell pepper, fennel seeds, and garlic, then sauté for 5 minutes.

Add potatoes, stock, tomatoes with their juices, and the tomato sauce, then bring to the boil. Reduce the heat and simmer for 20 minutes.

Return the mushrooms to the kettle, along with the fish pieces, then simmer until the fish is cooked.

Stir, taste, and adjust the seasonings with salt & pepper.

Ladle into individual heated bowls.

Garnish with the fresh parsley.

INGREDIENTS:

8 oz. halibut fillet, in 1-inch pieces
8 oz. red snapper fillet, in 1-inch pieces
8 oz. sole fillet, in 1-inch pieces

1 T. olive oil
6 oz. mushrooms, sliced thick
4 bacon slices, chopped
1 medium onion, chopped
1 cup fennel, sliced thin
1/2 red bell pepper, chopped
1 t. fennel seeds, crushed
2 large garlic cloves, chopped
1 pound red-skinned potatoes, unpeeled & diced into 1/2-inch pieces
3½ cups stock
2 cups canned tomatoes, diced & with their juices
3/4 cup tomato sauce
Salt & pepper, to taste
Parsley, chopped for garnish

233

Zuppa di Pesce
CROTONE, ITALY

Having noted the hint of the Mediterranean in the previous recipe, let me now settle into some serious regional tastes. Crotone is a coastal community located just about where the instep of the Italian boot becomes the sole; however, it is but one of hundreds of such places along this nation's coast where fishing has always been a ready source of food. As with any kettle of fish, this recipe provides but one interpretation of *zuppe di pesce*.

INGREDIENTS:

16 oz. assorted finfish (lean & oily), in 1-inch pieces

8 oz. lobster meat, cleaned & in 1-inch pieces

8 oz. uncooked shrimp, cleaned, deveined & in 1/2-inch pieces

8 oz. squid, cleaned & in 1/2-inch rings

1/3 c. olive oil
1 garlic clove, chopped
1 bay leaf
Dash thyme, crushed
1 t. basil, crushed
2 T. parsley, chopped
4 cups stock
1 cup wine
1½ cup canned plum tomatoes, with juices
2 saffron threads, crushed
Salt & pepper, to taste
4 slices grilled Italian bread

IN YOUR KETTLE, heat half of the olive oil, then sauté the garlic, bay leaf, thyme, basil, and parsley for 3 minutes.

Stir in the stock, wine, tomatoes, and saffron, then bring to the boil.

Reduce the heat, cover, and simmer for 10 minutes.

Stir, taste, and adjust the seasonings with salt & pepper.

Meanwhile, in a skillet heat the remaining olive oil and sauté the Italian bread slices until they are brown on each side.

Place a piece of grilled bread in the bottom of each individual heated bowl, then divide the fish and shellfish equally among them.

Ladle the soup into individual heated bowls.

Seafood Stew

TARANTO, ITALY

This seaport is in the lowland region of the peninsula that includes the heel of Italy's geographical boot. The Gulf of Taranto is on one side of the peninsula; the Adriatic Sea, on the other.

IN YOUR KETTLE, heat the oil, then sauté the onion and garlic for 5 minutes.

Stir in the basil, saffron, and orange peel and sauté another minute.

Add the wine and bring to the boil for 2 minutes.

Stir in the tomatoes and bring the kettle again to the boil. Reduce the heat and simmer for 10 minutes.

Meanwhile, in a separate pot cook the pasta *al dente.*

Add to the kettle the mussels and clams, then cover and simmer for 3 minutes.

Stir in the shrimp and fish, then cover and simmer for another 5 minutes

When the fish is cooked through and the mussels and clams have opened, remove and discard any shells that have not opened.

Stir, taste, and adjust the seasonings with salt & pepper.

Drain the linguine and divide it among the individual heated bowls.

Ladle the stew atop the linguine.

INGREDIENTS:

8 mussels, scrubbed & debearded
8 hardshell clams, scrubbed
4 uncooked jumbo shrimp, peeled & deveined
12 oz. halibut fillet, in 1-inch pieces

1 T. olive oil
1 onion, sliced thin
1 clove garlic, crushed
1/4 cup basil, chopped
1/4 t. saffron threads, crushed
2 T. orange zest
1 cup dry white wine
3½ cups canned plum tomatoes, peeled & with their juices
Salt & pepper
16 oz. linguine

Cioppino

SAN FRANCISCO, CALIFORNIA

In the dialect of those from Genoa, Italy, *cioppin* is the word for *chop*. This stew, though, is not from that region of the country, but is more closely associated with the Italian section of San Francisco, whose residents are credited with its creation in the 1930s.

INGREDIENTS:

2 Dungeness crabs, dressed
12 uncooked shrimp, peeled & deveined
12 mussels, scrubbed & debearded
12 hardshell clams, scrubbed
4 oz. bay scallops
4 oz. each of 2 or more kinds of fish fillets, in 1-inch pieces

2 T. olive oil
2 onion, chopped
4 garlic cloves, chopped
1 carrot, peeled & diced
1 leek (white & pale green), washed & diced
1 celery rib, diced
1/2 cup tomato paste
1/4 t. saffron threads, crumbled
1 cup white wine
2 cups stock
1 bay leaf
1/4 t. oregano
1/4 t. thyme
2 tomatoes, peeled, seeded & chopped
Salt & pepper, to taste

IN YOUR KETTLE, heat the oil, then sauté the onion, garlic, carrot, leek and celery for 3 minutes.

Stir in the tomato paste and the saffron, then simmer another minute.

Stir in the wine, stock, bay leaves, oregano, thyme, and chopped tomatoes. Cover and bring to the boil.

Add all the fish, then stir gently, reduce the heat, and simmer for 15 minutes.

Remove the kettle from the heat. Coax open any mussels and clams with a tap of your fingers. Remove and discard any that do not open, then remove all the fish to a large bowl. Remove the meats of the opened mussels and clams, then discard the shells.

Allow the stew to reduce for about 15 minutes, then return all the fish to the kettle and simmer for 10 minutes.

Ladle into individual heated bowls.

Seafood Stew

CATAUMET, CAPE COD, MASSACHUSETTS

This rockbound little inlet along Buzzards Bay on the western coast of the Cape provides neither native waters for shrimp, nor native soils for leeks, but is nonetheless the source of this simple, but exquisite kettle of fish. Aside from that of the lone leek, the only other texture is derived from this simple variety of seafood, each of which also brings its own special source of natural liquids to enhance the flavor of the stock.

IN YOUR KETTLE, heat the oil, then sauté the leek for 3 minutes.

Stir in the garlic, pepper, and thyme, then sauté another minute.

Add the stock and bring to the boil.

Add shrimp, scallops, cod, mussels, and clams, then reduce the heat, cover, and simmer until all the mussels and clams have opened.

Remove the kettle from the heat. Coax open any mussels and clams with a tap of your fingers. Remove and discard any that do not open.

Ladle into individual heated bowls.

INGREDIENTS:

6 extra large shrimp, peeled & deveined with tail on
8 scallops
8 oz. cod fillet
12 mussels, scrubbed & debearded
12 hardshell clams, scrubbed

1 T. olive oil
1 leek (white & pale green), washed & sliced thin
1 garlic clove, minced
1/2 t. black pepper
1/2 t. fresh thyme
2 cups stock

Fish Soup

AYIOS NIKOLAOS, CRETE

The variety found in a traditional *psarosoupa* is a combination of flavors and textures that can only be created with a mixture of lean fish with those that have a higher oily content. Your fishmonger will be able to suggest others, but these might include *carp, cod, hake, mackerel, salmon, skate, trout,* and *swordfish.*

Of some further interest to you might be the fact that this rugged Mediterranean island between Greece and northern Africa does not derive its main source of food from the sea, but by farming fruits and vegetables, as well as by raising sheep. As you can see, however, that does not mean that they do not know how to make a fine kettle of fish.

INGREDIENTS:

8 oz. lean fish fillets
8 oz. oily fish fillets

1/4 cup olive oil
2 scallions (white & pale green), chopped
1 carrot, peeled & chopped
1 celery rib, chopped
1 tomato, peeled, seeded & chopped
1 zucchini, unpeeled & diced
2 T. parsley, chopped
1/4 cup stock
2 T. flour
2 T. water
4 cups *court bouillon*
Juice of 1/2 lemon
Salt & pepper, to taste
Parsley sprigs, for garnish

IN YOUR KETTLE, heat the olive oil, then sauté the scallions for 3 minutes.

Stir in the carrot, celery, tomato, zucchini, parsley, and stock, then cover and bring to the simmer until the vegetables are just fork tender.

Meanwhile, in a small bowl combine the flour and water to make a thin paste. Stir this into the kettle and simmer until the stock becomes a light brown.

Meanwhile, in a small skillet bring the *court bouillon* to the simmer, then poach the fish fillets.

Remove the skillet from the heat, then remove and reserve the poached fish on a clean plate.

Strain the *court bouillon* through a sieve into the kettle, then stir and bring to the boil until thickened.

Remove the kettle from the heat. Strain the soup through a colander into a heatproof bowl, then use a pestle to force the vegetables through the colander. Discard any remaining solids.

Return the strained soup to the kettle and bring to the simmer.

Cut the poached fish into small cubes, then add to the kettle and simmer for 3 minutes.

Stir in the juice of the lemon, then taste and adjust the seasonings with salt & pepper.

Ladle into individual heated bowls.

Garnish each with parsley.

Fish Soup

PATMOS ISLAND, THE DODECANESE, GREECE

In the Aegean Sea, just along the western coast of Turkey stretches the Dodecanese group of Greek islands, the smallest of which is Patmos. Unlike the preceding island recipe, the variety in this kettle of fish is less explicit.

INGREDIENTS:

32 oz. assorted fish fillets, washed & cleaned

1/4 cup olive oil
2 onions, chopped
2 celery ribs, chopped
4 tomatoes, peeled, seeded & chopped
6 cups stock
2 bay leaves
4 potatoes, peeled & quartered
Salt & pepper, to taste
1/3 cup rice

IN YOUR KETTLE, heat the olive oil, then sauté the onions and celery for 5 minutes.

Stir in the tomatoes, bay leaves, potatoes, and stock, then cover and bring to the simmer until the vegetables are just fork tender.

Add the fish to the kettle and simmer for 10 more minutes.

Remove the kettle from the heat, then carefully remove the fish and reserve on a warm platter. Strain the stock through a colander into a heatproof bowl. Reserve the vegetables, then return the stock to the kettle and bring to the boil.

Add the rice to kettle, reduce the heat, and simmer until the rice is tender.

Stir, taste, and adjust the seasonings with salt & pepper.

Return the fish and vegetables to the kettle, then simmer for 5 minutes.

Ladle into individual heated bowls.

Seafood Stew

SANTA FE, NEW MEXICO

At last check, the city of Santa Fe had not slipped along any fault toward the sea. In fact, the desert sand was the closest thing to a beach. Nonetheless, this recipe brings together several of the regional tastes along with those of the distant ocean.

INGREDIENTS:

8 oz. uncooked shrimp, peeled & deveined
8 oz. crab meat, cleaned & picked

1/4 cup olive oil
1 zucchini, chopped
1 onion, chopped
3 garlic cloves, crushed
1 sweet pepper, diced
2½ cups canned plum tomatoes, peeled, seeded & chopped (reserve juices)
3 tomatoes, peeled, seeded & chopped
4 oz. mushrooms, sliced
1 T. chili powder
1 T. cumin
1 T. basil
1 T. oregano
Dash cayenne
1 t. black pepper
1 t. fennel seed
1/4 cup cilantro, chopped
1/2 cup kidney beans, rinsed & drained
1/2 cup chick peas, rinsed & drained
1 T. lemon juice
4 lemon slices, for garnish

IN YOUR KETTLE, heat 2 T. of the olive oil, then sauté the zucchini until tender. Remove the zucchini to a clean dish.

Heat 2 T. more of the olive oil in your kettle, then sauté the onion, garlic, and pepper for 10 minutes.

Return the zucchini to the kettle, along with the canned tomatoes and their juices, fresh tomatoes, mushrooms, chili powder, cumin, basil, oregano, cayenne, black pepper, fennel seed, and cilantro. Stir and bring to the simmer for 30 minutes.

Stir in the beans and chick peas, then simmer 10 minutes.

Stir in the shrimp and crab meat, then simmer until the shrimp just turn pink.

Stir in the lemon juice.

Ladle into individual heated bowls.

Garnish with lemon slices.

Shrimp & Crab Bisque

MONTEREY, CALIFORNIA

Whenever I used to think of this community, I was always reminded of Steinbeck's *Cannery Row*, as well as the gorgeous rocky waterfront that serves as a home to all sorts of sea life. The last time I visited was well before they transformed the canneries into a tourist attraction, but the majestic beauty of the water still remains. Since then, though, I have add yet another association to the mentioning of "Monterey," and it is the mouth-watering taste of this fine kettle of fish.

INGREDIENTS:

8 oz. uncooked shrimp, peeled & deveined
8 oz. crab meat, cleaned & picked

1 T. butter
1 onion, chopped
1 garlic clove, chopped
1 celery rib, chopped
2/3 cup dry, white wine
3 cups stock
Bouquet garni
1 bay leaf
Salt & pepper, to taste
1/2 cup cream
1 T. brandy
2/3 cup yogurt, for garnish

IN YOUR KETTLE, melt the butter, then sauté the onion, garlic, and celery for 5 minutes.

Add the wine, stock, *bouquet garni*, and bay leaf.

Stir, taste, and adjust the seasonings with salt & pepper.

Simmer for 10 minutes.

Add 1/3 of the shrimp and 1/3 of the crab meat, then simmer until the shrimp just turn pink.

Remove and discard both the bay leaf and *bouquet garni*, then remove the kettle from the heat.

With either a blender or a food processor, purée the vegetables, fish, and stock until smooth.

Return the bisque to the kettle, then stir in the cream and brandy, as well as the remaining shrimp and crab meat. Bring to the simmer until the shrimp just become pink.

Ladle into individual heated bowls.

Garnish each with a dollop of yogurt.

Baja Bouillabaisse

TODOS SANTOS, BAJA CALIFORNIA

To paraphrase Maurice Chevalier: "Thank heaven for *bouillabaise*, for without it what would other chefs do?" This particular variation comes from an old (but *not* aging!) classmate of mine who has now taken up residence in this southernmost community at the tip of the peninsula which parallels the Mexican mainland before dropping into the Pacific. Not quite a little latitude, Todos Santos appears to rival that of Havaña and Key West in both climate and ambition.

INGREDIENTS:

24 hardshell clams, scrubbed & in-shells
16 oz. uncooked shrimp, peeled & deveined
8 oz. red snapper fillets, in 1-inch pieces
8 oz. Dungeness crab meat, cleaned & picked

2 T. olive oil
1 onion, chopped
4 green chili pepper, seeded & chopped
2 garlic cloves, minced
2 cups dry white wine
1 T. orange zest
2 cups orange juice
3 cups canned plum tomatoes, peeled & chopped, with juices
1 T. sugar
1 T. cilantro, chopped
1 t. basil, chopped
1/2 t. oregano, chopped
Salt & pepper, to taste

IN YOUR KETTLE, heat the olive oil, then sauté the onion, green chili peppers, and garlic for 3 minutes.

Stir in the wine, orange zest, orange juice, tomatoes with their juices, sugar, cilantro, basil, and oregano, then bring to the boil.

Reduce the heat and simmer for 10 minutes.

Add the clams and mussels, then stir gently, cover, and simmer for 10 minutes.

Remove the kettle from the heat. Coax open any clams and mussels with a tap of your fingers. Remove and discard any that do not open, then remove and discard any shells.

Add the red snapper, shrimp, and crab meat to the kettle, then stir and simmer until the shrimp just turn pink.

Stir, taste, and adjust the seasonings with salt & pepper.

Ladle into individual heated bowls.

Defroster's Chowder

HOQUIAM, WASHINGTON

Hardshell clams from these local waters are as tasty as they come, and their luscious liquor can breathe new life into all those scraps of fish in plastic wrap that might have accumulated in in your freezer; hence, the name. Whatever you have collected deserves to be served-up in this fine kettle of fish.

IN YOUR KETTLE, heat the olive oil, then sauté the green pepper, carrot, onions, and garlic for 10 minutes.

Stir in the fish, tomatoes, bay leaf, and stock, then bring to the boil. Reduce the heat and simmer for 20 minutes.

Add the white wine, lemon juice, parsley, pimentos, and fennel, then simmer for 30 minutes.

Stir, taste, and adjust the seasonings with salt & pepper.

Ladle into individual heated bowls.

INGREDIENTS:

32 oz. assorted fish fillets, 1-inch pieces
12 hardshell clams, shucked & liquor reserved

1/4 cup olive oil
1/2 green pepper, chopped
1 carrot, peeled & diced
2 onions, chopped
2 garlic cloves, crushed
2½ cups canned tomatoes, with juices
1 bay leaf
6 cups stock
1 cup dry white wine
1 T. lemon juice
3/4 cup parsley, minced
4 T. pimentos, chopped
1 t. fennel seed
Salt & pepper, to taste

Pork & Shellfish Stew
RIBATEJO, PORTUGAL

One of the few recipes in this book which allows a hearty portion of meat, this traditional *cataplana* combines pork with shellfish in a red wine sauce. If at all possible, include the freshest paprika that you might find.

INGREDIENTS:

12 uncooked shrimp, peeled & deveined
8 hardshell clams, scrubbed
16 oz. boneless pork shoulder, in 2-inch pieces

1 ½ cups dry red wine
2 garlic cloves, minced
1 t. red pepper flakes, crushed
1/2 t. paprika
1/2 t. salt
1 ½ cups tomato sauce
1/2 cup pepperoncini, chopped for garnish
1/4 cup parsley, chopped for garnish

Before beginning this stew, prepare a marinade in a large bowl by combining the red wine, garlic, and red pepper flakes. Place the pieces of pork in the bowl and cover thoroughly with the marinade. Cover the bowl tightly with plastic wrap and refrigerate this overnight.

IN YOUR KETTLE, combine the pork and marinade, along with the paprika and salt, then bring to the boil. Reduce the heat, cover, and simmer for 1½ hours.

When the pork is tender, stir in the tomato sauce, then return to the boil.

Add the shrimp and clams to the kettle. Cover and cook until shrimp are just pink and the clams have opened.

Coax any clams that have not opened with a gentle pry from the point of a knife, then remove and discard any clams do not.

Ladle into individual heated bowls.

Garnish each with pepperoncini and parsley.

Three Sea-Fresh Treasures Soup

HAKODATE, JAPAN

Often compared to a *bouillabaisse*, this *Saam Sin Tong* can also be made with clams, fish fillets, lobster, oysters, sea cucumbers (*beche-de-mer*), shark's maw (a specially-prepared delicacy of shark stomach), and squid. Use whatever treasures you might find.

IN YOUR KETTLE, add the stock and bring to the boil.

Stir in the mushrooms, scallions, light soy, sesame oil, and abalone, then simmer for 5 minutes.

Stir, taste, and adjust the seasonings.

Meanwhile, in a small bowl dissolve the cornstarch in the water. Slowly stir the mixture into the kettle until the stock begins to thicken.

Remove the kettle from the heat.

Stir in the chopped lobster and shrimp, then cover and let stand for 3 minutes.

Ladle into individual heated bowls.

Garnish with green parts of scallions.

INGREDIENTS:

8 oz. cooked king crab meat, diced
8 oz. cooked shrimp, peeled, deveined & diced
1/2 cup canned abalone, diced fine

6 cups stock
4 dried Chinese mushrooms, soaked & diced
3 scallions (white & pale green), chopped, reserve green parts for garnish
1 t. light soy sauce
1/4 t. sesame oil
1 T. cornstarch
1/4 cup cold water

Sharkfin Soup

WENZHOU, CHINA

Listing here the most familiar species of shark would sort of be like naming the Seven Dwarfs or the members of the Supreme Court. None of them would have much to do with the ingredients in this recipe. That's because the species of shark used for this kettle of fish is *Galeorhinus zyopterus*, which is simply known as *soupfin* shark. Not mako. Not great white. Not blue. Not tiger. Just soupfin. (Gee, I almost got away with listing some anyway.)

For this esteemed and ancient Oriental dish, the pectoral and the dorsal fins are dried. They must be simmered for hours, then diced before you can actually prepare this soup.

INGREDIENTS:

8 oz. dried shark fin, washed well
4 oz. crab meat

1 t. oil
1 T. ginger, minced
2 scallions (white parts), sliced
1 T. dry sherry
6 cups stock
1 T. cornstarch
2 T. water
1/2 t. soy sauce

IN YOUR KETTLE, cover the shark fin with cold water, then bring to the boil. Reduce the heat and simmer for 3 hours.

Drain the kettle, then add water and repeat the process.

At the end of the second boiling, discard the water, remove the shark fin, and dry with paper towel. Dice the shark fin and set aside.

Wipe clean the kettle, then add oil and sauté the ginger and scallions over medium heat for 3 minutes.

Add the diced fin to the kettle, along with 2 cups of the stock. Bring to the boil for 10 minutes.

Remove the kettle from the heat, then strain the stock through a sieve into a heatproof bowl.

Return the vegetables and shark fin to the kettle, along with the remaining 4 cups of stock, then bring to the simmer.

Meanwhile, in a small bowl mix together the cornstarch, water, and soy sauce, then stir into the kettle.

Stir the crab meat into the kettle, then simmer until the stock begins to thicken.

Ladle into individual heated bowls.

Seafood Stew

LEPE, SPAIN

The recipe for this kettle of fish calls for 2 "dashes of paprika," my own personal taste is to add substantially more. If you've always tended to use paprika as little more than a colorful garnish, you ought to find some opportunity to experiment with its full range of flavors. This just might be the time to do that.

IN YOUR KETTLE, add the olive oil, then sauté the onion and garlic for 5 minutes.

Stir in the tomatoes and bring to the simmer until reduced to a paste.

When the tomatoes have reduced, sprinkle the flour into the kettle and stir to incorporate into the vegetables.

Gradually stir in the stock and wine.

Stir, taste, and adjust the seasonings with paprika, salt & pepper.

Add to the kettle the squid, shrimp, mussels, red snapper, clams, and lobster.

Stir, cover, then simmer until the mussels and clams have opened.

Remove the kettle from the heat. Coax open any mussels and clams with a tap of your fingers. Remove and discard any that do not open.

Ladle into individual heated bowls.

INGREDIENTS:

4 squid, cleaned & in 1/2-inch rings
8 uncooked shrimp, shells on
8 mussels, scrubbed & debearded
12 oz. red snapper fillets, in 1/2-inch pieces
8 hardshell clams, scrubbed
1 (1½-lb.) cooked lobster, separate claws & chop body (shell-on) into 6 large pieces

1/4 cup olive oil
1 onion, chopped
1 garlic clove, minced
2 tomatoes, peeled, seeded & chopped
2 t. flour
4 cups stock
2 cups dry white wine
2 dashes sweet paprika
Salt & pepper, to taste

Cotriade

BREST, FRANCE

The distinctive ingredients in this kettle of fish are not so much the eel or the sea bass, but the blend of aromatic herbs not found in any other combination in this book; most notably, mint and chervil.

INGREDIENTS:

1 eel, skinned & in 1-inch pieces
16 oz. haddock fillets, in 1-inch pieces
16 oz. sea bass, in 1-inch pieces

2 T. butter
1 onion, chopped
4 potatoes, peeled & cubed
2 cups dry white wine
4 t. mint, chopped
1/2 t. marjoram, crushed
1/2 t. chervil, crushed
1/2 t. tarragon, crushed
1/2 t. thyme, crushed
Salt & pepper, to taste
Garlic toast
Parsley, chopped for garnish

IN YOUR KETTLE, melt the butter, then sauté the onion for 10 minutes.

Meanwhile, in a separate saucepan cook the potatoes until fork tender. Drain, then add to the onions in the kettle.

Add the eel and the fish to the kettle, along with the wine, then bring to the simmer.

Stir in the mint, marjoram, chervil, tarragon, and thyme, then taste and adjust the seasonings with salt & pepper.

Stir, cover, and simmer for 20 minutes.

Place a piece of garlic toast in the bottom of each heated bowl.

Ladle the soup into the bowls.

Garnish with parsley.

Gulf Coast Bouillabaisse

PENSACOLA, FLORIDA

There might be a temptation to forego the rubbing and refrigerating by simply adding those ingredients directly into the kettle. The result, though, is simply not the same. The fish fillets take on a distinctive flavor when allowed to absorb the essence of the rub.

Before beginning this kettle of fish, use a mortar & pestle to prepare a rub with the garlic, cloves, allspice berries, sea salt, and black peppercorns. Thoroughly coat the pieces of finfish with the rub, then place them in a bowl covered tightly with plastic wrap. Refrigerate at least 1½ hours.

IN YOUR KETTLE, melt together the butter and oil, then sauté the onion, celery, and garlic for 10 minutes.

Place the refrigerated pieces of finfish on top of the sautéed vegetables in the kettle.

Add the tomatoes, saffron, red pepper flakes, and stock, then bring to the boil.

Reduce the heat, cover, and simmer for 15 minutes.

Add to the kettle the oysters and their liquor, along with the split crabs and the shrimp.

Cover and simmer for 5 minutes.

Add the lemon.

Stir, taste and adjust the seasonings with salt & Tabasco sauce.

Stir in the sherry, then simmer 5 more minutes.

Ladle into individual heated bowls.

INGREDIENTS:

24 oz. assorted firm-fleshed fish fillets, cut in 1-inch pieces & rubbed with spices
8 oysters, shucked with liquor
2 crabs, cleaned & halved
8 uncooked shrimp, shells-on

The Rub:
1 garlic clove, crushed
2 whole cloves, crushed
3 allspice berries, crushed
1/2 t. sea salt
12 black peppercorns, cracked

The Kettle of fFsh:
1 T. butter
1 T. oil
1 onion, diced
2 celery ribs, diced
2 (more) garlic cloves, minced
2 tomatoes, peeled, seeded & diced
2 saffron threads, crushed
1/2 t. red pepper flakes, crushed
4 cups stock
1 lemon, sliced thin
Salt, to taste
Tabasco, to taste
2 T. sherry

249

Seafood Stew

NETTUNO, ITALY

Again, the larger ingredients appear to be similar to those in many other recipes; however, this abundance of fish is embraced by a delicate stock laced with the flavor of sage.

INGREDIENTS:

1 (1½-lb.) cooked lobster, separate claws & chop body (shell-on) into 6 large pieces
8 oz. scallops
8 oz. haddock fillet, in 1-inch pieces
8 oz. halibut fillet, in 1-inch pieces
2 squid, cleaned & in 1/2-inch rings

1/4 cup olive oil
1 onion, diced
1 garlic clove, chopped
1/2 t. sage
1 cup dry white wine
1 cup stock
1 t. tomato paste
1 bay leaf
Salt, to taste

IN YOUR KETTLE, heat the oil, then sauté the onion, garlic, and sage for 5 minutes.

Stir in the wine, stock, tomato paste, and bay leaf, then bring to the boil.

Reduce the heat and simmer for 10 minutes.

Add the lobster to the kettle, cover, and simmer for 5 minutes.

Stir in the scallops, haddock, and the halibut to the kettle, then cover and simmer for 5 minutes.

Stir the squid into the kettle, cover, and simmer 5 minutes more.

Stir, taste, and adjust the seasonings with salt.

Ladle into individual heated bowls.

Seafood Stew

PARANAGUÁ, BRAZIL

Even though two-thirds of Brazil's population lives along a coastline that stretches nearly 4,500 miles, fish is neither a staple of their diet, nor a major component of their economy. For such things, they look to the soil and not the sea. No doubt, you'll recognize the Portuguese influence in this kettle of fish, which does require a little preparation several hours ahead of its actual cooking.

IN YOUR KETTLE, arrange the pieces of red snapper on the bottom.

In a bowl, combine the tomatoes, scallion, parsley, bay leaf, and coriander. Mix well and pour over the fish in the kettle.

Place the kettle in the refrigerator for at least 4 hours.

Remove the kettle from the refrigerator and place on the heat. Add just enough water to the kettle to cover the fish, then bring to the boil.

Reduce the heat and simmer for 15 minutes.

Remove and discard the bay leaf.

Stir, taste, and adjust the seasonings with Tabasco, salt & pepper.

Add the shrimp and simmer until they just turn pink.

Ladle the soup into individual heated bowls.

INGREDIENTS:

32 oz. red snapper, in 1-inch pieces
16 oz. shrimp, peeled & deveined

3 tomatoes, peeled, seeded & chopped
1 scallion (entire), sliced
1/4 cup parsley, chopped
1 bay leaf
1/2 t. coriander, crushed
Tabasco, to taste
Salt & pepper, to taste

251

Seafood Stew

CANET PLAGE, FRANCE

Both the mussel meats, and the flounder fillets in this recipe provide a relatively delicate texture to this kettle of fish, but the stock that emerges from the combination of ingredients is surprisingly rich.

INGREDIENTS:

24 mussels, scrubbed & debearded
16 oz. flounder fillet

1½ cups *court bouillon*
1 t. olive oil
1 cup white wine
Salt & pepper, to taste
1 onion, chopped
2 T. butter
1 garlic clove
4 slices grilled garlic bread

IN YOUR KETTLE, bring the *court bouillon* to the boil.

Add the mussels, cover, and cook until all the shells have opened.

Remove the kettle from the heat, then strain the broth through a colander into a heatproof bowl.

Coax any mussels that have not opened with a gentle tap of the finger, then remove and discard any that do not.

Remove the mussel meats and reserve on a clean plate.

Wipe clean the kettle, then heat the oil.

Sauté the flounder fillets about 1 minute on each side.

Add 1/2 cup of the wine and 1/4 cup of the reserved mussel broth to the kettle.

Taste and adjust the seasonings with salt & pepper.

Simmer for 5 minutes.

Remove the fillets and keep warm on a plate.

Add the onion to the kettle, along with the remainder of the wine and the reserved mussel broth, then bring to the boil until reduced to about 1½ cups.

Meanwhile, in a skillet melt the butter and sauté the garlic. Add the 4 slices of bread and grill on each side.

Place a slice of grilled garlic bread in the bottom of each bowl, then divide the mussels around the bread in the bowls. Divide the fish equally and set atop the bread.

Ladle the broth into the individual heated bowls.

Seafood Chowder

CAM RANH, VIETNAM

I doubt that we will ever associate the food from this nation as anything that resembles a gourmet dish, and yet the subtle flavors that meld together in this kettle of fish are nothing less than marvelous.

As for the finfish in this recipe, the *snook* is a species found throughout the waters of Florida, as well as along parts of coastal Texas. It's a fish that is sometimes found well inland when the currents from an estuary flow that distance.

INGREDIENTS:

12 oz. snook fillets, in 1-inch cubes
6 mussels, shucked
6 shrimp, peeled & deveined

1/2 onion, chopped
2 scallions (entire) sliced
1 garlic clove, crushed
2 T. peanut oil
1/2 t. anise seeds, ground
1 bay leaf
1 green chili pepper, seeded & chopped
2 t. orange zest
2 saffron threads, crushed
1/4 cup sherry
6 cups stock
2 T. soy sauce
2 T. cornstarch
1 cup pineapple chunks, drained
2 cups cooked rice, hot

IN YOUR KETTLE, heat the oil, then sauté the onion, scallions, and garlic for 5 minutes.

Stir in the ground anise seeds, bay leaf, green chili, orange zest, saffron, sherry, and stock, then bring to the boil.

Add the finfish, the reduce the heat, cover, and simmer for 10 minutes.

Meanwhile, in a small saucepan, cook the rice according to the directions on the package.

In a small bowl, make a paste by mixing the soy sauce and cornstarch, then stir into the kettle and simmer until the stock begins to thicken.

Remove and discard the bay leaf.

Stir the mussels into the kettle, along with the shrimp and the pineapple, then simmer for 5 minutes.

Divide the rice among the individual heated bowls.

Ladle the soup into the individual heated bowls.

Seafood Soup

CABO CREUS, SPAIN

As with several other recipes in this book, this kettle of fish depends upon that blend of oily and lean fish. Though some of the suggested species might sound unfamiliar to you, do not assume that they are unavailable. You just might be surprised what can be found in your local waters, be they fresh or salt.

INGREDIENTS:

16 oz. assorted small fish fillets (butterfish, smelts, crappies, sardines), in 1-inch pieces
16 oz. assorted large fish fillets (hake, cod, halibut, pollock, sablefish), in 1-inch pieces

1 T. sea salt
2 T. olive oil
2 garlic cloves, minced
1 onion, chopped
6 cups stock
1 bay leaf
4 peppercorns
Salt, to taste
1/2 cup fresh bread crumbs
Juice of 1/2 lemon
Juice of 1/2 orange
1/4 cup Spanish brandy

Before beginning this kettle fish, toss the pieces of fish together with the sea salt in a large bowl. Cover tightly with plastic wrap and refrigerate for 1½ hours.

After that, rinse the fish and drain in a colander.

IN YOUR KETTLE, heat the oil, then lightly brown the garlic.

Remove and discard the garlic, then add the onion and sauté for 3 minutes.

Add the stock, bay leaf, and peppercorns, then bring to the boil for 15 minutes.

Remove the kettle from the heat, then strain the stock through a sieve into a heat-proof bowl.

Return the stock to the kettle, then add the fish.

Stir, taste, and adjust the seasonings with salt.

Simmer for 5 minutes.

Meanwhile, in a small bowl mix the bread crumbs, lemon juice, orange juice, and brandy, then stir into the kettle and simmer 5 minutes more.

Ladle into individual heated bowls.

Seafood Stew

ST. ANNS BAY, JAMAICA

There is not any one ingredient in this recipe which makes this kettle of fish exclusively Jamaican, and yet I think that underscores the universality of this whole concept. While we might be able to trace the roots of some recipes back to a particular cultural origin, there clearly can be no trademark on catching a fish and cooking it.

IN YOUR KETTLE, bring the stock to the simmer, then poach the fish fillets.

Remove and reserve the fish fillets on a clean plate and keep warm.

Remove the kettle from the heat, then strain the stock through a sieve into a heatproof bowl.

Wipe clean the kettle clean, then heat the olive oil. Sauté the onion and garlic for 5 minutes.

Add the tomatoes and simmer for 5 minutes.

Stir in the parsley, basil, peppercorns, saffron, bay leaf, and salt, then simmer for 15 minutes.

Add the crawfish and simmer for 5 more minutes.

Stir in the shrimp, fish fillets, wine, and enough reserved poaching stock to cover the ingredients by 1 inch.

Simmer until the shrimp and fish are just cooked.

Ladle into individual heated bowls.

Garnish with lemon zest.

INGREDIENTS:

24 oz. whitefish fillets
12 oz. shrimp, peeled & deveined
8 crawfish, shell-on

6 cups stock
1/3 cup olive oil
1 onion, sliced
2 garlic cloves, minced
12 oz. canned tomatoes, chopped
1/4 cup parsley, chopped
1/2 t. basil, chopped
2 peppercorns
2 saffron threads, crushed
1 bay leaf
1/4 t. salt
2/3 cup dry white wine
Lemon zest, garnish

Seafood Stew

PORTO GARIBALDI, ITALY

Sage is one of those savory herbs that most of us more closely associate with the roasting of poultry or pork. By the same token, it is used by a great many cooks when baking fish, especially halibut. Perhaps the best known of all the herbs on earth, this native flavor of the south and central portions of Europe is also an excellent ingredient for any kettle of fish, as long as it is used judiciously. This recipe provides one of those occasions.

INGREDIENTS:

8 oz. halibut, cut into 1-inch pieces
16 oz. sea bass, cut into chunks
8 oz. scallops
1 (1¼-lb.) lobster, separate claws & chop body (shell-on) into 6 pieces

1/2 cup olive oil
2 garlic cloves, chopped
1 t. parsley, minced
1/4 t. red pepper flakes, crushed
Dash sage, crushed
2 T. tomato paste
4 cups stock
3/4 cup dry white wine
Salt, to taste

IN YOUR KETTLE, heat the oil and sauté the garlic and parsley for 3 minutes.

Stir in the red pepper flakes and sage, then add the lobster, cover the kettle, and bring to the simmer for 5 minutes.

Stir in the tomato paste, stock, and wine, along with the fish and scallops. Simmer for 20 minutes.

Stir, taste, and adjust the seasonings with salt.

Ladle into individual heated bowls.

Seafood Soup
PUNTO FIJO, VENEZUELA

Not long after Columbus made his first forays into this hemisphere, Alonso de Ojéda followed with his own exploration of the Caribbean. When he came to these shoreline villages built upon stilts, he called this land *Venezuela*, "Little Venice." But the watery environment was about all there was to be found in common with Italy. If anything, this particular recipe appears to have a Portuguese influence, and many of the same ingredients are in the recipe which follows this one.

IN YOUR KETTLE, melt the butter, then sauté the onion for 5 minutes.

Stir in the fish, shrimp, and ham, along with the stock, then bring to the boil.

Reduce the heat, then stir in the rice, almonds, and saffron.

Cover and simmer for 30 minutes.

Stir, taste, and adjust the seasonings with salt & pepper.

Add the egg yolks and stir.

Ladle into individual heated bowls.

Garnish with parsley.

INGREDIENTS:

12 oz. flatfish fillets, in 1-inch pieces
12 oz. shrimp, peeled, deveined & in 1-inch pieces

3 T. butter
1 onion, diced
3 oz. ham, diced
6 cups stock
1/4 cup uncooked rice
2/3 cup blanched almonds, ground
2 saffron threads, crushed
Salt & pepper, to taste
2 hard-cooked egg yolks, chopped
2 T. parsley, chopped for garnish

Seafood Soup

QUIBERON, PORTUGAL

This recipe does require a little work, but it is certainly not hard work. The thickening agent is not only a combination of fresh breadcrumbs, ground almonds, and hard-cooked egg yolks, but also the fish puréed through the sieve. The distinction between this kettle of fish and a bisque is a very, very fine one.

INGREDIENTS:

8 oz. flatfish fillets
12 oz. shrimp, peeled & deveined

2 T. olive oil
4 parsley sprigs
1/2 t. basil, crushed
4 onions, sliced
4 cups stock
4 slices fresh bread, crusts trimmed
4 hard-cooked egg yolks, mashed
2/3 cups almonds, ground
Salt & pepper, to taste
4 slices crusty bread, toasted

IN YOUR KETTLE, heat the oil, then brown the fillets.

Remove the fish to a clean plate and keep warm.

Stir into the kettle the shrimp, parsley, basil, and onions, along with the stock, then bring to the simmer for 10 minutes.

Meanwhile, break the fresh slices of bread into rough pieces.

Return the fillets to the kettle, along with the bread and mashed egg yolks. Stir and simmer for 15 minutes.

Remove the kettle from the heat, the strain the soup through a sieve into a heatproof bowl. Use a pestle to force through the solids, then return the soup to the kettle.

Stir in the crushed almonds and simmer until hot.

Meanwhile, toast the crusty bread.

Stir, taste, and adjust the seasonings with salt & pepper.

Place a piece of toasted bread in the bottom of each heated bowl.

Ladle the soup into the individual bowls.

Seafood Soup

CHIMBOTE, PERU

The ingredients in this recipe include more of the regional vegetables and flavors than in the previous Peruvian kettles of fish included in this book. Some of the combinations are rather commonplace, but it is unusual to find items such as rice and potatoes together in one kettle, let alone corn, cottage cheese, and poached eggs. Believe me, this one is well worth the attempt.

IN YOUR KETTLE, heat the oil, then sauté the onion, red chili pepper, garlic, tomato, tomato sauce, marjoram, and bay leaf for 5 minutes.

Add the stock, then bring to the boil.

Stir in the corn, peas, potatoes, and rice, then simmer until the potatoes are fork tender.

Add the sea bass, shrimp, and scallops, then simmer for 10 minutes.

Stir in the cottage cheese and evaporated milk, then simmer another 5 minutes.

Meanwhile, in a saucepan bring 2 cups of water to the simmer and poach the eggs.

Place a poached egg in the bottom of each heated bowl.

Ladle the soup into the individual heated bowls.

Garnish with sliced green olives.

INGREDIENTS:

16 oz. whitefish fillet, in 1-inch pieces
12 shrimp, peeled & deveined
12 scallops

2 T. oil
1 T. onion, chopped
1 T. dried red chili pepper, crushed
1 garlic clove, chopped
1 tomato, peeled, seeded & chopped
2 T. tomato sauce
1/2 t. marjoram, crushed
1 bay leaf
4 cups stock
1½ cups kernel corn
1/2 cup peas
2 potatoes, peeled & diced
2 T. rice, uncooked
1/4 cup cottage cheese
3½ cups evaporated milk
4 eggs
6 green olives with pimiento, sliced for garnish

Seafood Soup
OPOBO, NIGERIA

Most of us tend to think of the African continent as being either jungle or desert, and we would not be wrong. Still, every continent must have a coastline, and certainly Africa is no exception. Why, then, do we not think of fish when we think of these nations?

As with some other countries discussed briefly in this book, Nigeria is one of those whose economy has been driven more by the land: agriculture, petroleum, and minerals. In the delta where the Niger flows into the Gulf of Guinea, however, they do make use of whatever food the sea might provide.

What strikes me most about this particular recipe is that the ingredients seem to be the same as those found along the Mississippi delta, and the taste borders upon being Creole.

INGREDIENTS:
8 uncooked shrimp, peeled, deveined & chopped
24 oz. red snapper fillets, in 4 servings
8 crawfish, shell-on
8 uncooked shrimp, shell-on

1/4 cup corn oil
1 onion, sliced
1 tomato, peeled, seeded & chopped
4 T. tomato paste
1/2 t. Tabasco
1/2 T. salt
4 cups stock
1/2 cup cornmeal
2 cups spinach, washed & stemmed

IN YOUR KETTLE, stir together the sliced onion, chopped shrimp, tomato, tomato paste, corn oil, Tabasco, salt, and stock, then bring to the boil.

Reduce the heat, then simmer for 5 minutes.

Stir in the cornmeal and simmer another 15 minutes.

Add the red snapper and simmer for 5 minutes.

Stir in the crawfish, shrimp, and spinach, then cook until the crustaceans turn pink.

Ladle into individual heated bowls.

Long Island Seafood Stew

RIVERHEAD, LONG ISLAND

At this point in the book, we are probably due for another recipe billed as a *bouillabaisse*, but this one is but a humble stew . . . with a bit of white wine and a shot of Pernod! Toss in the mint and the basil, and you'll savor the subtle difference from the others.

IN YOUR KETTLE, heat the oil, then sauté the shallots and garlic for 3 minutes.

Add to the kettle the parsley, saffron, tomato purée, stock, wine, mint, and basil.

Stir, taste, and adjust the seasonings with cayenne, salt & pepper.

Bring to the simmer for 15 minutes.

Add to the kettle the cod and lobster pieces, then stir and simmer for 10 minutes.

Stir in the scallops, shrimp, and clams, then cover and simmer until all the clams have opened.

Coax any clams that have not opened with a gentle pry from the point of a knife, then remove and discard any clams do not.

Stir in the Pernod.

Ladle into individual heated bowls.

INGREDIENTS:

2 (1¼-lb.) cooked lobsters, separate claws & chop each body (shell-on) into 2 pieces
8 oz. scallops
8 uncooked shrimp, peeled & deveined
12 oz. cod fillet, cut in 4 pieces

1/4 cup olive oil
2 shallots, minced
2 garlic cloves, minced
1/3 cup parsley, chopped
2 t. whole saffron, crushed
2 cups tomato purée
3 cups stock
2/3 cup dry white wine
1/2 t. mint, crushed
1/2 t. basil, crushed
Cayenne pepper, to taste
Salt & pepper, to taste
2 t. Pernod

261

Lemon Fish Soup
KATÁKOLON, GREECE

This recipe provides a rich and refreshing change from many of the previous kettles of fish in this chapter. The ingredients are simple, yet elegant.

INGREDIENTS:
8 oz. halibut fillets
8 oz. tautog, fillets
12 shrimp, peeled & deveined

4 cups stock
1/4 cup dry white wine
8 small new potatoes, quartered
1 T. cornstarch
1 T. water
1 T. butter
2 eggs
Juice of 1 lemon
4 T. *aïoli*, for garnish
2 T. parsley, chopped for garnish

IN YOUR KETTLE, combine the stock and wine, then bring to the boil.

Add the potatoes and simmer until fork tender.

Add the fish and simmer for 5 minutes.

Add the shrimp and simmer until they just turn pink.

Remove the potatoes, fish, and shrimp to a clean plate and keep them warm, then bring the stock to the boil.

Meanwhile, in a small bowl make a paste by mixing together the cornstarch and water.

Reduce the heat, then add the butter to the kettle, along with the cornstarch paste. Stir until the stock begins to thicken.

Meanwhile, in a small bowl lightly beat the eggs and add the lemon juice. Gradually, add 1/2 cup of the stock from the kettle to temper the eggs, then stir the egg and lemon mixture into the kettle.

Simmer and stir until the stock has the consistency of a soft custard.

Divide the fish, shrimp, and potatoes among the individual heated bowls, then ladle in the soup.

Garnish each with *aïoli* and chopped parsley.

262

Fish Soup

PORTSMOUTH, DOMINICA

Some people mistake Dominica for the Dominican Republic, which shares the island of Hispaniola with the nation of Haiti. This tiny island republic, though, is in the Lesser Antilles between Guadeloupe and Martinique. Its very poor agricultural economy was even further devastated when Hurricane David struck back in 1979, and much of its income today comes from tourists attracted to its remote beauty.

IN YOUR KETTLE, add the oil and sauté the onions and garlic for 5 minutes.

Add to the kettle the lobster meat, fish, and rice, then cover and simmer 5 minutes.

Add the potatoes, tomatoes, cabbage, tomato paste, stock, and pimientos, then stir.

Add the salt, pepper, and oregano.

Cover and simmer for 30 minutes.

Ladle into individual heated bowls.

INGREDIENTS:

24 oz. assorted fish fillets, in 1-inch pieces
1 (1¼-lb.) lobster, cleaned, picked & in 1-inch pieces

1/3 cup olive oil
2 onions, diced
2 garlic cloves, chopped
2/3 cup rice, uncooked
3 potatoes, peeled & diced
2 tomatoes, peeled, seeded & diced
1½ cups cabbage, shredded
2 T. tomato paste
2 cups stock
2 pimientos, sliced thin
1 t. salt
1/2 t. black pepper
1/4 t. oregano, crushed

Vatapa

SÃO GONÇALO, BRAZIL

What I find most enjoyable about this particular kettle of fish is neither the meat, nor the spices, nor even the stock that's enhanced with lime and coconut milk. My favorite part is the cashews, most of which the rest of the world imports from Brazil or from India.

I suppose that a great many readers will find it easiest to substitute the peanut butter for the raw cashews, and I can understand that. Still, you will not know what you are missing until you are able to prepare this with the ingredient of preference.

As a final note on the subject, let me add that cashews are nuts that have no shells. Instead, they are the seeds of a pear-shaped fruit that is somewhat like an apple. Moreover, these seeds grow *outside* the fruit! Admit it, you've gotta like the cashews in this recipe.

INGREDIENTS:

6 oz. fish fillets, cut in 1-inch pieces
8 oz. shrimp, peeled & deveined

5 t. safflower oil
1/2 onion, chopped
1 t. ginger, peeled & chopped
3 jalapeño peppers, seeded & chopped
1/4 cup raw cashews, ground (or 1/4 cup cashew or peanut butter)
3 tomatoes, peeled, seeded & diced
Juice of 2 limes
4 cups stock
1 cup coconut milk
1 T. cilantro, chopped
Salt & pepper, to taste

IN YOUR KETTLE, heat the oil, then sauté the onion, garlic, ginger, and jalapeño peppers for 10 minutes.

Meanwhile, grind the cashews until they have the consistency of peanut butter.

Stir the cashews into the kettle, along with the tomatoes, lime juice, stock, coconut milk, and cilantro, then bring to the simmer for 5 minutes.

Add the fish fillets and bring to the simmer for 5 minutes more.

Add the shrimp and simmer until they just turn pink.

Stir, taste, and adjust the seasonings with salt & pepper.

Ladle into individual heated bowls.

Gumbo

Recipes for gumbo reflect the tastes of a variety of ethnic groups that converged upon the Louisiana region over the centuries: the Native American Choctaw Indians thickened this stew with ground sassafras leaves (filé powder) and Africans — many of whom came as slaves — had included *ochingombo* (okra). The French refugees whom the British had driven out of Nova Scotia brought their Arcadian customs to the backcountry, while the Spanish and European French were bringing theirs to New Orleans.

Creole Gumbo

NEW ORLEANS, LOUISIANA

Though the word *creole* itself was first used in Latin America in the 1500s to distinguish the sons and daughters of European settlers from Native Americans, blacks, and those who later came to the area, in colonial Louisiana it was applied to the American-born descendants of parents who had come from Europe and Spain. Gumbo made in the creole fashion with tomatoes and okra is a somewhat lighter kettle of fish preferred by the aristocratic settlers of the city, as opposed to that made by the cajuns in the rural areas. Some maintain that only the creole gumbo is made with tomatoes, and this recipe reflects that.

IN YOUR KETTLE, make a light brown roux by rendering the bacon fat.

Sprinkle the flour into the kettle and stir to incorporate with the fat. Continue to stir until the flour has cooked and the roux has become the color of peanut butter.

Slowly add the stock, stirring to mix with the roux.

Remove the kettle from the heat, then pour the stock into a heatproof bowl and reserve.

Wipe clean your kettle and render the bacon until crisp and browned.

Remove and reserve the bacon on a paper towel to drain.

Discard all but 2 T. of the drippings, then sauté the onion, garlic, and pepper 3 minutes.

Meanwhile, strain the tomatoes through a sieve and reserve the juices in a bowl.

Add the tomatoes to the kettle, along with

INGREDIENTS:

4 crabs, dressed
16 oz. uncooked shrimp, peeled & deveined
12 oz. firm fish fillets, cut in 1-inch pieces
12 oysters, shucked with liquor

2 bacon slices, diced
1 onion, minced
2 garlic cloves, minced
1 green pepper, minced
1½ cups canned tomatoes, with juices
4 cups stock
2 cups okra, chopped
1/2 t. salt
1/2 t. black pepper
2 dashes cayenne pepper
2 dashes Worcestershire
2 bay leaves
2 dashes Tabasco
1/4 t. filé powder
3 cups cooked rice, hot

the stock and the okra, then cover the kettle and simmer for 10 minutes.

Add the reserved tomato juices, as well as the salt, black pepper, cayenne pepper, Worcestershire, bay leaves, and Tabasco, then stir and bring to the boil.

Reduce the heat, cover, and simmer for 2 hours.

Add the crabs, then simmer for 10 minutes.

Stir in the shrimp and fish, then simmer another 10 minutes.

Meanwhile, in a saucepan cook the rice according to directions on the package.

Stir the gumbo, taste, and adjust the seasonings.

Add the oysters and their reserved liquor, then simmer until the edges of the oysters just begin to curl.

Use a custard dish cup or similar dish to mold each serving of hot rice, then turn into individual heated soup bowls.

Dust the rice with filé powder, then ladle the gumbo into each bowl. Divide the seafood as best as possible among them.

Cajun Gumbo

PARISH, LOUISIANA

Cajun gumbo is a darker, richer kettle of fish that reflects the tastes and provisions of the 'Cadian refugees who settled in the rural areas. There are those who will debate whether the cajun recipe ought to contain tomatoes; however, this one does not. If you wish to do so, then simply adjust the creole recipe to be made with a dark roux.

INGREDIENTS:

- 4 crabs, dressed
- 16 oz. uncooked shrimp, peeled & deveined
- 12 oz. firm fish fillets, cut in 1-inch pieces
- 12 oysters, shucked with liquor

- 1 T. bacon fat
- 2 T. flour
- 6 cups stock
- 2 bacon slices, diced
- 1 onion, minced
- 2 garlic cloves, minced
- 1 green pepper, minced
- 2 cups okra, chopped
- 1/2 t. salt
- 1/2 t. black pepper
- 2 dashes cayenne pepper
- 2 dashes Worcestershire
- 2 bay leaves
- 2 dashes Tabasco
- 1/4 t. filé powder
- 3 cups cooked rice, hot

IN YOUR KETTLE, make a dark brown roux by rendering the bacon fat.

Sprinkle the flour into the kettle and stir to incorporate with the fat. Continue to stir until the flour has cooked and the roux has become the color of milk chocolate.

Slowly add the stock, stirring to mix with the roux. Remove the kettle from the heat, then pour the stock into a heatproof bowl and set aside.

Wipe the kettle clean and render the bacon until crisp and brown.

Remove and reserve the bacon to a paper towel to drain.

Discard all but 2 T. of the drippings, then sauté the onion, garlic, and pepper for 3 minutes.

Return the reserved stock to the kettle and bring to the simmer.

Add the okra, then cover and simmer for 10 minutes.

Stir in the salt, black pepper, cayenne pepper, Worcestershire, bay leaves, and Tabasco, then cover and simmer for 2 hours.

Add the crabs, then simmer for 10 minutes.

Stir in the shrimp and fish, then simmer another 10 minutes.

Meanwhile, in a saucepan cook the rice according to directions.

Stir the gumbo, taste, and adjust the seasonings.

Add the oysters and their reserved liquor, then simmer until the edges of the oysters just begin to curl.

Use a custard dish cup or similar dish to mold each serving of hot rice, then turn into individual heated soup bowls.

Dust the rice with filé powder, then ladle the gumbo into each bowl. Divide the seafood as best as possible among them.

Seafood Stew

KEHENA BEACH, HAWAII

If you bother to look closely at this recipe, you'll discover that this kettle of fish from our 50th state is not that much different from the Brazilian Vatapa. The only addition is garlic, while the only substitutions are lemon juice for the lime juice, then macadamia nuts for the cashews.

Having given a few good words to cashews, I feel obliged to do the same for these fine nuts. Though we associate them with Hawaii (where they are grown commercially), macadamias are native to Australia, where they grow on an evergreen tree, as do the cashews.

INGREDIENTS:

8 oz. firm fish fillets (tuna, snapper, swordfish) in 1/2-inch pieces
8 oz. scallops
8 oz. uncooked shrimp, peeled & deveined

2 T. oil
2 onions, diced
1 T. fresh ginger, minced
3 garlic cloves, minced
2 jalapeño pepper, seeded & diced
2 T. lemon juice
2 T. paprika
2 cups canned plum tomatoes, peeled & diced with juices
1/2 cup macadamia nuts, ground fine
1/2 cup cilantro, minced
1/2 cup coconut milk
2 cups stock
Salt & pepper, to taste

IN YOUR KETTLE, heat the oil, then sauté the onions for 5 minutes.

Stir in the ginger, garlic, jalapeño peppers, lemon juice, and paprika, along with the tomato juices and half of the tomatoes, then bring to the simmer for 3 minutes.

Remove the kettle from the heat, then stir in the coconut milk.

In a blender, purée small batches of the cooked ingredients, then return to the kettle, along with the rest of the tomatoes, the macadamia nuts, cilantro, and stock.

Bring the kettle to the boil, then reduce the heat and simmer for 5 minutes.

Stir, taste, and adjust the seasonings with salt & pepper.

Add the fish, scallops, and shrimp, then cover and simmer another 5 minutes.

Ladle into individual heated bowls.

Seafood Gazpacho

NEWPORT, RHODE ISLAND

The origins of this particular kettle of fish are about as far as you might get — in time and space — from Aquidneck Island, at the tip of which sits this fabled summer resort of the rich. Forerunners of *gazpacho* are found in the pages of the ancient Greeks and Romans, while the name itself is derived from the Arabic for "soaked bread." The Spanish later claim it is a dish of their former province Andalusia, which was made with bread, oil, vinegar, onions, and garlic. And by 1796, when Mary Randolph wrote her recipe in her *Virginia Housewife*, it had become a layered salad of greens, tomatoes, cucumbers, onions, and bread crumbs. Since 1845, though, gazpacho has been prepared as a soup; sometimes hot, sometimes cold, and most often simply chilled. As with most other kettles of fish, there are countless variations among those which bear this name; this, then, is but one.

INGREDIENTS:

8 uncooked shrimp, peeled & deveined
8 scallops
8 hardshell clams, scrubbed & in-shells
8 mussels, scrubbed & debearded

2 T. olive oil
1 cup dry white wine
2 T. sherry vinegar
1 onion, chopped
2 garlic cloves, minced
1 cucumber, peeled & seeded
Tabasco, to taste
1 garlic clove, minced
3 cups tomato juice
1/4 cup mayonnaise
Salt & pepper, to taste
2 roasted red bell peppers, peeled, seeded & halved
Croutons, for garnish

IN YOUR KETTLE, heat the olive oil, then sauté the shrimp and scallops for 4 minutes.

Remove the shrimp and scallops, then reserve and chill on a clean plate.

Add the wine, vinegar, onion, and garlic, then cover and bring to the boil.

Add the clams and mussels, then stir gently, reduce the heat, cover, and simmer for 10 minutes.

Remove the kettle from the heat. Coax open any clams and mussels with a tap of your fingers. Remove and discard any that do not open, then remove all the shellfish to a large bowl and chill.

Meanwhile, ladle the contents of the kettle into a food processor, along with the cucumber, Tabasco, garlic cloves, and 1 cup of the tomato juice, then blend until smooth.

Add in the mayonnaise, then blend until it is incorporated.

Taste and adjust the seasonings with salt & pepper.

Chill in the refrigerator for at least 1 hour.

Place 1 roasted pepper half in each chilled bowl, then top each pepper half with 2 shrimp and 2 scallops.

Ladle the gazpacho into each of the individual heated bowls, then garnish each with 2 clams, 2 mussels, and croutons.

Seafood Stew

ITAJAÍ, BRAZIL

All too often, a great many people tend to misunderstand Brazilian cuisine as something resembling Mexican, and I'm not at all certain why. If anything, it takes on the influence of Portugal, Spain, and parts of Europe. I point that out not just to dispel that notion of a Mexican flavor, but also to underscore the fact that this is very much like a *caldeirada*, minus the squid and the green pepper.

INGREDIENTS:

16 oz. grouper fillets
8 oz. shrimp, peeled & deveined
12 hardshell clams, scrubbed & in-shells
12 mussels, scrubbed & debearded
8 oz. crab meat, picked & cleaned
8 oz. lobster meat, in 1-inch pieces

2 T. olive oil
2 scallions, (white & pale green), chopped
3 garlic cloves, minced
2 tomatoes, peeled, seeded & diced
1 T. coriander, chopped
1 cup parsley, chopped
Cayenne pepper, to taste
4 cups stock
Black pepper, to taste

IN YOUR KETTLE, heat 1 T. of the olive oil, then sauté the scallions and garlic for 3 minutes.

Stir in the tomatoes, coriander, and parsley, then taste and adjust the seasonings with cayenne pepper.

Simmer for 5 minutes.

Stir in the stock, then bring to the boil.

Add the clams and mussels, then stir gently, reduce the heat, cover, and simmer for 10 minutes.

Remove the kettle from the heat. Coax open any clams and mussels with a tap of your fingers. Remove and discard any that do not open, then remove and discard any shells.

Meanwhile, in a skillet heat the remaining 1 T. of olive oil, then sauté the grouper fillets until browned on each side. Break the browned fillets into pieces, then add to the kettle.

Stir in the crab and lobster meats, then bring to the simmer for 5 minutes.

Stir, taste, and adjust the seasonings with black pepper.

Ladle into individual heated bowls.

Hot & Sour Seafood Soup

YONG SATA, THAILAND

A good many of us are aware that this country was once known as Siam, and we also remember something of Anna and the King. As lovers of seafood, however, we ought to appreciate this nation's geography; in addition to its majestic mountains, Thailand has two distinct and beautiful coastlines. Because part of its land is upon the Malay Peninsula, one coast is on the Gulf of Thailand, and the other is on the Strait of Malacca.

Given this geography, the Thais have taken full advantage, developed a modern fishing fleet, and grown into one of the world's largest fishing nations. In fact, there is a great danger that the stocks in the gulf might well become overfished.

IN YOUR KETTLE, combine the stock, green peppers, lime zest, lime leaves, lemon grass, and reserved shells, then bring to the boil.

Reduce the heat, cover, and simmer for 30 minutes.

Remove the kettle from the heat, then strain the stock through a sieve into a heatproof bowl.

Discard the solids, then return the stock to the kettle and bring to the boil.

Stir in the fish sauce, lime juice, cilantro, red pepper, mushrooms, and scallions, then reduce the heat and simmer for 5 minutes.

Add the shrimp and scallops, then cook until the shrimp just turn pink.

Ladle into individual heated bowls.

INGREDIENTS:

8 oz. uncooked shrimp, peeled & deveined (shells reserved)
8 oz. scallops

6 cups stock
2 green serrano chili peppers, seeded & chopped
1 t. lime zest
3 kaffir lime leaves
2 lemon grass stalks, in 1-inch pieces
2 T. fish sauce
Juice of 2 limes
2 T. cilantro, chopped
1 red serrano chili pepper, seeded & chopped
4 shiitake mushrooms, sliced
2 scallions (entire), sliced

Clam & Shrimp Chowder
NEWBURYPORT, MASSACHUSETTS

Every year it seems that almost every seaside community presents a chowderfest of one sort or another. Were this kettle of fish put forth as a clam chowder, I would protest that its ingredients — aside from the shrimp — included too great a variety. In my own feeble mind, I just can't accept all of them in a clam chowder.

But once you toss in those shrimp, I shed all my neuroses and welcome the flavors that all those other things bring. Ralph Waldo Emerson said it best, even though he was not talking of chowder. "A foolish consistency is the hobgoblin of little minds." Oh, that all the world's problems were so small.

INGREDIENTS:

24 hardshell clams, steamed & chopped
8 uncooked shrimp, peeled, deveined & in 1/2-inch pieces

2 T. butter
1 onion, chopped
2 celery ribs, chopped
2 T. flour
2 cups stock
2 potatoes, peeled & diced
1½ t. fennel seeds
1 t. paprika
1 red bell pepper, seeded & chopped
1 cup kernel corn
2 cups cream
Salt & pepper, to taste

IN YOUR KETTLE, melt the butter, then sauté the onion and celery for 3 minutes.

Sprinkle in the flour, then stir to incorporate with the butter and vegetables. Cook for 1 minute.

Gradually stir in the stock, then bring to the simmer.

Add to the kettle the potatoes, fennel seeds, and paprika, then cover and simmer until the potatoes are fork tender.

Stir in the red bell pepper, corn, and cream, along with the chopped clams and shrimp, then simmer for 5 minutes.

Add in the cream.

Stir, taste, and adjust the seasonings with salt & pepper.

Simmer for 5 more minutes.
Ladle into individual heated bowls.

Things that Go *Splash!* in the Water

Though the focus of this effort has been — until now — fine kettles of *fish*, I thought I'd add a final page or 3 on kettles of other things that spend some time in the water.

While I discovered that a great many people whose initial reaction to eels was that they (the *eels*, that is) were really snakes and not fish, there are others whose first thoughts were that turtles and frogs should be considered fish. The truth of the matter, as we all really know, is that turtles are reptiles, while frogs are amphibians. I'm certain that you'd like me to carry on about all these differences, but I don't want to have flashbacks to Biology 101; we've got to decide whether we want to eat these things or to dissect them. My suspicion is that most will vote for the latter.

Still, I am certain that somewhere in your life you have heard mention of some of these things. In the case of turtle soup, you've probably heard more references to *mock* turtle soup than to the real thing; however, there was a time when turtle was such a popular item in the diet that the demand endangered the species. The same could be said for alligator and crocodile, but the demand was more for their hides than for their steaks.

Of course, there is the seal, the walrus, and so on, which the Eskimos and the Tlingit Indians of Alaska do boil in a 50/50 mix of fresh- and saltwater, but it is not served as a soup or a stew.

Finally, there is that reference to frog soup. I know of no one who has either served or eaten such a thing, but it most certainly exists. And, no doubt, it tastes like chicken, right?

Turtle Soup

BALTIMORE, MARYLAND

When turtles became so scarce that turtle meat was affordable only to wealthy males who belonged to private social clubs, the proper preparation of turtle soup then became the topic of debate among those who had too much free time on their hands. The members of Baltimore's Maryland Club insisted that the recipe should be essentially a consommé to which the meat was then added.

INGREDIENTS:

16 oz. turtle meat, chopped

1 T. oil
2 celery ribs, chopped
2 carrots, chopped
1 onion, chopped
2 garlic cloves, chopped
2 cups cabbage, chopped
8 whole peppercorns
3 parsley sprigs
2 bay leaves
1½ t. salt
5 cups water
1 T. oil
1 cup water
1/2 cup sherry

IN YOUR KETTLE, heat the oil, then sauté the celery, carrots, onion, garlic and cabbage for 3 minutes.

Stir in the peppercorns, parsley, bay leaves, salt, and the 5 cups of water, then cover and bring to the boil.

Reduce the heat and simmer for 1 hour.

Meanwhile, in a saucepan heat the second 1 T. of oil, then brown the turtle meat.

Add to the saucepan the 1 cup of water, then bring to the boil. Reduce the heat, cover, and simmer until the meat is tender.

After the kettle has simmered for an hour, remove it from the heat.

Strain the stock through a sieve into a heatproof bowl, then discard all the solids.

Return the strained stock to the kettle and bring to the simmer.

Add the turtle meat and its liquid to the kettle, then stir in the sherry. Simmer for 5 minutes.

Ladle into individual heated bowls.

Cream of Terrapin Soup

PHILADELPHIA, PENNSYLVANIA

The difference between *terrapin* and *turtle* is simply that the former refers to any edible turtle. The difference, however, between a Maryland recipe and those prepared in the men's clubs of Philadelphia was the key issue in the debate among the clubs. At the Rittenhouse Club in the City of Brotherly Love, the recipe called for a cream base.

In an attempt to settle the dispute in a gentlemanly manner, a jury of impartial males tasted the soups made by the respective clubs. The Baltimore recipe won; however, the proof of the kettle remains in the tasting.

INGREDIENTS:

32 oz. terrapin meat, chopped

8 T. butter
4 T. flour
4 cups milk
Salt & pepper, to taste
1 cup heavy cream
1/2 cup dry sherry
2 T. parsley, chopped for garnish

IN YOUR KETTLE, melt the butter, then remove from the kettle from the heat.

Sprinkle the flour into the kettle to make a white roux and stir to incorporate into with the butter.

Return the kettle to the heat and allow the flour to cook, but be careful not to let it become brown.

Slowly stir the milk into the roux, then bring to the simmer.

Stir, taste, and adjust the seasonings with salt & pepper.

Add the terrapin meat, then simmer for 5 minutes.

Stir in the heavy cream and simmer until thickened.

Add in the sherry and simmer another minute.

Ladle into individual heated bowls.

Garnish with parsley.

Alligator Stew
TALLUHLA, LOUISIANA

There is a physical difference between an alligator and a crocodile. If you ever get close enough to tell them apart, however, it's probably too late to benefit from such knowledge. Let's just say that they both are capable of eating humans, but humans eat more alligators than crocodiles. The American alligator can be found from the Carolinas down through the Gulf coastal states, including the Rio Grande, and since 1973 they have been protected by the Endangered Species Act. Those who savor the tasty meat of the tail can do so legally by purchasing alligator which is farm-bred for the market. Otherwise, if the Feds don't get you, then the 'gators just might.

INGREDIENTS:

24 oz. alligator meat, in 1-inch pieces

3 T. olive oil
2 onions, chopped
2 celery ribs, chopped
1 green bell pepper, seeded & chopped
4 garlic cloves, chopped
4 cups canned plum tomatoes, peeled & chopped (reserve juices)
1/2 cup basil, chopped
3 T. oregano, chopped
3 t. thyme, chopped
Cayenne pepper, to taste
Salt & pepper, to taste
3 t. Worcestershire sauce
5 cups stock
3 scallions (white & pale green) chopped
12 T. butter
3 T. parsley, chopped for garnish

IN YOUR KETTLE, heat the olive oil, then sauté the onions, celery, and pepper for 3 minutes.

Stir in the garlic and sauté for 2 minutes.

Add the tomatoes and their juices, basil, oregano, and thyme.

Stir, taste, and adjust the seasonings with salt & pepper.

Add the Worcestershire and the stock, then bring to the boil.

Stir in the scallions and alligator meat.

Reduce the heat, cover, and simmer for 10 minutes.

Stir in the butter, then remove the kettle from the heat and let stand for 5 minutes.

Ladle into individual heated bowls.

Garnish each with parsley.

Finishing Touches

Aïoli

The principal ingredients of egg yolk and oil lead many to conclude that this Italian condiment is nothing more than mayonnaise with garlic. When made properly, however, with olive oil and with a mortar & pestle, the result is exquisite. If you do not have a simple mortar & pestle among your kitchen utensils, my first advice would be to get them; otherwise, you must blend the egg yolks and olive oil in a bowl with a wooden spoon — *never* with a blender or food processor.

Adding too much oil at any time will cause the aïoli to break. Begin by adding just a drop or so, then continue at that pace for the first tablespoon. After that, drizzle the olive oil down the side of your mortar in increments of 1 T., then work that into the paste before drizzling the next.

This recipe yields 2 cups.

IN YOUR MORTAR, sprinkle the salt on the garlic cloves to help release their moisture, as well as to provide your pestle with some friction, then work the ingredients into a smooth paste.

Add in the lemon juice and egg yolks, then continue to work the paste.

Gradually, incorporate the olive oil into your mixture.

Cover and reserve, or use as directed in your recipe.

INGREDIENTS:
1 t. kosher salt
3 garlic cloves, peeled & whole
2 egg yolks
1 T. fresh lemon juice
1¾ cups extra virgin olive oil

277

Butter Crackers

INGREDIENTS:

4 cups all-purpose flour
1 cup cold butter, cut in pieces
1/2 t. soda
1/2 t. of salt
2 T. water
2 cups milk

IN YOUR MIXING BOWL, combine the flour and butter, then cut together with a fork.

Dissolve the soda in 2 T. of hot water, then add to the mixing bowl, along with the salt, water, and milk. Mix together well and work into a ball.

Lay the ball upon a floured surface, then *beat* with a rolling pin for 30 minutes. Turn and shift the mass often.

Preheat the oven to 400°F.

Roll the pastry into a sheet no thicker than 1/4-inch.

Place upon an ungreased baking sheet and prick the surface throughout with a fork. Lightly spray the top surface with water.

Bake until the sheet is hard, then remove from the oven and allow to cool.

Place the crackers in a muslin bag, then hang to dry for 2 days.

Crustacean Butter

This butter will keep well in the refrigerator for at least a month and will last indefinitely in your freezer, all of which is a blessing, for the recipe is somewhat time-consuming. Nonetheless, the rich flavor and dynamic color lends an elegant garnish if you swirl 1 T. of crustacean butter into each individual bowl.

There are two keys to this recipe. First, you must have shells from about 5 lobsters; for shrimp or crawfish butter, the shells from about 7 pounds. Keep in mind that shells can be frozen until you have what you need. Second, you need a heavy duty electric mixer with a paddle blade. A hand mixer will not do.

This recipe yields about 1 lb. of butter.

INGREDIENTS:

Reserved shells from 5 lbs. of lobster, or from 7 lbs. of shrimp or crawfish, chopped into 3-inch pieces
1 lb. cold butter, cut into chunks
8 cups water

IN THE LARGE BOWL OF YOUR ELECTRIC MIXER, combine the pieces of shell with the chunks of cold butter, then run the mixer at slow speed for 20 minutes.

When the shells have broken apart and the butter is pink, add them to your kettle.

Place the kettle over low heat for 45 minutes, but be careful that the butter does not burn.

Meanwhile, in a separate pan bring the water to the simmer.

Remove the kettle from the heat, then stir in the hot water.

Allow the kettle to cool to room temperature, then refrigerate it overnight. By morning, the congealed butter will have become red and floated to the surface of the kettle.

Carefully remove the congealed butter with a slotted spoon and reserve it in a saucepan. Discard the shells and liquid.

Melt the butter over low heat, then strain it through a fine sieve into a heatproof container.

Cover and refrigerate/freeze, or use as directed in your recipe.

Hardtack (Ship's Biscuit)

This wheat-based cracker is the historical precedent for the so-called pilot cracker made by a handful of companies throughout the United States, such as Alaska's Sailor Boy Pilot Bread, Bent's Pilot Crackers, and Hawaii's Saloon Pilot Crackers, but most notably by the National Biscuit Company (Nabisco). The recorded history of pilot cracker sales dates back to the era of George Washington's first administration. Measuring 5" x 2½" x 3/16", the Crown Pilot Cracker was first baked by John Pearson of Newburyport, Massachusetts, some hundred years or so before his and other bakeries joined together as the National Biscuit Company.

Though Nabisco eventually produced its Crown Pilot Crackers on a scale much larger than other bakeries, in recent years it had confined their distribution simply to Maine, New Hampshire, and Massachusetts. Then, in May of 1996, the company announced it would cease production of this New England staple altogether.

The news was not met well by the residents of Chebeague Island (population: 325) in Casco Bay, just off the southwest coast of Maine. Spearheaded by Donna Miller Damon, whose own roots on the island go back to 1756, a campaign was waged to convince the newly-merged companies of Nabisco and R.J. Reynolds not to abandon this product. And on February 4, 1997, Nabisco announced it would continue production of their product whose package once bore the slogan: "The Famous Chowder Cracker."

Though not the exact same thing, hardtack is that cracker that was kept well in barrels aboard ships upon the oceans and in general stores across the young nation. A fairly bland cracker free of fat and most salt, they serve as the perfect thickener for chowders.

This recipe yields 12 servings.

IN YOUR MIXING BOWL, combine the flour, salt, sugar, and water. Mix well, then turn out onto a floured surface.

Use your hands or a rolling pin to flatten the dough into a sheet 1/4-inch thick.

INGREDIENTS:

4 cups flour
1 T. salt
1 T. sugar
1 cup water

Place on a cookie sheet and score with a knife to create crackers of the desired size.

Bake in a 350°F oven for 30 minutes.

Allow to cool, then break into pieces as needed.

Mushroom Ketchup

Eventually known as *catsup* and *catchup,* this thick and well-seasoned sauce takes its name from the Malaysian *ketjap,* a fish sauce made from salted and spiced mushrooms. When British sailors brought the sauce back from the China trade, they not only Anglicized the name, but also the recipe. That is when tomatoes became a primary ingredient.

This recipe yields 6 cups .

INGREDIENTS:

4 lbs. mushrooms, cleaned & chopped
8 onions, chopped fine
1 cup salt
1/2 cup mustard seed
2 T. black pepper
2 T. celery seed
1 cup vinegar

IN YOUR KETTLE, combine the mushrooms and onions.

Add the salt and let stand 30 minutes.

Pour into a colander and press out the liquid that has drained from the salted mushrooms.

Return to the kettle and add the mustard seed, pepper, celery seed and vinegar.

Ladle into sterilized jars, but do not fill to the top.

Fill with vinegar and seal.

Picada

Depending upon the region of Spain, the recipe for this flavorful sauce might include hazelnuts in lieu of some of the almonds. Unlike some of the other Old World condiments, picada can — and most likely *should* — be made with a small food processor. Because there are more dry ingredients and no eggs whatsoever, using a mortar & pestle would require much more time and effort.

This recipe yields 1 cup.

INGREDIENTS:

6 1/2-inch slices of French bread
1 cup extra virgin olive oil
1 cup blanched almonds, toasted
1 ancho chili, blanched, seeded & chopped coarse
8 garlic cloves, chopped
1 jalapeño chili, seeded & diced
Salt, to taste

IN YOUR SKILLET, heat 1/2 cup of the olive oil, then sauté the slices of bread of each side.

IN A SMALL PROCESSOR, combine the remaining olive oil, nuts, ancho chili, garlic, and jalapeño chili, then process 30 seconds.

Break the sautéed slices of bread into pieces, then add to the processor and process for 3 minutes.

Scrape the sides and process another minute. If the mixture is too thick to process, thin with a little stock or olive oil.

Taste and adjust the seasonings with salt.

Cover and refrigerate, or use as directed in your recipe.

Rouille

Though you will find this intense sauce used in the finishing of some soups from Spain and Portugal, its origin is in the Provence. As with *aïoli*, the recipe could be made with a food processor; however, using a mortar & pestle not only makes use of a traditional method, but also produces the traditional texture. Moreover, when extra virgin olive oil is processed or beaten, it can take on a bitter taste.

This recipe yields 2 cups.

IN A SMALL BOWL, soak the saffron in the warm water for 20 minutes.

Meanwhile, in your mortar combine the red pepper, jalapeno peppers, and garlic.

Sprinkle in the salt to help release their oils, as well as to provide your pestle with some friction, then work the ingredients into a smooth paste.

In another bowl, soften the slices of bread in warm water. Squeeze the water each slice, then add the bread to the other ingredients in your mortar.

Add in the saffron and water, then continue to work the paste.

Gradually, add the olive oil into your mixture until all has been incorporated into the paste.

Cover and reserve, or use as directed in your recipe.

INGREDIENTS:
1/8 t. saffron threads, crushed
1 t. warm water
3 roasted red bell peppers, peeled, seeded & chopped
3 jalapeño chili peppers, seeded & chopped fine
4 garlic cloves, minced
1 t. kosher salt
4 1/2-inch slices of French bread, trimmed of crusts
2 cups warm water
3/4 cup extra virgin olive oil

Bibliography

ANDERSON, JEAN. *The Food of Portugal.* William Morrow and Company, Inc. (New York: 1986)

ANDERSON, KEN. *The Gourmet's Guide to Fish and Shellfish.* William Morrow and Company (New York, NY: 1984)

ANDOH, ELIZABETH. *An Ocean of Flavor: The Japanese Way with Fish and Seafood.* William Morrow and Company, Inc. (New York, NY: 1988)

ARESTY, ESTHER. *The Delectable Past.* Simon & Schuster (New York, NY: 1969)

ARMSTRONG, ALISON. *The Joyce of Cooking: Food & Drink from James Joyce's Dublin.* Station Hill Press (Barrington, NY)

BEARD, JAMES. *American Cookery.* Little, Brown & Company (Boston, MA: 1972)

BOYD, LIZZIE, ed. *British Cookery: A Complete Guide to Culinary Practice in England, Scotland, Ireland and Wales.* Overlook Press (Woodstock, NY: 1979)

BROTHWELL, DON & PATRICIA. *Food in Antiquity.* Thames & Hudson (London, EN: 1919)

CARSON, JAMES. *Colonial Virginia Cookery.* Colonial Williamsburg (Williamsburg, VA: 1968)

CHADWICK, MRS. J. *HomeCookery: A Collection of Tried Recipes, both Foreign and Domestic.* (Reproduction) Arno Press (New York, NY: 1973)

CLAYTON, JR., BERNARD. *The Complete Book of Soups and Stews.* Simon & Schuster (New York, NY: 1984)

CUMMINGS, RICHARD OSBORN. *The American and His Food.* (Reproduction) Arno Press (New York, NY: 1970)

DAVIDSON, ALAN. *North Atlantic Seafood.* Viking Press (New York, NY: 1980)

DUMAS, ALEXANDRE. *Le Grand Dictionnaire de Cuisine.* Tchou (Paris, FR: 1965)

EICHLER, LILLIAN. *The Customs of Mankind: With Notes on Modern Etiquette and the Newest Trend in Entertainment.* Nelson Doubleday, Inc. (New York, NY: 1924)

EUSTIS, CÉLESTINE. *Cooking in Old Créole Days.* (Facsimile reproduction) Arno Press (New York: NY 1973)

FEIBLEMAN, PETER S. *American Cooking: Creole and Arcadian.* Time-Life Books (New York, NY: 1971)

FISHER, M.F.K. *The Art of Eating.* World Publishing Company (Cleveland, OH: 1954)

GIBBONS, EUELL. *Stalking the Blue-Eyed Scallop.* David McKay (New York, NY: 1964)

GRUVER, SUZANNE CARY. *Cape Cod Cookbook.* Little, Brown (Boston, MA: 1930)

HARLAND, MARION. *Common Sense in the Household.* Scribner, Armstrong & Company (New York: 1873)

HESS, JOHN L. & KAREN. *The Taste of America.* Penguin Books (New York: 1977)

KAPE, JESSIE, ed. *The Anthropologist's Cookbook.* Routledge and Kegan Paul (London, EN: 1977)

KNIGHT, JACQUELINE. *The Cook's Fish Guide.* E.P. Dutton (New York, NY: 1973)

LEE, JIM. *Jim Lee's Chinese Cook Book.* Harper & Row (New York, NY: 1968)

LEONARD, JONATHAN NORTON. *American Cooking: New England.* Time-Life Books (New York, NY: 1970)

LINCOLN, JOSEPH C. *Cape Cod Yesterdays.* Little, Brown (Boston, MA: 1935)

MARIANI, JOHN F. *The Dictionary of American Food & Drink.* Ticknor & Fields (New Haven: 1983)

McCULLY, HELEN. *Things You've Always Wanted to Know About Food & Drink.* Holt, Rinehart & Winston (New York, NY: 1972)

MELVILLE, HERMAN. *Moby Dick.* W.W. Norton (New York, NY: 1967)

NEY, TOM. *The Healthlover's Guide to Super Seafood.* Rodale Press, (Emmaus, PA: 1989)

NGO, BACH and ZIMMERMAN, GLORIA C., *The Classic Cuisine of Vietnam.* Barron's Educational Series, Inc., (Woodbury, NY: 1979)

ROOT, WAVERLEY & de ROCHEMONT, RICHARD. *Eating in America: A History.* William Morrow and Company (New York, NY: 1976)

SCOTT, GENIO C. *Fishing in American Waters.* Harper & Brothers, (New York: 1869)

SHAY, EDITH & FRANK, ed. *Sand in their Shoes: A Cape Cod Reader.* Houghton, Mifflin (Boston, MA: 1951)

SIMCONS, FREDERICK J. *Eat Not This Flesh: Food Avoidances from Prehistory to Present.* (2nd Ed.) University of Wisconsin Press (Madison, WI: 1994)

SPARKS, ELIZABETH HEDGECOCK. *North Carolina and Old Salem Cookery.* Dowd Press (Kernersville, NC: 1964)

TANNAHILL, REAY. *Food in History.* Stein and Day (New York, NY: 1975)

THOMPSON, SIR HENRY. *Food and Feeding.* Frederick Warne & Co. (London, EN; 1896)

THOREAU, HENRY DAVID. *Cape Cod.* The Peninsula Press (Cape Cod: 1997)

TUPP, JULIE SPENCER. *Gifts of the Earth: 55 Authentic Recipes from 15 Tribes.* Pruett Publishing Company (Boulder, CO: 1982)

ZACHARY, HUGH. *The Beachcomber's Handbook of Seafood Cookery.* John F. Blair (Winston-Salem, NC: 1969)

Index

A

aïoli 168, 232, 277
abalone 161
Adriatic Sea 235
Africa 69, 265
Alabama 192
Alaska 55, 65, 71, 206
alligator 273, 276
Anchor Bay, CA 189
andouille 79
Antilles, Lesser 185
Antoine's Restaurant 147
Aquidneck Island, RI 269
Arcadians 265
Australia 121, 128, 172, 219, 268
Austria 86
Azores 230

B

Bahama Islands 67, 166
Baja Peninsula 71, 242
Baltimore, MD 274, 275
base flavors 15-6
Bass River, MA 38, 87
Beaufort, NC 214
Beaufort, SC 214
beche-de-mer 245
Bergeron, Vic 138
bisque 20
blender 11-2
Block Island, RI 157
B.O.'s Fish Wagon 164

Bongo Bong 112
Booke of Cookery 129
Boston 40, 115
Boston Cooking School Cook Book 101
bouillabaisse 63, 80, 121, 223, 225, 226, 228, 249, 261
bouillon 20
bouquet garni 22, 168
bourride 80-1
bowls 9-10
Brazil, SA 83, 85, 172, 251, 264, 268, 270
Bristol, RI 118
British Columbia, Canada 53, 55, 212
broth 19, 20
butter crackers 278
Buzzards Bay, MA 64, 177, 237

C

Cajun 265, 267
caldeirada 229, 230, 270
California 46, 161, 162, 189, 218, 236, 241
Canadian Maritimes 41
Cannery Row 241
Cape Ann, MA 115
Cape Cod, MA 38, 42, 47, 71, 84, 87, 103, 150, 170, 223-4, 230
Cape Cod Bay 38, 123

Cape Disappointment, WA 51
Cape Fear, NC 149
Cape Hatteras, NC 150
Cape May, NJ 195
Casablanca, Morocco 72
Cataumet, MA 237
catfish 76*ff.*
catsup 280
caviar 54
Cedar Key, FL 204
cephalopod 91, 161
Charleston, SC 205, 209
Chatham, MA 174
Chebeague Island, ME 279
cherrystone 92
Chesapeake Bay 88, 139, 206
Chevalier, Maurice 242
Chicago, IL 138, 233
China 75, 142, 188, 198, 246
China cap 11
chinois 11
chinook 51
chourice 104
chowder 20
cioppino 236
clams 91*ff.*
"Clams and Quahaugs" 94-102
conch 161, 162, 163

Coffs Harbour, New South Wales 122
Cohasset, MA 38
colander 11
Colombia, SA 85
Columbia River 51, 54
Connecticut 109
consommé 20, 47
Coos Bay, OR 144
coquille 156
Cornelius, Mary 40
Cotuit, MA 135
Count of Monte Cristo, The 120
court bouillon 28, 73
crackers (see also pilot crackers) 278
crawfish (crayfish) 182
cream, first recorded use in chowder 40
cream soup 20
Creole 73, 231, 260, 265ff.
Crete 238
crocodile 273
crustacean 91
crustacean butter 278
Cuba 84
Cummaquid, MA 103
cuts of fish 30

D

dash 14
dashi 20, 25
Dauphin Island, AL 192
debeard, mussels 119
Delaware 107, 216
Denmark 206
dijon 107
Dijon, FR 127
Dodecanese Is, Greece 239
Dominica 263
Dominican Republic 263
dress a fish, how to 31-2
Dumas, Alexandre 120, 202
Dutch oven 10
Duxbury, MA 140

E

Ecuador, SA 85
Edgartown, Martha's Vineyard 89, 179
eel 88
Emerson, Ralph W. 272
Endangered Species Act 276

England 52, 90, 156, 211
English House-keeper 129
Eskimos 65
evaporated milk 13, 38

F

Fairhaven, MA 177
Fall River, MA 169
Fanny Bay, Vancouver, BC 212
fillet a fish, how to 33
Finnan Haddie 59
"Fish Chowder" 35-7
flavors 16-7
Florida 163, 164, 165, 186, 204, 206, 249, 253
fonds de poisson 21
food processors 11-2
France 43, 80, 82, 113, 127, 156, 158, 159, 183, 223-4, 248, 252
freshness of fish 30
frog soup 273
fumet 21

G

Galilee, RI 125
Gardners Bay, Long Island NY 110
Gay Head, Martha's Vineyard 148
gazpacho 269
Georgia 154, 208, 209
Glasse, Hannah 18
goby 29
Grand Isle, La 183
Great Lakes 76
Greece 63, 225, 239, 262
Guadeloupe 263
Gulf of Guinea 260
Gulf of Mexico 76, 141, 172, 206
Gulf of Naples 106
Gulf of Taranto 235
Gulf of Thailand 271
gullah 205
Guyana 199

H

Haiti 263
hana-katsuo 25
hardtack 279
Havaña, Cuba 242
Hawaii, 45, 268
Hemingway, Ernest 84
hominy 191
Hyannis Port, MA 47

I

India 264
Ireland 114, 124, 160
Italy 106, 113, 126, 234, 235, 236, 250, 256

J

Jamaica 105, 255
Japan 25, 62, 74, 153, 180, 190, 245
jugged 61

K

kakavia 63, 225, 226
ketchup 280
kettles 10
Key West, FL 163, 230, 242
kippers 61
Kitty Hawk, NC 215
konbu 25
Korea 116

L

Lake Charles, LA 73
ladles 10
Le Grand Dictionnaire de Cuisine 120, 202
Lesser Antilles 185, 263
Lincoln, Joseph Crosby 94-102, 103
linguica 104
littleneck 92
liquor 92
lobster 172ff.
Long Island, NY 110, 145, 261
Louisiana 73, 79, 147, 182, 183, 265ff., 276
Louisiana court bouillon 73

M

MacDonald, John D. 204
Madeira Island, Portugal 72
Magellan, Ferdinand 203
Maine 108, 172, 175, 176, 186
Manchester-by-the-Sea, MA 115
Manhattan, NY 110
Marblehead, MA 40
Marion, MA 177, 197
marlin 84
Martha's Vineyard 42, 87, 89, 179

Martinique, Lesser Antilles 185, 231, 263
Maryland 111, 274, 275
Mattapoisett, MA 177
McGee, Travis 204
Melville, Herman 35-7
Mexico 66, 143, 191, 242
milt 23
Minnesota 212
Mississippi 76, 192, 194, 260
molcojete & tejolete 12
mollusk 91
Monaco 113
monkfish 48, 49
Montana 69
Monte Carlo, Monaco 113
Monterey, CA 161, 241
mortar & pestle 12, 62
muddle 71
mushroom ketchup 58, 280
mussels 119
mutton stock 136
Mystic, CT 109

N

Nantucket 87, 151, 152
Nantucket Sound 38, 135
Native Americans 144, 148, 191, 212, 265, 273
New Bedford, MA 38, 152, 168, 177
Newburyport, MA 272
Newfoundland, Canada 48, 230
New Hampshire 40
New Jersey 71, 195
New Mexico 240
New Orleans, LA 147, 223, 265*ff.*
Newport, RI 269
New South Wales 122
New York 110
New Zealand 69, 112, 138
Nigeria 260
North Bend, OR 56
North Carolina 71, 78, 117, 149, 213, 214, 215
North Dakota 57
Norway 50, 54, 69, 172, 178
Nova Scotia 41, 175, 206, 265

O

Oak Harbor, WA 217
Ocean City, MD 111

Ojéda, Alonso de 257
Old Man and the Sea, The 84
Onset Island, MA 64
Oregon 55, 56, 144, 182
Orleans, MA 123
Ossabaw Island, GA 208
Outer Banks, NC 117, 172, 213
oysters 128*ff.*

P

Pacific Grove, CA 218
Padre Island, TX 141
Page, Patti 174
Pamlico Sound 213
Pennsylvania 70, 74, 275
periwinkle 91
Peru 200, 259
Philadelphia, PA 110, 275
Phillipines, The 203
picada 232, 280
pike
pilot crackers 39, 40, 108, 279
Plymouth, MA 220
Poland 184
pompano 85
porgy
Point Arguello, CA 162
Port Renfrew, BC 53
Portugal 44, 72, 171, 193, 196, 201, 229, 230, 244, 258, 277
Poverty Bay, NZ 112
pozole 191
Provence 63, 80, 223, 277
Provincetown, MA 104
puréed soup 20

Q

quahaug 92
Quebec, Canada 68, 137
Queensland, Australia 219

R

Randolph, Mary 269
ratatouille 43
Rhode Island 83, 118, 125, 157, 269
Rockport, MA 181
roe 23, 86
romesco 232
rouille 218, 227, 232, 281
"Rules for Making Soops or Broths" 18
Russia 54, 55

S

salmon 51
salt cod 42
St. Anns Bay 255
St. Catherines Island, GA 154
St. Helena Island, SC 205
St. James (St. Jacques) 156, 157
St. Lawrence River 88, 150
San Francisco, CA 236
Santa Fe, NM 240
Santa Catalina Island 46
sardines 63
Sardinia 63
Savannah GA 209
scallops 150*ff.*
Scandinavia 54
Scituate, MA 155
Scotland 58, 59, 60, 211
Seven Dwarfs, The 246
ship's biscuit 279
shrimp, peel & devein 186-7
Siberia 69
sieves 11
simmer 19
skink 59
sockeye 51
solianka 55, 56, 57
soup 20
South Africa 172
South America 69, 76
South Carolina 77, 205, 209, 214
South Dartmouth, MA 38
South Yarmouth, MA 87
Spain 49, 128, 229, 232, 247, 254, 265, 277
spoons 10
steaks, how to cut 34
Steinbeck, John 241
stew 20
stifle 89
stock 16, 19*ff.*
Supreme Court, The U.S. 246
suribachi & surikogi 12, 62
Sweden 128
Switzerland 127

T

Tennessee 194
terrapin soup 275
Texas 128, 141, 253
textures 16-7
Thailand 271

Thistle Island, South Australia 121
Thoreau, Henry David 130-4
Three Musketeers, The 120
Tidewater, VA 210
Titicaca, Lake 29
Tortugas 186
Trader Vic (Bergeron) 138
tuna 44
tureen 10
Turkey 54
turtle soup 273

U

Uruguay 206

V

Vancouver Island, BC 53, 212
Venezuela 199, 257
Vietnam 253
Virginia 139, 210
Virginia Housewife 269

W

Wales 136
Washington state 51, 55, 217, 243

Wellfleet, MA 135
"Wellfleet Oysterman," 130-4
West Africa 205
West Indies 85
Westport, MA 146
whale shark 29
wild rice 212
Windward Islands 185
Woods Hole, MA 170

X, Y & Z

Young Housekeeper's Friend, The 40
Yucatan Peninsula, Mexico 143
zuppa di pesce 106, 234

Acknowledgments & Credits

This is *the* page that most people see when first they pick up a book to flip through it. And so, it is not by accident that *this* is where I want to thank all those who have helped me to compile, edit, and design this book. Many of them know that I will write this; some will be very surprised. Still, there are many to whom I wish to express my appreciation.

Thanks, of course, to all my friends at The Peninsula Press who have guided me through this project. Thanks not only to Andy Scherding at Quarterdeck Communications in Chatham on Cape Cod for helping us with the cover image, but also to Jason Paul in Manhattan for his research on the subject. No one could have done better, and we could not have asked for anything more.

On a similar subject of research, thanks to Richard Graydon Tasker for his geographical guidance and to Jean-Marie Fraser in the Reference Room at Cape Cod Community College. Modern technology aside, there are some things that can *never* be replaced or surpassed, and a good reference librarian is among those.

Finally, my thanks to all of those who have assisted in trying to locate and contact Kurt J. Wallace. They include Michelle Smalling at William Morrow and Company in New York, Helen Johnson and Chris Baines at the Friedman Fairfax Publishing Group in New York (formerly Quarto Marketing, Ltd.), and almost everyone else who worked with Mr. Wallace on *The Gourmet's Guide to Fish & Shellfish*; especially, Naomi Black, Mary Forsell, and Liz Trovato, all of whom searched their memories and databases. And thanks to every other Kurt Wallace nationwide who accepted our uninvited phone calls with courtesy and grace. Perhaps we shall find him, yet.

D. B. McG.